Consulting with NLP

Neuro-linguistic programming in the medical consultation

Lewis Walker

Forewords by

Ian McDermott
and
John Duncan

Radcliffe Medical Press

Radcliffe Medical Press Ltd
18 Marcham Road
Abingdon
Oxon OX14 1AA
United Kingdom

www.radcliffe-oxford.com
The Radcliffe Medical Press electronic catalogue and online ordering facility.
Direct sales to anywhere in the world.

British Library Cataloguing in Publication Data

A catalogue record for this book is available from the British Library.

ISBN 1 85775 995 8

Typeset by Advance Typesetting Ltd, Oxfordshire
Printed and bound by TJ International Ltd, Padstow, Cornwall

Contents

Foreword

Some years ago I was asked to create a training programme on *Improving Bedside Manner*. One sceptical physician who declined a colleague's invitation to attend made his position quite clear: 'Look, one of the best things about being a surgeon is that I have most contact with my patients when they are unconscious.'

Certainly working with patients – conscious or unconscious – can be demanding and sometimes extremely stressful, and over time it can take a heavy toll. One of the real contributions I have seen NLP make to those physicians with whom I have worked was to give them both new ways to manage the stress of their calling and new protocols to use with patients.

In fact, it was these twin concerns that gave rise to my first meeting with Lewis Walker. He and his colleagues invited me to work with them on the application of NLP to working with difficult patients. In the training that ensued we explored examples of patients who seemed to be very 'stuck' and kept coming back, but with no real change. It became very clear that it was not just the patients who were stuck – their GPs were, too. Feeling stuck is disempowering. The most effective intervention is to free the GP. To do this we used many of the NLP tools outlined in this book. Once they were 'unstuck', these physicians felt empowered again and their consultations changed dramatically.

What 'unstuck' them was a different way of thinking, combined with specific practical techniques which they could adapt to particular patients. This combination of approach and technology is known as NLP. You will find it expertly delineated in the pages that follow.

This book is called *Consulting with NLP* – dictionaries tell us that to consult is to seek the advice of another, to confer or take their counsel, and that a consultant is someone who gives professional advice. Certainly patients do consult their doctors in order to seek advice. However, the finest doctors do so much more than simply dispense advice when consulting, because they engage with much more than just a physical ailment. They enter into a relationship with someone who is troubled and vulnerable, and they attempt to remedy or at least alleviate distress.

I know from personal experience that this can happen in the space of a brief, single consultation. In December 1997, I started experiencing a pain in my left testicle. It was a time of acute stress, as I thought I might be witnessing the financial meltdown of the training organisation I had founded and nurtured over many years. My GP did a thorough examination, of course, and told me that there was nothing untoward organically. This was a huge relief – but what made my visit of such value was what happened next. First, he told me how men can register stress in this way and so put my experience in a larger context. Then he asked me 'How long is this stress going to continue?'. I said that I would know the score by mid-February. He suggested that I should contact him if the pain worsened before or continued after this time. In fact, it disappeared very quickly – because, I think, his question had suddenly given me a time perspective on my crisis. Now I could see that I had been too wrapped up in it, and I now realised that I would emerge from the tunnel one way or the other, and I knew when.

It struck me at the time that my GP had not just examined me – he had also given me reassurance, information and a more healthy perspective. Without the examination I would not have felt safe. However, if that had been all he had done I would have left mystified and uneasy. I would have had a physical symptom which had no explanation or, to put it another way, no meaning. This would have left me disconnected from myself, like an examined object. I was instead able to make sense of my experience – I felt engaged with, and was able to renew my engagement with myself in a more healthy way. So often, I think, it is this combination of physical and psychological aspects that makes for effective interventions and allows maximum healing to take place.

However, with many ailments such explanation and meaning are not so easy to come by. Our level of knowledge still seems to be rudimentary, and medical science may just not know why some disease has occurred in this person at this time. The consequent feeling of helplessness which many doctors have described to me can be profoundly stressful and debilitating, causing some to retreat into the role of a technician. However, on talking with patients it becomes very clear that these are the times when a doctor's capacity to engage with their patient as a person is what makes all the difference. In the face of an incomprehensible experience, the reassertion of care and relationship means that the patient no longer feels alone. If patients are to be believed, this is a powerful intervention in its own right.

Building on the Calgary–Cambridge model, Lewis Walker has outlined some of the NLP tools that are most useful to physicians who wish to engage their patients' physical and psychological ability to self-heal. In addition, he has also demonstrated the way of thinking that makes NLP so effective. In my experience – both as an NLP trainer and as a patient – the results speak for themselves. There is less wear and tear for all concerned, and better and more effective practice. This is why it is truly a pleasure to introduce a book that offers pragmatic tools in the service of that highest calling, namely the desire to alleviate suffering and promote healing.

With this technology, that surgeon I mentioned earlier might even have come to enjoy his patients while they were conscious!

Ian McDermott
Director of Training
International Teaching Seminars
May 2002

Foreword

Cum Scientia Caritas (the motto of the Royal College of General Practitioners) meaning care with science, or sometimes care with compassion, sums up the dual nature of the work in general practice – applying the science of therapy within the empathetic environment of the doctor–patient relationship. The consultation is the framework within which this relationship is developed and increasingly has become patient centred.

This approach allows for the exchange of information between patient and doctor and enables decisions to be reached that are realistic, shared and agreed. The limits of professional responsibility can then be negotiated. In this way, the practitioner can apply evidence-based medicine within the context of the patient's needs, wants and experience. Doctor and patient can decide *together* the most appropriate therapeutic action that will have meaning and purpose for the patient.

It is important for the doctor to be self-aware through reflection since the therapeutic relationship is likely to be influenced by the practitioner's own personality and his/her perceptions of his/her task.

Consulting success therefore relies on the willingness of both parties to share their views so that the doctor can attain a fuller understanding of what the patient is going through and offer acceptable options for change.

To achieve this goal is a complex undertaking and requires competence and expertise in communication skills as well as capabilities in effecting change. Lewis Walker combines his experience of consulting as a general practitioner in the North-East of Scotland with his undoubted abilities and knowledge gained from extensive training in neuro-linguistic programming (NLP) to illustrate how these capabilities and expertise might be realised.

Whilst much has been written on the structure of the consultation, less attention has been paid to the dynamics of communication at work during a doctor–patient interaction and how this might influence the therapeutic outcome. Dr Walker aims to open up the *process* of consulting and employ the tools and techniques of NLP to show how a better understanding of what is going on in the consultation can lead to greater benefits for the patient and, in turn, provide deeper job satisfaction for the doctor. The educational value of this book lies in the achievement of these aims for the reader.

The author covers all aspects of the consultation and acknowledges the impact that the doctor's own story might have on the proceedings. Special attention is paid to those situations that require particularly skilful communication such as dealing with anger and aggression, breaking bad news and the heartsink patient.

This is a book packed with practical advice and a welcome feature is the way the author relates his message to everyday problems and concerns that patients bring to the surgery. It contains powerful tools for change to be used ethically and with compassion.

The visionary thoughts and ideas of Dr Walker in integrating the field of NLP into the current models of the consultation may lead doctors to transform the way they conduct their consulting with patients.

Dr John Duncan
General Practitioner
Woodside Medical Group
Aberdeen
May 2002

About the author

Dr Lewis Walker FRCP (Glas) graduated from Aberdeen University in 1981, and spent the next five years training in hospital general medicine, initially at Glasgow Royal Infirmary, where he obtained the MRCP (UK) in 1984, then subsequently at Raigmore Hospital, Inverness. In 1986 he began vocational training for general practice, and in 1989 joined what is now a seven doctor training practice at Ardach Health Centre, Buckie, on the Moray Firth Coast. He was elected Fellow of the Royal College of Physicians of Glasgow in 1998.

In the early 90s, fascinated by what makes people 'tick', he developed a keen interest in behavioural change mechanisms, which led him to study both classical and Ericksonian hypnosis, together with neuro-linguistic programming (NLP). To date he has undertaken certified courses at the level of Practitioner, Master Practitioner, Health Practitioner and Trainer of NLP. With numerous other short courses in addition attesting to his wide experience, he has also trained with many of the leaders and developers in the NLP field. He holds the Certificate of Accreditation of the British Society of Medical and Dental Hypnosis (Scotland), and is also a Trainer of Hypnosis.

Acknowledgements

The field of NLP first came into being through the creative genius of Richard Bandler and co-founder John Grinder. As originators, they have contributed much to the technology that you will read about here. Although many people have added to their work, Robert Dilts stands out for his extensive modelling and further developments, especially in the area of beliefs.

I wish to thank UK-based trainer and author Ian McDermott, who kindly read the manuscript, provided very useful feedback and wrote one of the forewords. Over the years I have benefited greatly from his training expertise and personal advice.

I am also grateful to prolific author Joseph O'Connor – not only have his books provided an extensive information base about NLP, but also his writings set the standard for the field. In this domain he has been a model of excellence.

Although I have never yet trained with John Overdurf and Julie Silverthorn, I have gained immensely from both their tape-assisted learning material and their writings. You never know how far a change will go!

Over the years I have trained with and learned a great deal about how to utilise NLP (and also how not to) from the following world-renowned trainers (from first to most recent): Willie Monteiro, Ian McDermott, Tad James, Robert Dilts, David Shephard, Tim Hallbom, Suzi Smith, Richard Bandler, Paul McKenna and Michael Breen. My thanks to one and all.

A very special thank-you must go to my general practice partner Bill Jaffrey, who has read each chapter hot off the press, and also the whole manuscript meticulously from beginning to end. His comments and feedback have been invaluable in helping me to keep things as simple as possible ... yet without being simplistic. He is living proof that reading a book like this can effect profound behavioural change.

My other partners, Gordon Pringle, Colin Menzies, Angus Gallacher, Berny Welsh and Kathleen Schrader, together with retainers Clare Hood and Kathryn Arnould, have put up with my somewhat different perspectives on persuasion and behavioural change for a long time now. They probably do not yet realise how useful our many and varied discussions have been.

For almost eight years now there has been a group of doctors trained in NLP in North-East Scotland who have met regularly during the winter months. We have swapped case histories, practised much of the material you will read here, and generally had a great time debating the applications of NLP in general practice. My thanks and warm memories go to James Beattie, John Duncan (with special thanks for his foreword) Gavin Stark, Pat Mulcahy, Hilary Johnstone and Colin Harris.

I would also like to acknowledge four people whom I have never met, yet whose writings have had a major influence on this book. Way back in 1987, Roger Neighbour wrote *The Inner Consultation*, which has helped to fuel and motivate my further exploration of NLP and Ericksonian behavioural change mechanisms. In their book *Skills for Communicating with Patients*, Jonathan Silverman, Suzanne Kurtz and Juliet Draper have drawn together all of the evidence-based material for each phase of the consultation. Their explanation of *what* works and *why* it works has laid an extensive foundation for me to use NLP in expanding their *how to's* of effective communication.

On a very personal note, I have had a great deal of support from my wife Pam and my children Lindsay and Kerry, to whom I dedicate this book. The innumerable evenings and weekends that are eaten into by a venture like this have given me a ready excuse for failing to participate in household chores! And my 'hogging' of the computer, thus preventing access to various CD-ROM games, was incredibly well tolerated. I promise that the second computer will be up and running before the next book.

I must also give thanks to the countless patients who have sat in the consulting chair, allowing me to hone my skills further. They have sown the seeds for the various case vignettes throughout the text. Most importantly, however, their details have been altered sufficiently to protect their identity, thereby preserving anonymity yet allowing you to experience the full flavour of the fruits of the NLP approach.

Lastly, I have attempted to give all due and deserved credit to those NLP trainers and various authors who have developed specific exercises or particular approaches. Please let me know of any glaring errors, misattributions or indeed non-attributions, and I shall set the record straight in future editions.

CHAPTER I

Before we start ...

Introduction

Something attracted you to this book – perhaps something you have seen or read already, or maybe an idea in your mind. Perhaps you have been told a little about it, by friends or colleagues. Maybe you have been browsing through bookshelves, or found it in a catalogue, or maybe someone gave it to you. A present! Now you have picked it up, settled down to read through it, and perhaps you are wondering 'What is it that makes good doctors turn into really great communicators?' And perhaps also 'What is it that these doctors are doing differently, that makes them stand out from the rest?' And maybe even 'How can I excel in the same way? How can I learn these skills easily and effectively?'

So why are *you* reading this book? Why have you picked it up? Why is it really important for you to know about this material? What are the benefits for you in utilising this knowledge? What reasons do you have that will ensure not only that you complete it, but also that you will also incorporate everything from your learning into your ongoing behaviour?

Perhaps, like me, you have had experiences that do not bear repeating. You know, the kind of dysfunctional consultations where the door slams, the chair is empty, and you are left bewildered, wondering 'What on earth is going on here?' You have not seen eye to eye, you are tuned to a different communication frequency, and things just do not seem to fit. Uncomfortably so. And you have thought to yourself 'How can I really make a connection?'

And yet there are times when consultations flow, and they really flow. You know, the ones when you not only make an empathic connection, but you intuitively come up with the right diagnosis, almost as if no thinking is involved. You are there, in present time, paying attention to the here and now. And afterwards you wonder 'What would it be like if I could do this every time?'

So what are *your* reasons for reading this book?

Perhaps you are a GP trainer or you are interested in education. You probably know the ins and outs of the various models of the consultation that have evolved thus far. You are likely to be the kind of person who is really enthusiastic about teaching and learning, and you are already beginning to think about how you can best incorporate what you are going to learn here for the good of your trainee registrars, your patients and even yourself. I promise you that there is a lot you can look forward to incorporating into your practice.

Maybe you are a GP registrar, fresh out of a hospital post and thrust into the world of general practice where uncertainty seems to be the order of the day. It is still early days, yet you may well be feeling overwhelmed, with so much to learn, so much to do and so little time. Ten-minute consultations – a complete contrast! Why are they here? Why now? And the vagaries of summative and formative assessments. Video recordings. Argh!! In these pages there is much that will help you to weather the seas of uncertainties and to cope with whatever happens.

Perhaps you view yourself as an ordinary GP (whatever that is!). You have been in the job for a number of years, and you can handle most things, or you know a man (or woman) who can. Although you may not be an 'old dog', you still wonder whether there really are any new tricks to learn. Perhaps you have browsed through other 'consultation skills' books before, but they have not exactly set the heather on fire. This book will help you to re-experience what you already do well in a way that will stimulate you to do more, and let it ripple into other areas of life as well.

Perhaps you are on the retainer scheme. Maybe you work part-time or have come back after some time off. You have several other demands on your time, and you may feel a bit like a juggler, which is OK until someone throws you an extra ball! Sometimes confidence can be an issue. Maybe you do not feel fully part of 'the team'. Perhaps you occasionally question your ability to keep up with what is going on, and all of the new developments. I can assure you that the skills you will learn here will free you up to be more effective on many fronts, and to feel good in the process.

You may be a medical student, fresh from the life sciences, about to enter the world of therapeutic relationship for the first time. Your head is buzzing with scientific facts and data, details of examination and investigation, pathology and taxonomy of disease. So much to think about, yet on the wards and in your attachments to general practice you wonder about the wider aspects of illness and just how to approach this unique individual in front of you as a person, rather than as a collection of physical and psychological symptoms and signs. Breathe easy – the following pages will illuminate your path and help to integrate both task *and* relationship.

Are you a health professional from another discipline, perhaps a nurse, a counsellor, a psychologist, or from one of the many professions allied to medicine? Maybe you have started to flick through these pages and wonder if any of this applies to you in your own particular field. What exactly can you learn from *Consulting with NLP*? Well, you may or may not be surprised to find out that the deeper aspects of the processes involved in getting your message across apply to you, too. Be ahead of your field. Read on.

Lastly, you may be a brave hospital doctor reading something outwith your specialist field – someone who wonders whether there really is anything to be learned from how effective GPs communicate with patients. Maybe you are interested in how to break bad news in a more caring way, or how to deal with angry or aggressive patients. Or perhaps you are one of those growing numbers of physicians, surgeons, obstetricians, gynaecologists, mental health professionals, paediatricians, and so on, who are gradually realising that whatever the speciality, the core fundamentals of effective communication are applicable across the board. Who knows, you may already be the one who has gained the most by choosing to read this now.

So what is *your* purpose in reading this book?

Once upon a time ...

For the last eight years or so I have been using neuro-linguistic programming (NLP) in my daily consultations, with excellent results. In the rest of this book I shall be explaining exactly what NLP is, and just how you can use it to consult more effectively. You require no previous knowledge of the subject, as all will be revealed. As an overview, NLP is mostly an attitude of mind which has spawned a host of different techniques and approaches. It is an attitude that involves getting really curious, and wondering just how effective people get results. And wondering, too, just how you can change your world by expanding your possibilities, exploring new ways of thinking and enhancing what you already do well.

NLP is composed of three parts:

* *neuro* – how we use our neurology to think and feel
* *linguistic* – how we use language to influence others *and* ourselves
* *programming* – how we act to achieve the goals that we set.

I can still remember the intense feeling of excitement running through my mind and body when I read my first book about NLP, *Frogs into Princes* (Bandler and Grinder, 1979). You know that kind of feeling, when you have stumbled on something that you suspect may change your perspective forever. I just couldn't put the book down. I read page after page after page. I had always wondered about what made people 'tick', why they did what they did, how we could exchange information more effectively and, most importantly, how we could change behaviours easily. From that first day no patient was safe from my wanton experimentation with this new model of communication!

I remember one patient who walked in, sat down, looked at me intensely and said *'I want you to* **hypnotise me now** *to stop smoking!'* Now I knew that this guy was a polarity responder – someone who usually does the opposite of what other people say (more on this later). I viewed this, in the words of NLP co-founder Richard Bandler, as *'an unprecedented opportunity to* **learn something new***'.*

So, as you can imagine, I looked him in the eye and, utilising my newly read and acquired language patterns, said *'I don't know if you're the kind of person who can* **get really comfortable** *in that chair. And I'm really not certain whether you can* **begin to go into a deep trance. Now** *you probably won't be able to* **let your breathing slow down***, and feel the* **developing relaxing in your limbs***. And I really don't know if you can stop preventing yourself* **learning the kinds of things here that will last a lifetime***.'*

Anyway, he got a glazed kind of look in his eyes, stopped blinking and seemed to consider very carefully everything I said from then on. Now I don't know about *you*, but for me it is important to find out what a particular symptom does for a person, before helping change to occur. So I asked him *'What's the best cigarette of the day, the one that you* **enjoy** *the most?'*

He seemed to *go inside himself*, thinking for a moment, his eyes looking up to his left, and taking a deep breath before answering, *'Well, the best one is when I'm rock-climbing, and I sit at the bottom, looking up,* **contemplating**, **planning** *my route, getting there* **safely***.'*

At that point I said in a voice tone that startled him *'Well, after hearing that I'm not going to* **help you** *stop smoking. You could be on the rockface, not* **completely safely!** *I don't* **want that** *on my conscience. In fact smoking, if you* **really, really think about it***, could save your life!'*

He looked at me completely bemused – you know, like times when you have been deeply confused about something, and he said *'Call yourself a doctor? How could you say that? Is this some kind of reverse psychology?'*.

To which I replied *'Of course not (nodding yes with my head). What kind of a doctor do you take me for? Now just go and close the door behind you.'* And he left looking very puzzled.

Now the late great Milton Erickson MD, upon whose teachings much of NLP has been built, used to say that *'Confusion is the gateway to learning'*. He would get his patients into exactly the right kinds of states of mind and body that would allow them to learn what is really important. And there are many tales of how he helped his patients in unusual ways (described in *My Voice Will Go*

With You by Sidney Rosen (Rosen, 1982). Here is one that I especially like. It highlights Erickson's almost legendary ability to *notice fine distinctions* in behaviour patterns.

One day, Erickson's wife Betty announced that there was a beautiful young woman waiting to see him – a striking blonde in a dark, two-piece suit, and stockings with seams that went all the way up. He said *'Show her in my dear, show her in.'* As she came in, just as she was sitting down, she picked some lint off her sleeve. She then proceeded to tell him about all of the other doctors she had consulted, many of them his colleagues, none of whom had been able to diagnose or treat her condition. She finished by saying *'I've come here to find out if you are the right doctor for me.'*

Erickson looked her directly in the eye and said *'Yes Madam, I am the right doctor for you.'*

She looked back, equally directly, and replied *'Isn't that just a bit conceited, Dr Erickson?'*

And he said *'No, I'm just stating a fact. And the fact is,* **I am the right doctor for you.***'*

She still thought that he was terribly conceited, so he added *'It's not conceit, simply fact. And I can prove I'm the right doctor for you by asking one, simple, direct question. And the question is ... (pause) ... how long have you been dressing up in women's clothes, sir?'*

Erickson was a master at noticing detail! He always told his students to *'open your eyes and ears to the information that is there all around you'.*

I began to follow Erickson's advice one day when I saw a woman who was less than 5 feet tall, weighed 120 kg and wanted to lose weight. However, she had been unable to lose any, despite trying hard over the years. In fact, the harder she tried, the more her weight imperceptibly increased! She had tried diets, aversion therapy, hypnosis with time distortion for meals, aerobic exercise classes and even medically prescribed drugs, but all to no avail. Yet she seemed so desperate. So I set up a longer appointment with her, saying *'Listen and note carefully. I am going to tell you some things of great importance that will help you to achieve your most cherished goals.'*

When the day came, I went over in great detail all of the things that she had done that had not yet worked for her. Then, somewhat intriguingly, I mentioned that in my research I had come across an approach which would guarantee success. The only drawback was that she had to *agree* to do what I was going to prescribe for her *before* I let her know what it was she had agreed to do! A real double-bind situation. And of course I built up the tension somewhat by wondering out loud if I could really do this to her. The crux of course was that she had a choice. If she did not take on the task, I would no longer be able to help her with her weight problem. If she did, she would have my full support.

I wrote out a contract, which she agreed to sign without reading it first. You can imagine the look on her face when she found out what she had agreed to do. It said '*You presently weigh 120 kg. Over the next 8 weeks your task is to gain 5 kg, so that you weigh 125 kg. Then your weight issues will be resolved.*'

She found it one of the hardest things she had ever done. Yet she managed to stick to the task assiduously, with weigh-ins at two-weekly intervals. At the final weigh-in she had become an overachiever, by 1 kg! In a funny sort of way, she was really proud of herself, as this was the first time that she had ever reached a weight target. She said that she felt she could now put her mind to '*mastering anything and everything!*'.

Building blocks

I remember when I was a trainee in general practice, in the days before the name change to GP registrar, when the main guide to the consultation was *The Consultation: an approach to learning and teaching* (Pendleton *et al.*, 1984). This was the subject of many tutorials, and active debate ensued after various video-recording sessions. For a long time afterwards, this was the skeleton which I fleshed out with the meat of many, many consultations. However, I did personally find it a somewhat 'dry' approach and, like others, went on to develop my own style.

When I came across Roger Neighbour's delightful book, *The Inner Consultation* (Neighbour, 1987), I had just started to explore NLP. It made an immediate impact on me, connecting deeply. Beautifully written in an Ericksonian style, intermingled with Eastern philosophy (especially Zen), I found it simultaneously challenging and liberating. It led me to believe that, above all else, establishing a rapport with the unique individual in front of me was the foundation of effective consulting, and also trusting my intuitions to make the occasional leap into the dark, to go with the flow.

During the succeeding years I trained extensively in NLP with a variety of world-class trainers, yet something was missing. Although I recognised that I was consulting far more effectively, NLP itself did not yet have a large enough evidence base to prove its efficacy as a useful tool in medicine. In fact, most people in the NLP world eschewed evidence. They followed the dictum '*do whatever it takes to get the result you want*'. Great for the unique individual sitting in the consulting chair, but making meaningful research a challenging task. However, help was at hand.

One of my partners, Gordon Pringle, in his guise as clinical tutor, introduced me to *Skills for Communicating with Patients* (Silverman *et al.*, 1998). The rest, as they say, is history! This provided a complete evidence base for the five stage

Calgary–Cambridge model of the consultation, a model that was being taught to undergraduates and postgraduates alike, and to both GPs and hospital doctors. Each section, as well as giving the phase-specific skill sets, also provided the clinical and research evidence to back up each skill – *the very communication skills that were shown to **actually make a difference** in clinical outcomes.*

They showed clearly and categorically how communicating effectively significantly improved health outcomes, namely patient satisfaction, adherence to management plans (concordance), symptom relief, and even improved psychological and physiological outcomes. Not only that, but also these same skills helped doctors to become less frustrated and more satisfied with their work!

Box 1.1: Calgary–Cambridge framework

1 *Initiating the session*
 • Establishing initial rapport
 • Identifying the reasons for the consultation
2 *Gathering information*
 • Exploring problems
 • Understanding the patient's perspective
 • Structuring the consultation
3 *Building the relationship*
 • Continuing developing rapport
 • Involving the patient
4 *Explanation and planning*
 • Providing the correct amount and type of information
 • Aiding accurate recall and understanding
 • Achieving a shared understanding by incorporating the patient's perspective
 • Planning and shared decision making
 • Discussing and negotiating mutual plans of action
5 *Closing the session*
 • Safety-netting and final checking
 • Next steps

I remember feeling very excited for quite some time thereafter. This was the evidence base that I had been looking for. I began to map over the key NLP processes and techniques to the five stages and 70 individual skill sets of the Calgary–Cambridge model. The evidence had shown *what* skills worked and *why* they worked. Silverman, Kurtz and Draper had begun to look at the underlying *process* of effective communication, the *'how to's'* of a skills-based approach (Silverman *et al.*, 1998). And in my view NLP, being perhaps the ultimate process-driven behavioural technology to date, has so much to offer – and not only in terms of further elucidating, expanding and simplifying the *'how to's'*. In addition, by utilising NLP's accelerated-learning formats, you can more rapidly acquire, assimilate and spontaneously use these skills in everyday practice.

So you don't need to cut anything out, leave past skills behind, or do anything completely new. At the end of this book you will still have all of your current skills ... and more. Much more! The NLP approach sits very comfortably on the shoulders of all the past models of the consultation. It is evolutionary rather than revolutionary. It is a model of increased choice, of expanding possibilities, of enriching and cross-fertilising every field of enquiry. So sit back, enjoy the ride, and delightfully surprise yourself in the pages that follow.

How to get the most out of this book

If you are astute, and even if you are not yet, you will already have begun to notice that there is far more to this book than immediately meets your eye. I have written it with both your conscious *and your unconscious* in mind. Many people struggle to overload their conscious, rational, logical, 'thinking' mind with the facts and figures of supposed learning. In reality, most 'true' learning actually takes place quite *automatically*, mostly outwith our conscious awareness. If I were speaking to you as an accelerated-learning specialist, I would say that all learning is state dependent. That means that *what* you learn and *how* you learn it depends on the state of mind and body that you are in at that particular time. Pleasure, fun, curiosity and positive anticipation are all good learning states to be in as you continue reading.

There are some questions that, if you keep them in mind as you digest each section, will allow your curiosity to both broaden and deepen your rapid skills acquisition, allowing it to spread by association into multiple areas simultaneously.

Box 1.2: Learning questioning

Why is he writing this section in that particular way?
Why does he think that this topic is important? What is in it for me?
What is the key information he is getting across here?
What are the associated and linked areas?
How does this actually work?

How do I implement it?
What will happen if I use this material in the future?
What are the benefits for me? And for others?

I have structured this book in a similar way to the flow of a normal con-sultation, based on the Calgary–Cambridge model. This chapter and the next one set the essential frames for your learning easily. The following five chapters deal with the detailed skills that are pertinent to each phase of the consultation. There are several exercises in each chapter and it is important that, as well as reading through them, you actually *make time to do them thoroughly* to the best of your ability. Doing them in your mind's eye, in passing, may satisfy your intellectual curiosity. However, in order to really *master the skills* you need live practice. Only you can decide if you want to simply learn about the skills, or actually to be able to use them in the real world.

Of course there are always occasions when things don't necessarily go according to plan, or you require a slightly different approach. We shall take a closer look at special situations and specific ways to handle particular challenges in Chapter 8. One area that in my view has not yet had the exposure it deserves is developing personally. In Chapter 9 you will have an in-depth experience about what is really important to you in your work and vocation, together with an opportunity to develop your *compelling future*.

Making your learning easy

There are several tips from the various fields of learning that can help you to get the best results.

- Ensure that you are in a good state before starting (curious, open to learn-ing, and relaxed).
- Have a 10-minute break after every 45 minutes of reading.
- Jot down notes that come to mind in the margins or on a separate sheet.
- Vividly imagine, using all your senses, being in each experience as it is described.
- Think about where, when and with whom you would use each skill as you go along.

- Briefly review the previous section before starting the next one.
- Find a colleague and make a firm agreement to work through the exercises together.
- Utilise every opportunity to use this material both in consulting *and* in everyday life.

What if I get confused?

Then congratulate yourself, because confusion is the gateway to new learning! You can only have total clarity if you are completely ignorant of a subject or have complete cognisance – a closed book. Confusion can only occur *when you are learning something new*. It is that feeling which lets you know that cross-fertilisation of ideas, new with old, is actually taking place *at this very moment*. It is a time when your internal map of the world is being updated and expanded, giving you more flexibility and more choices.

Think of it as con-fusion. That means 'with joining together'. Like a chemical reaction, two relatively inert substances can come together to form a new compound, and the energy that is released can be harnessed to do useful work. This is exactly what happens as you allow yourself to be open to learning new things. So if you get that feeling of confusion, and you know personally how that feels, you can feel pleased that you are learning a great deal. If you don't get that feeling ... beware! Confusion is the signal that integration is occurring ... *now*.

What if I feel uncomfortable when doing the exercises?

Great! Yes, you've guessed it – that uncomfortable feeling is the pivotal point when you are actually beginning to embody the new skills. The new mental and physical patterns are being laid down in the software of your brain. Remember what it was like when you learned to drive a car. You probably passed through the kangaroo petrol stage initially, followed by intense focus and concentration to keep the car on the road, and now you drive to your destination automatically whilst thinking about a host of other things. In so doing you passed through the following four stages of learning:

1 *unconscious incompetence* – when you didn't know what you didn't know! It was all a mystery, blissful ignorance

2   *conscious incompetence* – when you know *what* you want to do, but your capabilities don't yet match up to your expectations. You may make many miss-takes!

3   *conscious competence* – when you know *how* to do it, yet you need to keep focused on all of the steps. You still have to think *about* what you're doing. You need to practise

4   *unconscious competence* – when you do it automatically, skilfully, without needing to pay conscious attention to any of the steps.

Many people may feel uncomfortable in steps 2 and 3. Yet because this is where the most learning and change are taking place, that discomfort can be *your signal* to let you know that you are on the right track. Intriguingly, because NLP is an accelerated-learning technology, it is possible, just as when you were a young child, to jump directly from step 1 to step 4 without the intervening steps being apparent. You may find yourself becoming delightfully surprised at your rate of skills acquisition as you read through this book.

NLP also recognises a fifth step, that of *mastering*. This is the stage where not only can you do things automatically with skill, but you can also describe the process that you are using as you go along. You are conscious of your *unconscious competence*. You can teach what it is that you do. We use the word 'mastering' rather than 'mastery' to show that this is still an ongoing process, *a never-ending spiral of improving skill.*

So, what do you want from this book?

By this I mean, like the Spice Girls said, 'what do you really, really, want?'. One of NLP's most important contributions to goal setting and achievement of outcomes is to begin with the end in mind. Think back for a moment to the reasons why you are reading this book. What purpose do you have? What is important to you about what you are doing? What is it that you want to achieve?

You see, before embarking on any venture, great or small, you want to be able to stack the odds up in your favour so that not only will you reach your destination and have a great time getting there, but you will also achieve results way beyond your expectations. So how is this possible? Well, you need to ask yourself some questions, and ask them in a particular way. Not only that, but it is really useful to write down the answers. And also, think **BIG,** be *greedy*, be unreasonable, and ask for much more than you think you currently deserve. Set your aims, aspirations and goals beyond any limitations, higher than any self-imposed ceiling. Yes, I know that this is terribly un-British, and possibly even – heaven forbid – grandiose. But set that feeling aside for now as you get on and *do the following exercise.*

Exercise 1:   My goals and outcomes

1   What are *your goals and outcomes* for reading this book? Before writing them down, consider this question modelled from trainers Tad James and David Shephard:

> What are my goals and outcomes, such that having successfully finished this book, having successfully completed all the exercises, and having successfully gone beyond my expectations, achieving all my goals, I would have to say 'That was the best book I have ever read on developing and improving my consulting skills?'

2   Now *write down* as many goals and outcomes as possible that come to mind. Take at least 5–10 minutes right now. Aim to have between *10–20 goals* or more. Be greedy. Think **BIG**! You can keep adding to this collection as you continue to read through the book.

3   As you look over all of your goals now, take a moment to *imagine them coalescing into one giant outcome*. Sit back in your chair and begin to contemplate. Imagine how you would look having successfully completed them all. How would you walk, talk, stand, sit, breathe and move differently? How would others know, just by seeing you, that you have achieved it all, and more? As you allow that picture to become brighter, closer and more colourful, step inside it and *experience the feelings of really getting what you want.*

You can come back to this exercise as many times as you want, adding new goals and building up a collage, a kaleidoscope of successful outcomes. The more you do it, the more streamlined it will become. The more you do it, the better the chances of having it all. The more you do it, the more likely it is that this will automatically spread into many other areas of your life, becoming second nature.

You are now ready to start your journey in earnest. And it is too serious a venture to take too seriously. By that I mean have fun, amuse yourself, have a rollercoaster ride, let go, be childlike in your curiosity, and enjoy yourself in the process. And I will see you again at destination's end – wiser, well travelled, more skilful and more naturally able to be the best communicator that you can possibly be.

CHAPTER 2

Overview of neuro-linguistic programming

Introduction

Have you ever seen someone who displays a skill so elegantly and gracefully that you wonder just exactly how they do it? Perhaps someone who seems to be able to deal effectively with an angry and upset person without losing their cool. Maybe someone who has excellent influencing skills and can persuade people, with integrity, to go in a direction of mutual gain. Possibly you marvel at the minor surgical skills of a colleague. It could be that your practice manager has the best planning and negotiating skills on the block. Perhaps you have a partner with a relaxed, laid-back attitude to the vicissitudes of on-call work. You may have a mentor, a person you respect immensely, and you hope that in time you can develop similar characteristics. You may ask yourself *'How do they do that?'*

And what of the people you know in other careers? The businessman who has great creative thinking skills. The trainer who can hold an audience spell-bound *and* make learning fun, almost effortless. The fireman who can keep calm in the most difficult of rescue situations. The nurse who seems to exude empathy and caring to all. The tennis player with great hand–eye co-ordination. The driver of a huge articulated lorry who can reverse into seemingly impossible spaces. The accountant who can make head *and* tail of complicated financial figures. *Just how do they do that?*

You could of course put it all down to natural talent. They were probably born that way. It runs in the family. That's just the way they are, like it or lump it. It is a personality thing. Or else it took years for them to get that way, to learn that skill, and you just don't have the time anymore, nor the same starting point. Maybe it was all luck anyway. Maybe they were in the right place at the right time and that's all there is to it.

But is that really true? What if it weren't true? What if there was a way to learn skills far more easily and effectively, regardless of your starting point? What if these skills actually had a structure, and there was a process by which you could assimilate them easily? Interested? *Just how do you do that?*

I remember in my early NLP training seeing a trainer work with a demonstration subject. All her life she had felt inferior to other people – she couldn't look them in the eye, she didn't match up. She had experienced episodes of depression, and had been on treatment, yet still felt low. I watched entranced as the trainer, using verbal and non-verbal skills exquisitely, found out just precisely how this woman structured her problem state. But he did not stop there. He used extremely effective communication skills to lead her elegantly and respectfully through a process of change to a different outcome, to a different solution. And she did – *change*, that is. And over the next few months of this modular course we heard first hand her reports of continuing wellness.

I remember thinking at the time, '*Just how did he do that? How did he seem to know the right things to say? How did he structure his communication to get that result?*' Of course that was quickly followed by the thought '*I want those skills. And I want them now!*'

NLP is the study of the structure of subjective experience. Wow! What a mouthful. Just exactly what does that mean? Well, according to NLP everything that we think, say or do – our behaviours of excellence, our talents and skills, our behaviours that we wish we could change, and our troublesome problems, all of this – has an underlying, recurring pattern. An underlying template, if you will, which when brought to the surface, can be changed, rearranged, even taught to someone else. NLP is really all about having an attitude of curiosity, intense curiosity. Getting really curious about *how* people do what they do. Wondering how they manage to maintain their problem, doing it over and over again. Wondering how they can perform differently, competently, in other situations. Wondering how the skills that some people have that help them to cope well, or even excel, can be extracted and put into a format that can be easily acquired by others.

The methodology that is used to do all this is called modelling. NLP builds cognitive and behavioural models of how successful people do what they do – how they behave, how they say what they say, how they think, and how their beliefs and values fit together in an enabling way. And in this book we shall be studying how, using NLP, successful communicators can get results in medical practice. *Just how do you do that?*

A brief history of ... NLP

NLP originated in the early to middle 1970s at the University of California in Santa Cruz, when mathematician Richard Bandler and linguistics professor John Grinder become interested in how people change. Bandler had been keenly studying how Fritz Perls, a medical doctor, outstanding psychotherapist and the founder of Gestalt therapy, got results with clients. An intuitive modeller, Bandler was able not only to reproduce these results, but also to do so with ease. He asked Grinder to help him to decode the patterns of language and behaviour that Perls employed. He reputedly replied to the effect: '*Teach me* **what** *you are doing, and I'll tell you* **how** *you're doing it.*' From this initial collaboration the field of NLP developed.

Neither Bandler nor Grinder were interested in abstract theories or esoteric claims about *why* people did what they did. They wanted to build practical models of how successful people in any domain achieved results, and how they could teach these models so that others could learn easily and quickly. They focused on what people actually did, rather than on what they claimed that they did. Very soon they had discerned the linguistic patterns and behavioural techniques of Perls, and both were obtaining equally high-quality results. They decided to turn their attention to other successful therapists, as they wanted to explore other patterns of change, and this led them to Virginia Satir.

Virginia Satir was at that time the doyen of family therapy. She had a reputation for taking on difficult, complex family and relationship problems that many thought were insoluble, and solving them. What Perls did for individuals, Satir did for families. Although they were completely different personalities, Bandler and Grinder found that their underlying linguistic processes and patterns were very similar. From modelling these two therapeutic giants, the *meta-model* (see later), a specific language model for communication and change, was developed.

John Grinder and Richard Bandler also conversed with Gregory Bateson, a British anthropologist who was living and working in California at the time. From a medical perspective, Bateson was the first to propose the double-bind theory of causation in schizophrenia. He had been part of the Palo Alto group, an influential mental health research group working on the application of communication and systems theory in therapy. Interested in patterns of change, he suggested that the duo should visit Milton Erickson in Arizona.

Milton Erickson, a medical doctor, was also a trained psychiatrist *and* psychologist! The founding President of the American Society of Clinical Hypnosis, he was profoundly interested in the mechanisms of deep and lasting change. His linguistic and observational skills were legendary. He had developed the art of conversational trance whereby, without any overt trance induction, merely talking with his patients would somehow facilitate the changes that they needed. Bandler and Grinder, in modelling his language patterns, his voice tone and his gestures, found a completely different way of using communication skills therapeutically. If Perls and Satir were masters of using very specific language, Erickson was the opposite. He was a master of artfully vague language that allowed patients to *'change in your own way'*.

From the initial modelling of these three outstanding therapists, the field of NLP has grown considerably. Bandler and Grinder, using the tools of modelling, have gone on to explore many other fields of excellence, including business, law, sport and education, to name but a few. Many other patterns have been developed. One of the key developers and innovators in the last two decades has been American trainer Robert Dilts. A student in the early days of Bandler and Grinder, he has worked extensively in the area of beliefs, producing many useful models. Interested in concepts, cognitive mapping and categorisation, he has also applied these models to health issues with intriguing results. And of course Bandler himself has continued to develop and refine his work, principally in the areas of accelerated-learning strategies and formats, making more available in less time.

This is of necessity a brief history of NLP's formation and growth. Other books will give more depth and breadth of coverage (*see* Bibliography on page 273). NLP is still an open book – it is not a complete body of knowledge. It is still growing, evolving and changing. What stands out for me is that much of the foundation on which NLP rests is *derived from a medical background*. I believe that now is the time to come full circle and bring the fruits of NLP back into the medical world, so that both our patients and we ourselves can greatly benefit.

So what really is neuro-linguistic programming?

Neuro-linguistic programming is a bit of a mouthful. How about breaking it down into its component words and examining these in a little more detail?

The *neuro* aspect is all about the mind and how it takes in and processes information. If you really think about it, the basic building blocks of all our experiences are composed of what we see, hear, feel, smell and taste – our five senses. Of course, to be different, and set the field apart somewhat, NLP tends to use the jargon words visual (V), auditory (A), kinaesthetic (K), olfactory (O) and gustatory (G) instead. Whatever (!), information coming from the outside world can only reach us in this way. Once inside, it passes through our various *internal filters*, such as our beliefs, values, memories and life experiences, among other things. Mostly we are unaware of this process taking place, apart from the end result. And this is our internal representation, our internal images, sounds, feelings, smells and tastes *about* the outside event.

The *linguistic* element is all about how we use our language, how we label things, how we interpret things, and how we talk, both with others *and* with ourselves. The sixth thing that we can do inside our heads (after VAKOG) is to speak to ourselves *about* what is happening. We often have a running commentary in our mind about what is happening right now. Sometimes, perhaps in a consultation, we may pay more attention to that commentary than to our patients, sometimes to the detriment of both of us. Language, both spoken and unspoken, verbal and non-verbal, has a definite structure, and a set of rules for use, or even abuse. NLP has uncovered many useful language patterns which we shall meet in due course.

Programming is a word left over from the early days of the personal computer, which has mirrored NLP's dramatic rise in usage over the years. Patterning might be a better word. Having taken in outside information (*neuro*), talked to ourselves or others about what to do (*linguistic*), we then run a series of actions or behaviours designed to achieve our particular goal in that situation (*programming*). Our behavioural programmes may stem from the skills of excellence, doing things really well. However, we may run a pattern over and over again that leads to depression, or worse. This patterning element of NLP is the *order and sequence* of internal representations that leads to that particular behaviour – good or bad, liked or disliked, wanted or unwanted. If you know the sequence you can change the order, and thereby change the behaviour.

Universal filters

In doing all of the above, we use the universal filtering processes of *deletion*, *generalisation* and *distortion*. We delete, generalise and distort massive amounts of information which would otherwise overwhelm us. Psychologists reckon that about two million pieces of information bombard our nervous system *every second*. Yet we can only be consciously aware of about seven pieces at any one time. We have deleted the rest. If you have ever mislaid your car keys, and then found them right under your nose, that is an example of *deletion*. If you are having an enthusiastic conversation with someone and fail to hear someone else calling your name, that is another.

We take the rest of the information that remains, and generalise from it. *Generalisations* are useful short-cut rules to help us to navigate the world without having to think too much. Most doors work the same way, as do most pens, auriscopes and stethoscopes. Sometimes the rules are not so helpful. If you make one mistake and from this believe that you will never learn, that is *not* a useful generalisation. Miss a case of meningitis and you may find yourself checking every febrile child.

What is left of the information is distorted by us in some way. The process of *distortion* involves giving labels to our experiences so that we can interpret them, make meanings out of them, evaluate them and even judge them. For example, suppose that one of your patients gives you a present to thank you for what you have done. You could think that they really appreciate you. Or, if you are cynical, you might assume that they want something more in return. You distort the experience to fit your beliefs. You are alone at the health centre at night, catching up on paperwork. You hear a noise and think that there is an intruder. You start at the shadow of a large potted plant. You find that a colleague has left his Dictaphone running and that is what is making the noise!

Figure 2.1 shows an NLP model of communication.

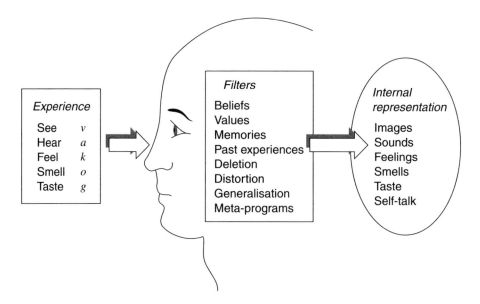

Figure 2.1: NLP communications model.

Communicating meaning

How do you say what you mean and mean what you say? Many people believe that words themselves carry all of the meaning when communicating. However, try saying the following words out loud:

'You can't do that here.'

First, imagine that you are really, really angry with someone. Get in touch with that feeling, point your finger blamingly, and then say the words emphasising '*you*'. Now shake that state off and calm yourself down.

Now imagine that someone has told you off for doing something, and you are quite incredulous about it. Put both hands out, palms up, as you say the words, emphasising '*here*' in a questioning tonality. Now shake that state off. Let me ask you, given that the words were the same each time, what conveyed the meaning?

In a classic study in the 1970s, Albert Mehrabian showed that, in face-to-face communication, only 7% of the meaning was conveyed by the actual words used. Voice tonality accounted for 38%, and physiology (our posture, gestures and facial expression) a whopping 55%! Our *non-verbal* behaviours – how we say what we say, and what we are physically doing at the time – make a major contribution to the overall meaning of our utterances. In fact, we cannot *not* communicate. Even when we say nothing at all we are still communicating something.

Cartoonists, of course, have known this forever. They use posture and gesture to convey a wide variety of meanings at a glance. Actors and actresses practise saying words like 'no' in such a way that it conveys yes, no, maybe, oh go on then, incredulity, seductiveness and myriad other meanings. So in any communication we must learn to pay attention to the non-verbal components.

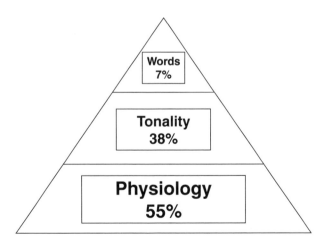

Figure 2.2:   Communicating meaning.

What Mehrabian and others found was that the emotional content of a communication tended to be expressed non-verbally. This includes information about our deeper beliefs and values which will 'leak' spontaneously as we talk.

They will be 'given away' by tonality and gestures, *emphasis* on *certain* words, repetitive movements, etc. This occurs mostly out of conscious awareness – we usually don't know that it is happening, it is unconscious. Yet there is much valuable information here.

When we are *congruent*, aligned, our words, tonality and physiology match up. When we are *incongruent*, our words say one thing, and our tonality and physiology say another. Remember a time when you met someone and what they said seemed right yet ... later ... you felt that there was something about them – you couldn't put your finger on it ... but ... you had that recurring feeling of unease. In a mixed non-aligned message like that, the non-verbals win out each time. This is so important that we shall return to it again later.

Beliefs of excellent communicators

No matter which field of endeavour NLP has studied, time and time again the following beliefs about how to communicate effectively have always come to the fore. They are sometimes called the *presuppositions of NLP*. These are the underlying assumptions which, when acted upon, ensure that communication flows in an active, dynamic, recursive loop. They are not necessarily 'true' or 'correct' or the 'right way'. However, if you *act as if* they are true, if you try them on for size, and if you use them as a filtering lens for all your communication, then you will begin to experience exceptional results.

Everyone has their own unique model of the world

If you look again at the NLP communication model, you will see clearly that because we all have different filters, different life experiences, and different beliefs and values, then any two or more people who share the same external experience will each have a different internal representation. Your internal map – your model of what is going on 'out there' – is unique to you. So is that of your patient. In a sense, their interpretation is absolutely right – for them! So we need to give them information in a way that best fits their map, not ours.

An adolescent once told me about the excruciating pain he had from a bee sting. We got nowhere until I acknowledged that what was an irritation for most people was painful for him. Another patient was upset when he was told that his chest pain was not significant. He thought that he was being disbelieved. In fact the consultant cardiologist was only trying to reassure him that his heart was fine!

Ask yourself *'Am I communicating this in a way that fits for them?'*

Behind every behaviour is a positive intention for that person

This presupposition states that no matter what the behaviour, it is always trying to do something of positive value for *that* individual. Sometimes the behaviour itself can be a problem, but we can always find an underlying positive intention. Consider the binge drinker who drinks to escape from his personal difficulties. At the time of drinking, he feels a massive sense of relief, freedom and comfort. His behaviour is positively intended for himself *at that time*. The same is true for the anxious person who avoids the difficult social situation and now feels calm.

It is a good idea to ask yourself what could be the positive intention behind any recurring symptom or behaviour. Separate the intention *behind* the action from the action itself. Sometimes it can be difficult for a patient to give up a behaviour until the positive intention is satisfied in some other way. The classic example of this is the smoker, who smokes to relax, yet has no other way to reach that goal. Preserving the positive intention and providing other avenues for relaxing is the key.

Ask yourself *'What is the positive intention behind this behaviour?'*

The meaning of your communication is the response it gets

When two people communicate, messages are being sent and received by both parties simultaneously. Each filters the message in their own unique way. Sometimes the message sent out is received in a different way to that which was intended. You may get a response that you did not bargain on. Whatever your intentions were, the *interpreted message* was different. No one is 'wrong' in this situation – there is no blame. You simply need to accept this as feedback and put your message in a different way.

A woman in her forties started to cry when I asked about her mother's recent death. I said I was sorry if that had made her feel sad again. She said that, on the contrary, they were tears of relief, that after her long-drawn-out illness her mother was finally at peace. A woman in her fifties who was dying of cervical cancer told me she did not have the heart to tell her husband that she was too nauseated to eat the meals he had lovingly cooked. He thought that she had to eat in order to get better and that she didn't like his cooking. Explaining this to them both helped him to express his love and caring in other ways.

Ask yourself *'Are they interpreting my message in the way I intended?'*

Present behaviour is the best choice available at this moment in time

Whatever someone is doing at this point in time is generally the best response that they have available in these circumstances. That is not to excuse anyone's behaviour, but simply to say that, given their history, their previous experiences and their current internal map, it is impossible for them to behave any differently. What we can do, of course, is to help them to update their map and expand their choices. This presupposition applies to us, too. Whatever *we* are doing as doctors today is the best we can do given the circumstances. And we can expand our choices, too, which is perhaps one of the reasons why you are reading this book.

One of my patients had been abused as a child. Now 32 years of age, having kept it secret for all this time, someone else had named the perpetrator. She was exposed and had to go to court. Memories flooded back, overwhelming her. She couldn't bear her husband to touch her. She felt like a child again, unsafe, and her husband got upset, too. We ran a simple NLP mental process, distancing the troublesome images and allowing her to be more resourceful. She was able to keep the events at arm's length as she dealt with them.

Ask yourself *'If this is their current best choice, how can I help them to expand their choices?'*

There is only feedback

Good communicators know that in every situation, what you do next moves you either towards or away from your goal. They use every response from their patient as feedback for what to do next. They have honed their *calibration* skills – their ability to 'read' people. They ensure that they only take the next step after securing agreement to the last step. If they do not obtain agreement to the next step, verbally or non-verbally, they backtrack to the previous step. They refuse to wallow in the word 'failure'. They know that this kind of thinking takes their attention off the other person. It is not that they don't make mistakes. They may make plenty of them! But they use them as feedback instead.

A patient came in and sat down. I said something that was intended to be flippant, an off-the-cuff joke that went wrong. Unfortunately, the patient became quite upset instead – not what I'd hoped for. I jumped up, pointed back to my seat and said *'You're right, that kind of behaviour is totally out of order. I apologise on his behalf.'* Then I moved my chair slightly, sat down and asked if we could start again. With the patient now bemused rather than upset, we went on to have a satisfactory consultation!

Ask yourself *'How can I utilise this response as feedback?'*

Resistance is a sign of lack of rapport

If, as an excellent communicator, you sense that you are having some difficulty getting your message across, and you recognise that you are not 'getting through' and that they are 'resisting', this means that you have lost rapport with your patient. You need to back off and re-establish rapport before moving on (we shall deal with the specifics of rapport more fully later on).

I was telling a 40-year-old man about treatment options for his back pain and noticed a glazed, far-away look come into his eyes. I stopped speaking, adjusted my body posture to mirror him, and waited to get his attention again. When I had it, he became much more receptive to my comments.

There is a saying that *'there are no resistant patients, only inflexibly communicating doctors'*. True or not?

Ask yourself *'How can I best re-establish rapport?'*

Everyone has, or can acquire, all of the resources that they need

This is sometimes a 'challenging' one. Essentially this presupposition states that there are no unresourceful people, only unresourceful states of mind and body. Many people actually have, in other life contexts, the skill that appears to be lacking in this, the troublesome context. Finding it and bringing it to bear changes the situation. In a medical context, a prescription for medication is an external resource that is brought to bear on disease and illness.

A 43-year-old smoker who wanted to stop smoking searched his mind for an aversive past experience. As a child he hated the smell and taste of castor oil. We re-vivified that experience and with NLP anchoring techniques (see later) attached the negative feelings to cigarettes, and he stopped smoking!

Ask yourself *'Which resource can I bring to bear on this situation?'*

Mind and body are one unified system

Changing our thoughts changes our physiology, and changing our physiology changes our thoughts. In medicine, psychosomatic illness reflects one part of the link. Yet perhaps we should coin another term, *somatopsychic illness*, for the reverse. Patients who are depressed may have physical symptoms as a result, and others with chronic physical illness may become depressed. Our verbal expressions can tell one side of the story, yet much information is presented non-verbally in posture and gesture. We need to pay attention to the whole message – mind and body.

A 55-year-old man, stooped with ankylosing spondylitis, became quite depressed. A prescription for exercise not only cleared his depression, but also he became stronger and more mobile as a result.

Ask yourself *'What is the total message – mind and body – that they are communicating?'*

When you consult other NLP literature, you will find that there are several more presuppositions of NLP in addition to those that we have dealt with here. By and large, they say the same things in a slightly different way, from a slightly different viewpoint – which is fine. We all agree, though, that starting off any process of communicating with these in mind will reap dividends both for us and for our patients.

The pillars of NLP

If the beliefs of excellent communicators, the presuppositions of NLP, are the guiding principles, then the *pillars of NLP*, coined by Ian McDermott, are the operating rules in any given situation. If you pay close attention to these five rules then you will significantly increase your chances of a successful encounter. I believe that it is true to say that the whole of NLP is encapsulated within them. And *every* consultation will benefit from them. They will repay your close study a hundredfold!

1   *Your state of mind and body*
    Your state is the sum total of your thoughts, emotions and feelings, and everything that is going on for you right now. We give states names, such as happy, sad, depressed, ecstatic, bored, tired, curious, fascinated, etc. You will have your own personal favourites, some of which you inhabit more frequently than others. It is vital to be in the right state for the job in hand. The right state and you flow with the task. The wrong one ... well!

    And whilst you might not have recognised this yet, each state is the container for certain specific skill sets embedded within it. Being in the right state accesses the right skill most easily. Think of morning consultations after a long, tiring night on call, and three difficult cases to start with. You may find your thinking and diagnostic skills hard to access. Yet if you were fresh, and had just heard that partnership profits were up ... what a difference!

    Your state is important. You need to check that it best fits the current situation, and if it doesn't, choose another. We shall deal more specifically with how to do this throughout the rest of this book.

2   *Rapport – relating to other people*
    Once you are in the right state, you need to turn your attention to the other person. Rapport is also a state – one of empathic communication, a dance of mutual responsiveness. You are 'in sync' with the other person, seeing eye to eye, on their wavelength, making a felt connection. It is the state wherein mutual influence occurs. Over time, with certain patients, it may develop into deep trust.

Rapport is the *sine qua non* for effective communication. It is not necessarily about agreement, but more about *respecting* the other person's position, expressing your thoughts in ways that they can understand and act upon. You can probably recall times when rapport was lacking and meaningful communication ceased, and other times when consultations flowed. Rapport is vital life's blood to medical practice, and we shall deal with it in much greater depth and breadth later.

3   *Outcomes – what do you want?*
    NLP is an outcome-focused technology. If you don't know what you want, that is exactly what you'll get ... don't know. We need to be really clear about our outcomes in any particular communication situation. NLP is solution centred. Sure, we have to start with the current problem in any given consultation, but we need a direction, a target, a goal to move towards – and the action steps that will get us there. The more clearly defined the outcome, the easier it is to identify which resources are required to complete the journey – resources that we either have or can acquire.

    How many times have you had a consultation during which neither you nor the patient was clear about what was really wanted? Or perhaps what was wanted just seemed rather vague, or fuzzy. How did that feel? It is very useful to have a set of criteria for a *well-formed outcome*. Because outcome setting is a major skill in NLP, and there are several aspects to it, formulating what you want in the right way is tackled in depth in Chapter 4 on gathering information.

4   *Feedback – developing sensory acuity*
    Suppose that you are in the right state, have great rapport and have an outcome to work towards. How do you know that you are headed in the right direction? It is a bit like driving a car. You know your destination, but there may be several routes that you can take. And no matter which route you choose, you need to pay attention to other road users, speed limits, weather conditions and destination signs, and to drive accordingly. You drive differently in the depths of winter on snow-covered roads to the way you drive on an 'open road' in summer. Feedback like this helps you to change tack when necessary and get there in one piece.

    It is the same with any other outcome. We need to open up our senses, our eyes, ears and feelings to the information that patients are displaying from moment to moment. NLP calls this developing our sensory acuity, *calibrating* to the patient's responses. Everything we need for feedback is there in front of us. We shall hone these skills further shortly.

5   *Flexibility – doing something different*
    If we stay with the car metaphor a little longer, what happens if the route you have chosen has road-works or, worse still, is completely blocked? Of

course you just go home again. *No you don't!* You find another way – a detour, another route, a side road, or another form of transport altogether.

NLP calls this *behavioural flexibility* – ensuring that you have other choices, other ways to achieve your outcomes. If you believe in the 'one way fits all' type of thinking then, with this approach, some people will achieve their outcome but many others won't. NLP believes that it is more useful to have a high-quality outcome and to help that individual to get there as flexibly as possible using whatever route best fits the unique circumstances pertaining to them at that time.

So, to summarise this section, first pay attention to your own state. Ensure that it is the best one for the current situation. Then establish the depth of rapport necessary to get both your own and the other person's outcomes met. And in the setting of those outcomes, use whatever feedback you can to stay on track. If that track is closed, be flexible enough to find another one. Do this regularly and you will notice your results improving, perhaps markedly.

Logical levels of experience

The *logical levels* model (sometimes called the neurological levels model) was developed by American trainer Robert Dilts and based on Gregory Bateson's levels of learning and thinking. It is widely used in the NLP world, although some would say that it is not necessarily either a logical or a hierarchical level as first conceived. Nevertheless, as is usual with NLP, we are not concerned so much with 'truth' as with pragmatic usefulness in the real world. When applied to health, this model can give some very interesting insights about the level at which an intervention can take place and its likely effect on the rest of the system.

Although often laid out in a hierarchy, I sometimes prefer a circular approach to show that all of the levels interact as a system, influencing one another equally (*see* Figure 2.3).

Let us examine each level in turn.

Environment – where and when?

This is the selected context and the time frame. Here you will have the places and any other people involved in the action. For instance, this could be your consulting room or health centre, or anywhere else you care to imagine that is pertinent to the situation under consideration. You can compare and contrast environments *where* you have a problem and ones *where* you don't. You

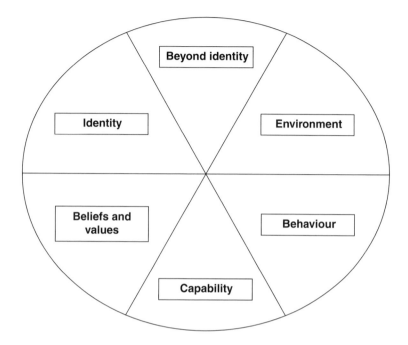

Figure 2.3:   Logical levels ('Beyond identity' courtesy of Ian McDermott).

might feel pressurised in your work environment and relaxed at home, or you might feel pressurised at work only *when* you are on call.

Behaviours – what?

These are the things that you actually *do* in that environment – how you walk, talk, breathe, move, and your posture and gestures, the very things that an external observer of the situation could comment on. You can compare and contrast your behaviours in different environments, as described above. *What* you do may be a troublesome behaviour, one that you want to change. However, changing behaviour *per se* is more intimately connected to changing at the other levels.

Capability – how?

Capabilities are the skills that you bring to bear in that environment. They answer the question *'How are you doing that?'* The skills can be mental skills, such as making a hypothesis or a diagnosis, which involve internal thinking strategies. They may also be physical skills such as performing minor operations or cardiac resuscitation. Your practice manager will display many organisational skills in the day-to-day running of your practice. Business people call these *competencies*.

We can apply this to disease and illness. For example, we could view depression as a series of thinking skills leading to feeling down. How might you think instead? Thinking in this way about illness can open up new avenues for exploration.

Beliefs and values – why?

If values are the things that are really important to us, *why* we do what we do, then our beliefs are the operational rules that express our values in action. You can think of them as guiding principles for our daily lives and deeds, letting us know what we can and can't do. When people say *'Actions speak louder than words'*, they are drawing attention to the fact that what we *say* we believe and value may be different from the underlying reality of what we *do*. Our deeply held beliefs may, more often than not, be below the level of our normal conscious awareness.

Beliefs and values also operate at an organisational level. You may not have considered that, whether you know it or not, your practice partnership operates out of shared beliefs and values, some of which are aligned together while others are not. How does this apply to the rest of the NHS? What about your family? What other organisations do you belong to?

When patients come with behaviours that limit them or cause illness, the solution may actually be at this level rather than the others. If health, which is a values-based word, is low down in their hierarchy of importance, it will be difficult to get them to sign up to healthy behaviours. However, profound change can occur when you make an intervention at this level.

Identity – who?

Your identity is your sense of self, *who* you are at the deepest level. It encompasses your core beliefs and values and expresses itself in why you are called to do what you are doing. Usually this sense of self is very robust and resilient, and change tends to occur slowly and in an evolutionary way. Change can occur more quickly when people explore their sense of purpose, their vision and life's calling in more depth.

Occasionally, however, after severe physical or psychological trauma we can lose this sense of self for a time, and this can be very troubling – a deeply felt anomie. Prolonged meditation and fasting without adequate preparation can also have this effect. Dissociative identity disorder is an example of differing identities being present in the same individual but with little or no internal connection. This can follow very severe childhood abuse. It is a rarity in general practice.

Organisations also have an identity, which reflects the business culture to which they belong. Manufacturing companies have a completely different ethos and feel compared with the creative whiz-kids in marketing.

Beyond identity – who else?

This level is all about connection – connection to other people, and connection to religion and spirituality. It is about who you are in the world and how you relate to others – your patients, partners and the wider community. And not only you, but also your practice has a place in the community, and you may have a vision of how you want that connection to be. In a sense we have come full circle, stepping back into the environment that we started in.

Language of the levels

It is often useful to map out the language that patients use to describe their problems in terms of the *logical levels*. This can give you a better idea not only of the various facets involved but also of the particular level at which an intervention might be more successful. Table 2.1 lists some examples of patients' statements showing which level they fit.

Table 2.1: Examples of patients' statements in relation to their identity

	Identity		
	I am an alcoholic	*I am a cancer victim*	*I am a smoker*
Beliefs	Drinking helps people to cope with life's problems	No one survives this kind of illness	Smokers are more sociable people
Capability	I can drink a bottle of whisky a day easily	I don't know if I have the strength to go on	It's the only way I can really relax
Behaviour	I like chatting to my drinking buddies	Chemotherapy makes me sick	I spend £30 a week on cigarettes
Environment	The Rose and Crown is my favourite pub	I want to die at home	We have a smoking area at work

You can use this to explore the levels of solutions as well. A patient complaining about stress might go on holiday for two weeks – a change of *environment*. He could do something different, such as take up jogging – a new *behaviour*. He might learn some new thinking skills, such as meditation, so that he is *capable* of relaxing at will. He could adopt the *beliefs* of successful communicators, and influence his boss to change working practices. Learning from all of his experiences so far he might find a new role (*identity*) as the company's 'stress buster'. There is no one right solution that fits all cases, yet some solutions (*meditation – capability*) will provide longer-term beneficial effects than others (*holiday – environment*).

Let me be quite clear about this. All of the levels interact with each other, and all of the levels can provide the means for a solution. Because they are part of a system, change at one level may lead to changes at all levels. Sometimes these collateral changes will be too small to notice, but sometimes a small change will cause a huge ripple effect. The trick is to find the one small change that gives most leverage for your patient.

The structure of subjective experience

How do you know the difference between something that you are going to do next week and something you did last week? What is the difference between thinking about your summer holiday of last year and the one that you are planning to go on this year or next year? Think of something you definitely did *yesterday*, you're certain of it. Now think of something you could have done but didn't do yesterday. How do you know the difference? (Hint: think of your mental pictures, sounds and feelings).

Think of something that you believe in 100%, such as 'breathing is good for you'. Now think of something that you are not sure of, such as what you might have for tea next Friday. What is the difference? Think of a good, happy, pleasant memory. Now think of one that is a bit unpleasant. What is the difference?

Experience has a *structure*. Whether we know it consciously yet or not, our brains code our experiences in such a way that we can retrieve them without getting them mixed up. We have codes for past, present and future, certainty and uncertainty, real and unreal, good and bad, like and dislike, belief and disbelief. We code all of these things by organising our internal pictures, sounds and feelings in particular ways.

Exercise 2:   Exploring mental perspectives

Think of a *really good pleasant memory from the past*, perhaps a time when you achieved something of importance at work, in sport, etc., maybe a *memorable* holiday, a place you visited, a *dramatic* sunset. Perhaps a time when you were *having fun*, with family, friends or relations. When you have the memory now, think about the following.

Visual
- Create a mental picture of the event. If you can't yet see it clearly, just pretend that you can. A glimpse is enough.
- Is it in colour or black and white?
- Is it close or far away?
- Is it a movie or a still framed photograph?
- Where do you see it in your visual field? Up, down, left, right or straight ahead?
- Is it fuzzy or in sharp focus?
- Are you inside it, seeing it as it is happening (associated), or outside it, watching yourself from a distance (dissociated)?
- Is it framed or unbounded, with single or multiple images, two-dimensional or three-dimensional?

Auditory
- Now listen to the sounds of the experience. If you can't yet hear them clearly, just pretend that you can.
- Is the volume loud or soft?
- Does it come from close by or far away? Which direction? Up, down, left or right? Point to it.
- Is it surround sound or more easily heard in one ear? Which ear?
- Is it clear or muffled, soft or harsh, high or low pitched?

Kinaesthetic
- How does this experience feel in your body? Pay attention to the feeling.
- Where is the feeling located? Put your hand on it.
- How intense is it? Is it high or low? Does it feel light or heavy?
- Does it start in one place and move to another? Does it move quickly or slowly?
- Is it hot or cold? It is continuous or discontinuous?

Well done, you have begun to find out more about the building blocks of all experiences. You can *repeat the exploration* with a neutral or less than positive experience for comparison, although not your worst memories! Use something of mild to moderate intensity only.

If visual, auditory and kinaesthetic are the *modalities* of experience, then the subdivisions that you have been exploring are the *submodalities*, the actual building blocks themselves. No matter what we experience, our brain codes this with a particular sorting code, a combination if you will, that locks it away for easy retrieval. If you experimented with the less than good memories as well, you will have noticed that your brain has coded them in a different way. Comparing in this way is called *contrastive analysis* – finding out the points where things differ. You can try this out with like and dislike, certainty and doubt, belief and disbelief, past and future.

Why is this so important? What are the benefits of knowing the structure of experience in this way? What if you could change the structure and thereby change the meaning of the experience? Would that be useful? And how could you begin to apply this now?

Let us do another thought experiment.

Exercise 3:   Changing perceptions

Think back to the pleasant experience in the last exercise. We are going to change the submodalities of that experience and notice what happens. After each shift, put the memory back the same way before experimenting with the next shift.

Visual
- Turn the brightness of your mental image up and notice what happens. Now turn it way down. What happens now? Now put it back to the original way.
- Bring the image really close. Then push it way into the distance. What happens? Put it back.
- Continue in this way.
- Make it much larger. Now make it tiny.
- Make it more colourful. Now drain all of the colour away.
- Change the location. If it was up right, put it down left, etc.
- If you are 'inside' (associated), step outside and see yourself over there. If you are 'outside' (dissociated), step inside and pull the image all around you.
- Adjust the image until it gives you the best feeling possible.

Auditory
- Listen again to the sounds.
- Turn the volume up and notice what happens. Now turn it way down.
- Bring the sound closer. Now push it away into the distance.
- Make it 'surround' sound. Now have it come from a point source.
- If it was louder in the left ear, change it to the right ear.
- Now adjust the sounds to give you the best feeling possible.

Congratulations, you have just changed an experience for the better by altering its structure through sub-modality shifts.

Now do the same for the previously less than good experience, finishing up with the changes which let you experience it more comfortably.

In this exercise you have found out just which submodalities affect your experience most, those which can enhance your good memories even more, and those which reduce the intensity of less than good memories. You may also have found that certain ones are *critical* or *driver* submodalities. Changing one of them in one direction also spontaneously changes others. For example, bringing your image closer may have brightened it up and made it more colourful at the same time. Knowing these drivers can help you to change any experience quickly.

Many people find that they can enhance good memories by stepping inside them (associated), making them bigger, brighter, more colourful and closer. At the same time you can turn up the volume of the sound, bringing it closer and making it 'surround' sound. Notice where the feelings start in your body, intensify them and loop them round to start again and again.

You can also markedly reduce the intensity of negative feelings associated with less than good memories. Step outside the image, seeing yourself over there (dissociated). Shrink it down into a small, still-frame, black-and-white photograph away in the distance. Turn the volume of the sound down until it is inaudible. Reverse the feelings back into a tiny area from which they came.

I wonder if you can think of certain patients, coming to mind now, who might benefit from experiencing things anew in this way, as well as yourself.

If you have not already done these exercises, I suggest that you *go back and do them now*. They may seem a bit 'off the wall', quite different from anything you have done before. Yet it is very important that you have the experience. You are the only one who will miss out if you don't (do the exercises, that is). The exercises in this book build on one another. Not only *you will benefit*, but your patients will, too.

Association and dissociation

We have mentioned these in passing several times already. They are two of our brain's most fundamental coding mechanisms and operate on every experience that we have. So what are they, and what effect do they have?

Association means that you are fully *inside* the experience, having a first-hand awareness. You are 'all there', looking out through your own eyes, hearing with your own ears, and feeling the feelings that are intimately connected with the experience. You are fully engaged emotionally, mentally and physically. This applies to events that are happening right now as well as being associated with past memories and future imaginings.

Dissociation, on the other hand, means that you have 'stepped out' of the experience and distanced yourself in some way. You see yourself over there, somewhat detached, like an observer. You may be hearing what you are thinking *about* the event, like a running commentary. Your feelings will be disengaged. You may feel something *about* the event, but not the feelings *of* the event itself. You can have this perspective about past memories and future imaginings as well.

Think of a patient who was telling you about a past unpleasant event and then became upset and tearful. They are back inside that memory reliving it as if it was happening now, feeling the discomfort once again. Remember how when someone is telling you about a past success that they had they seem to light up and feel excited, bubbling with energy. You catch that excited feeling and feel good, too. Think of a future event that you are really looking forward to, so much so that you feel good right now. These experiences are typical of varying degrees of association.

Think of a patient who was telling you about a harrowing experience. Yet they remain 'deadpan', with little expression and a somewhat monotone voice, describing it as if it had happened to someone else. Remember a time when you were consulting, trying out a new approach, a different way of doing things. As you were doing it you commented to yourself about your performance, criticising your apparent ineptitude. Think of a time when you were making strategic plans for the future, taking into account different perspectives. These experiences are typical of varying degrees of dissociation.

In and of themselves, association and dissociation are neither good nor bad. Yet each is useful with different types of experience. Look at the following patterns of possibility with regard to positive and negative events. Do you recognise anyone? Patients, colleagues, family or friends? Yourself?

Associating with both positive and negative

When you feel good, it's great. When you feel bad, it's awful. Life can be a bit of an emotional roller-coaster. You feel all feelings intensely, and it's difficult to step back and get some perspective on the situation. Sometimes you can't see the wood for the trees.

Dissociating from both positive and negative

You can easily handle difficult circumstances by distancing yourself. However, you have the same strategy for events that should be happy. You may feel like a spectator – not really engaged. A bit like a 'Mr Spock', you may feel that life is passing you by.

Associating with negative, dissociating from positive

Life seems painful most of the time. Happy events are fleeting, ephemeral, and you can't hold on to them. You may not even notice them slipping by. Episodic misery is punctuated by bouts of neutrality. The future may look bleak, and you may ask yourself if it's all worth the effort.

Associating with positive, dissociating from negative

You have lots of choice. You can feel really good about something if you want to. You can distance yourself from negative events and find some positive aspects to take away from them. Your future seems bright, and you are confident that you can handle whatever happens.

A cautionary word. Beware! Dissociation is a good way to handle painful events that are happening now. However, keeping the disconnection in the longer term is not such a good idea. Keep the events dissociated only until you have learned from them what you need to, and can integrate this into your everyday life.

You will find many suggestions throughout this book for you and your patients to associate and dissociate in helpful ways. Be patient!

Anchoring

Does the name Pavlov ring any bells? He was the Russian psychologist who conditioned dogs to salivate in response to the sound of a bell. He waited until they were hungry, salivating for the food that they saw in front of them, and then rang a bell at the peak intensity of the experience. After doing this several times, he found that ringing the bell without any food being present could make the dogs salivate again. This is called *associative conditioning*, whereby the natural salivatory response to *seeing* food was paired to a completely different stimulus, the *sound* of a bell. NLP calls this *anchoring*, whereby a particular trigger can fire off a particular response.

Anchors occur all around us – they are everywhere. They occur in every representational system – visual, auditory, kinaesthetic, olfactory and gustatory. This trigger can be something external in the environment, or something internal in our mind and body. Anchors happen automatically, outwith our conscious thinking processes, like knee-jerk reflexes. Just think, how do you respond to the sound of an ambulance siren? A flashing blue light? The sound of a cardiac arrest bleep? The feel of a scalpel in your hand? The smell of hospital disinfectant? The taste of post-consultation coffee?

What feelings do the memories of all these things generate in you right now? Box 2.1 lists some other examples in all of the representational systems.

Box 2.1:   Common anchors

Visual
The face of a 'heartsink' patient!
The entrance to your health centre
Blue sky and sunny day, or grey
sky and rain
A photograph from a great holiday

Auditory
Your name
The voice of a 'heartsink' patient!
Your favourite music
The sound of skidding tyres

Kinaesthetic
The feel of your consulting-room
chair
Rubber gloves
The touch of a clammy, shocked
patient
A massage

Olfactory and gustatory
The smell of coffee
The local bakery
The smell of ether
The taste of your favourite food

Anchors are universal, and they are used universally. Look at adverts in the various GP and medical magazines. The advertisers are attempting to pair their product to a particular induced feeling, a particular emotional state. Listen to the music that accompanies adverts on the television. It is there to change your state to make you more receptive to what they want you to buy. Smells are the 'express train to the brain' because they have a direct one-step connection to our emotional centres. The smell of newly laid tar takes me right back to being a child. I used to love that smell, and would get down on my hands and knees to sniff even more. Yes, I confess, I'm an addict.

Recall how your mother used to call your name in a particular tone of voice, and you knew that you were in trouble! How different when someone you love says it in *that* special way. How do you react when a patient who you hardly know calls you by your first name? It's the same name each time, an anchor for your identity, who you are, yet the different voice tones evoke differing responses. Auditory anchors tend to be mostly out of conscious awareness, and we may respond completely automatically, for good or ill, without knowing why.

What is a phobia? This usually occurs when an intensely negative feeling is paired with an external stimulus, usually a visual one. Simple phobias, such as fears of spiders, dogs, etc., are examples of one-trial learning. Often a single event is enough to set up a lifetime's fear – a very powerful visual–kinaesthetic link. Sometimes even just *imagining* being in the presence of the stimulus is enough to trigger the response. It has become hard-wired to our internal circuitry. NLP has techniques for dealing with simple phobias and other more complex psychological traumas.

Kinaesthetic anchoring, or touching, is also very powerful. If someone is in an intense state, if you touch them in a particular way in a particular place (e.g. on the arm or shoulder), that touch may become a trigger for that state. Touching again, in the same place, in the same way, can reactivate the feelings. This is great if it is a joyous state, but not so great if it is one of sadness or grief. So be careful how you touch people when they are in the grip of powerful negative emotions. Of course, you can deliberately set up touch anchors for yourself and your patients for really good, positive states. And you can deliberately use anchors for these powerful states to neutralise negative states. More on this later.

Anchors in health and disease

Phobias can begin with one intense emotional traumatic episode. However, many anchors are set up by repetition, over time, of mild to moderately intense states. This accumulative effect, out of conscious awareness, can cause certain anchors to run our lives. Just think of the number and variety of states that you go through each day as you respond to patients, phone calls, road traffic, meetings, music, food, coffee, etc.

Yet anchors can also, almost imperceptibly over time, damage our health. States such as depression, anxiety, anger, hostility and helplessness have all been shown to cause physiological and chemical changes that can lead to further disease and illness, shortening life expectancy. These states are negative anchors. The growing field of psychoneuroimmunology shows how our very thoughts can affect our immune system for better or worse. Some allergies may have a stimulus–response cause and effect on the immune system that can be modified by anchoring techniques. We can think about anchors at the various logical levels.

Many negative anchors are *environmental* responses. Chemotherapy-induced nausea and vomiting have a conditioned element to them which can be reduced by desensitisation techniques, as can certain allergies.

Our posture is a potent physiological anchor for certain *behaviours*. Depression has a characteristic posture which further anchors the state. That is why exercise, which significantly changes posture, can be helpful. Try it for yourself. Any time you feel down, dance for 15 minutes to upbeat music. Your state will definitely change quickly.

The *capability* level is all about our thinking styles and strategies. Worry, anxiety and panic are usually caused by associating into imagined future negative consequences and feeling the feelings now. The images trigger the response. Learning to dissociate can change the response.

Beliefs and *values* act as frames for experience which can lead to self-fulfilling prophecies. Negative beliefs such as 'Nobody gets better from cancer' can trigger profound immunological responses derived from 'learned helplessness'. Changing the frame changes the response.

At the *identity* level, the various roles that we play in life can trigger differing effects. The so-called 'sick role', where the secondary gain derived keeps the problem going, is another ill-health anchor.

Anchors are pervasive. Yet looking at disease and illness through this type of lens can open up many more opportunities for lasting, health-improving change. Keep this in mind as you read on.

Achieving what you want

NLP is an outcome-focused, solution-oriented behavioural technology. We look towards *outcomes*, rather than simply identifying problems to move away from. Think of a particular challenging situation and ask yourself the questions in Box 2.2 in turn.

Box 2.2: Identifying problems and outcomes

Problem frame	*Outcome frame*
Why is this a problem?	What do I really want here?
Why does this always happen to me?	How will I know when I have
What is my worst experience with	that?
it so far?	What can I learn from the
Who is to blame for it?	situation?

Why have I failed to resolve it?	What am I assuming about it?
What does that mean about me?	What else is possible here?
What should I do about it?	What resources do I already have
Who ought to solve it for me?	which I can bring to bear?
What if it can't be solved?	What example is there of something like this that I have previously succeeded with?
	What is the next step?

Which set of questions are the most useful ones to ask? Which ones leave you feeling more resourceful, that something can be done, that there is a potential solution? Yes, people do have problems. And yes, we do need to start from where they are at before moving on. We shall explore the setting of outcomes in more detail in Chapter 4 on gathering information.

However, there are three things that need to be in place before we can even begin to move in the direction of getting our goals met:

- *motivation* – we believe that the goal is achievable and worthwhile. We *want* to get there
- *means* – we know which resources we need to achieve it. We know *how* to get there
- *opportunity* – we can deal with any interference. We have a *chance* to get there.

Some people may want to get there, but may not know how to, or may not believe that they have a chance to do so. We can help them with the means and the opportunity. Others may know how to, and have the chance to, but they just don't want to! It can sometimes be comfortable staying as we are, letting someone else (e.g. the doctor) sweat about providing the motivation. Robert Dilts has put together the following general model for change.

We start from our *present state* – where we are right now, the problem as formulated. We then set up our *desired state* – our potential solution, our goal, where we want to end up. In order to get there, two things must happen. First, we must remove any *interference* that prevents us from reaching our target. Secondly, we must add the necessary *resources*. Remember that this all happens within the framework of the patient's existing *beliefs* about him- or herself and the world. Finally we must add *ecology* – the study of consequences, what will happen if the goal is actually met or not.

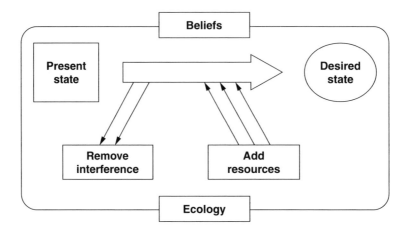

Figure 2.4: NLP model of change.

Over the next few chapters we shall find numerous ways not only to deal with the possible types of interference, but also to add resources at the appropriate *logical level*.

Consulting with NLP

We are going to draw this chapter to a close by having a look at a flow diagram (*see* Figure 2.5) which gives a useful overview of how you can use NLP to promote change within the consultation. This is a model that has been used extensively in business and education with excellent results, and is now being utilised with equal vigour in therapeutic and health contexts. It is a model which sits very comfortably with all of the other models of the medical consultation to date. And in fact all of your current skills and favourite approaches can be nested within it. The beauty of the NLP approach is that it *adds* to the choices which you already have. You don't have to give up anything. The rest of this book will put the meat on to the skeleton's bones.

The main aspects of each stage are summarised below. We shall cover them in depth in succeeding chapters.

1   *Your state* – your own state of mind and body – how you are in yourself before you start – is so important that we shall devote an entire section to this in Chapter 3 on initiating the consultation. And of course your state at the end of each consultation, and between consultations, is worth paying attention to as well.

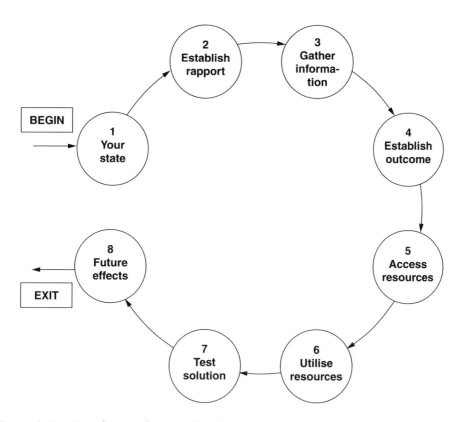

Figure 2.5:   Consulting with NLP (adapted from Ian McDermott).

2   *Rapport* – this is vital to any flowing consultation. Rapport needs to be
maintained throughout the consulting process, at *every* stage. And not only
the current consultation – it can be built up and deepened over a series of
consultations.
3   *Gathering information* – high-quality information about how this person
structures their experience of illness and disease will allow you to find the
levers for effective change. We need to pay particular attention to patients'
health beliefs and expectations and, of course, to both their verbal and non-
verbal communications.
4   *Outcomes* – you must find out what your patients really want for this
situation – their outcomes – and what you want, too! Both can be dovetailed
together. Specific outcomes can be set for achievement over one consultation
or, by a process of review, over several consultations.
5   *Access resources* – what does this particular person need now in order to
best get what they want? Which resources fit the bill? Perhaps they simply

need more information, or a particular kind of intervention, or maybe onward referral.

6   *Utilise resources* – no matter what resources are potentially available, they need to be brought to bear on the current situation. You must use your explanation and planning skills to give this information sensitively in a way that best fits the patient's unique worldview. There are myriad ways to do this, and you will find examples in every chapter.

7   *Test solution* – have you and your patient successfully achieved your outcomes? Has there been a significant difference in the patient's condition? Matching up where we want to go with the evidence that we have actually got there means that what we have done has worked. If it hasn't, you need to know that, too, so that you can do something different.

8   *Future effects* – whatever you do in the consulting room, the proof of the pudding is in the external world of future actions and behaviours. Does the patient actually take their prescribed medication? Has their behaviour really changed? Are they doing things differently? You will find out one way or the other on their return.

These are the eight stages that NLP has used over the years with excellent results. In the real world, all of these stages flow into one another, and may loop recursively back on themselves prior to successfully concluding. You may complete them all in a single consultation, or you may find that they spread out over several consultations, each aspect coming to the fore at the appropriate time. As we explore each phase of the consultation in the succeeding chapters, you can use this flow diagram as a framework in which to connect the detailed skills.

CHAPTER 3

Initiating the session

Introduction

A patient's perspective

Picture the scene, if you will. Jean, a 35-year-old mother of two, is in the rather full waiting-room. It is now some 20 minutes past her appointment time. She wonders what is keeping the doctor. The last patient seems to be taking ages. It is nearly lunchtime, and the kids are due home from school soon. She looks at her watch with a pained expression, and she rehearses what she is going to say – problems with her periods, coming twice a month, irregular, a real nuisance. And the spasms in her stomach – a tight knot, coming and going. Bloated, and a sick feeling. And the rows with her husband. Are they connected? She feels an answering spasm. Should she mention this, or not?

'Mrs Williams?' And in she goes, as a tearful patient brushes by on the way out. The doctor looks a bit distracted, harassed even. 'Hold on a sec,' he says, as he finishes off at the computer, a few hasty keystrokes. The phone rings. He answers it. Jean looks around and sees the large pile of notes on the floor behind him. An in-tray stacked high, its papers balancing precariously. Two coffee cups on the bookshelf.

'Sorry, sorry ... what can I do for you?' She looks briefly at the floor, takes a breath and starts to tell him about her periods. After a short time he interrupts mid-sentence. 'Twice a month ... ? How many days do you bleed ... ? Any bleeding after intercourse ... ?'

A bit thrown by the rapid fire, she says 'No, not after sex.' And inside she thinks '*how could it be? That's part of the problem.*' She looks up and he's already back at the computer. She decides to save the stomach knot for another day ...

An apocryphal tale? Maybe, or maybe not. When consultations start badly and then fade, there are a number of potential causes – failing to disconnect adequately from the last patient, poor initial rapport, interrupting the patient too early, before she's told her story, focusing on the first issue that arises, to the detriment of other perhaps more significant issues, or failing to elicit underlying concerns.

We shall concentrate on the remedies in due course. But next ...

A doctor's perspective

Beginnings are important, very important. And each patient consultation is a new beginning, both for them and for you. A good beginning and everything starts to flow well. A poor beginning ... well! I'm sure that, like me, you can remember times when you wish you could have started all over again. Times when you have not been entirely focused on the patient in front of you, for a variety of reasons. Maybe the previous consultation was an emotionally trying one, and you feel drained already. Perhaps you have had several like this in a row. Maybe you have taken a telephone call in between patients and you are still mulling over the new information. Or you are running late and that particular 'heart-sink' is next in line. You know, the one who insists on telling their tale in extreme detail from beginning to end, together with what their old 'granny' used to say thrown in for good measure. You may be contemplating missing coffee. Or worse still lunch!

At times like these our minds seem to be far away from the task in hand. There is that feeling of frustration, even irritation, or worse, combined with a chattering inner dialogue telling us what we *ought* to do, *should* do, definitely *must not* do, etc. I'm sure that you get the picture by now.

And yet there are times, probably less fleeting than we initially think, when things start off and continue really well, consultations that really flow. There are patients with whom I remember having an almost *instant rapport*. You can probably remember such ones, too. I can see them in my mind's eye again now – times when internal chatter seems to cease, or we are unaware of it, the focus of attention being entirely on the other person, time forgotten about (at least for a spell). A deeper felt sense of connection, of almost intuitively doing the right thing, making the right diagnosis, saying the right words – a state of mind and body that sports people would call being *in the zone*. The type of inner alignment that helps us to tap into our resources almost effortlessly. And afterwards, the satisfaction of knowing that we made a difference, we performed well, and we lived up to the best of our potential.

So what would it be like if you had more frequent access to your states of *consulting flow*? What differences for the better would that make for you *and* your patients? What if you had a simple process, available at your fingertips, which would allow you to be increasingly in the right state at the right time? How would that enhance your looking forward to your next series of consultations? Of course, only you can make the decision as to whether to utilise this right now.

Aims of this chapter

So what is it that we want to achieve in this opening phase? The consultation actually starts *before* the patient even comes in through the door. We must therefore ensure that we are well prepared prior to their entry. Then, whilst focusing on the initial stages of developing rapport, we move on to identifying the reasons for this particular patient's attendance here today.

So what are the skills involved in this phase? They include the following.

Section One: your state

- Accessing and having repeatedly to hand a *consulting flow state.*
- The ability to 'break state' or *go neutral.* This is particularly useful if you are already stuck in a negative state.

Section Two: getting connected

- Developing the ability to go quickly and deeply into a state of *rapport* with anyone you meet.
- Special tips for connecting with children.
- The way your room is set up, and how it influences consulting.

Section Three: initiating

- Allowing patients time to make their *opening statement*, identifying all relevant issues.
- Using a *backtrack frame* to help to establish a mutually agreed agenda.
- Initial attunement to *non-verbal communication* (NVC), calibrating to and eliciting *yes-sets*.

Section One: your state

Preparation

There are several things that we need to consider between the ending of one consultation and the beginning of another. It is really important – indeed vital – to finish off the mental and physical tasks left over from the previous patient, or at least to put them on hold. The next patient deserves our full and undivided attention without any residual clutter. We may need to take care of our own comfort needs. We must certainly also ensure that we have the necessary notes, documentation or computer record available. This is as far as most authorities on the consultation go. However there is, I believe, something even more important.

And that is having a method that allows us easily and repeatedly to enter and re-enter a state of *consulting flow*. Just like the times when we know, intuitively, that we are performing at our best, times when it all flows easily, times when we know that we have made a deep, meaningful connection, so much so that it becomes an *automatic* accompaniment every time we consult, just like using your stethoscope or auriscope – instantly available at the tip of your fingers.

Just think about it now. When you look down your consultation list for the morning or afternoon, there may be many names. Some of them you know, and some you don't. Some you like well, while others ... well, to put it nicely, they may be 'challenging'! And *your* internal state may change appreciably depending on whose name your eyes alight on. Isn't it interesting how one name can have such an effect? And they're not even in the room yet.

Yet among those names there are those whom you look forward to meeting. It may be because of the memory of previous successful encounters. Perhaps a particular look on their face, or a twinkle in their eye, maybe the sound of their voice, or the kind of things they say, and the way in which they say them. Maybe you have built up a strong relationship that encompasses a deep-felt sense of rapport over many years, or maybe over just a short period of time. Perhaps there are many trials and tribulations that you have faced successfully together, storms that you have weathered. No matter what has gone before, you know that each time you meet there is a strong, really strong feeling of connection.

So what would it be like if you could look forward to starting off each consultation, with every patient you see, no matter who they are, having already tapped into this state? If you were able to give them your full attention in a relaxed yet focused way? If you were able to connect deeply, to tune into their wavelength, to see eye to eye? Is that something that you are interested in? Would that be a useful way to begin?

As we shall go on to see and experience, the *consulting flow state* is really an amalgam of several different types of state, each of which is pertinent to different phases of the consultation. And in time we shall be adding different states, with different qualities and differing effects. However, as the ability to *make an immediate connection* is so vital at this stage – so important as a foundation for what is to follow – we shall concentrate initially on states of rapport.

Please give yourself 10 minutes to go through the following exercise. Allow yourself the freedom to participate fully, in the knowledge that this will have a major and continuing beneficial effect on all of your future consultations.

Exercise 4:   Consulting Flow state – initial rapport

1   Think of a patient with whom you know that you have a deep level of rapport, someone that you have an *instant connection* with as soon as they come into your room, or perhaps a friend or family member with the same quality of connection.

2   Now think of a time when you were last with that person, a *specific instance* that you can remember clearly. Perhaps it was in the recent past, maybe further back. It is important that this memory begins to *re-connect* you now to the feelings you were having then.

3   Now imagine yourself fully back in that experience as if it is happening here and now. *Step right into it*, and wrap it all around you. See what you're seeing in the experience, hear what you're hearing, and allow the feelings to grow and spread all over your body with every breath you take. It may help to imagine the picture being *bigger, brighter, more colourful* and *closer*. Adjust the volume of the sounds until it feels just right.

4   Now you can set your anchor or trigger. While you are fully in that state:
   • choose a word or phrase that best typifies that state – for example, 'flow' or 'deep connection' or some other word that fits for you. *Say* it in a particular way that fits the state (e.g. '*floooooowwwww*')
   • choose a *visual trigger*, something that is always in that situation – for example, the chair that the patient sits on, the door of your room, the carpet on the floor, etc. Make it even more specific by focusing in on part of the finer detail of the chosen object – perhaps a particular pattern that catches your eye
   • now choose the *kinaesthetic trigger* – something that you don't usually do, such as squeezing the tip of your index finger or knuckle

with your other hand. Time this to coincide with the peak of the feeling.

You can *repeat all of the above several times*, ensuring that you are fully associated into the memory each time. This will condition the response even more fully.

5   Once conditioned, you can mentally rehearse using your triggers just prior to future consultations. Imagine yourself in your consulting room as you prepare to meet your next patient. *Imagine using your triggers*, really stepping into the experience as if it is happening now. This will help you to remember to use your triggers at the right time.

6   Remember to *use your triggers consistently*! The more you practise this short ritual, the more easily it will become second nature, happening *automatically*, without your thinking about it consciously. You will then find yourself increasingly able to *connect effectively* with anyone who comes through your door!

Once you have mastered having the state of rapport at your fingertips, you can add other useful states to the same trigger (*see* Appendix 1 for a list). You might like to practise now with states such as curiosity, calmness, confidence, enthusiasm, fun, pleasure, etc. The more positive states of well-being you add, the better you will feel in every consultation. Repeat the exercise now with these states. We shall revisit this topic in Chapter 5 on building relationships, adding more depth to *consulting flow*.

So what happens if, having done the exercise, you are one of those people who have found that your triggers don't *yet* have the desired effect? Do you simply give up now because it has not yet worked? After all, you've tried it at least once! There are four main reasons why anchors may not work immediately.

1   The memory or event you chose did not have *sufficient emotional intensity*. It is important to step fully into a specific event which has strong feelings of rapport associated with it. The stronger the state, the better the effect.

2   You only did it once! This exercise benefits from *repeated practice*. Five to ten repetitions sufficiently close together will build a strong stable state.

3   The timing of the trigger was too early or too late. Too early and the state is not strong enough. Too late and you are already going out of the state. The trigger should be set *as the state peaks* and begins to plateau.

4   You may have been trying to fire your trigger in a situation in which you are already in some negative emotion, such as anger, upset, deep concern

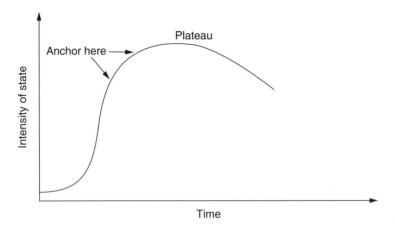

Figure 3.1:   Anchoring states.

or irritation. These negative states may be so strong that they overwhelm the state you wish to develop.

Because any state – positive or negative, empowering or disempowering – can be anchored and triggered it is important, if you want to be in the right state at the right time, to be aware of the laws of state sequencing. You must *disconnect* from any strongly negative state first before using your trigger. Otherwise your positive anchor may be neutralised by more intense negative emotions. Even worse, because the laws of associative conditioning (Pavlov) apply to all states, you could find, over time, that your trigger for rapport, contaminated by these other states, actually triggers the negative state instead. This is definitely *not* what you want. You may even conclude that the whole process simply doesn't work when it is actually working perfectly well, in reverse – the opposite direction to the one you intended!

So what is the answer to this potential conundrum? The answer is to ensure that you have a mechanism for a *break-state*, to allow the setting of a neutral state – a state which can consistently interrupt any negative feeling, quickly, easily and effectively. So how do people do this?

One way is to *change your physiology*, your posture or position by movement. I know of one GP who, after a difficult consultation, stands up, goes into a karate stance and performs two or three brisk moves. Within less than ten seconds his state changes significantly. Turning your eyes and head upwards to look at the ceiling, with a big grin on your face, is another simple yet powerful action that disconnects strong feelings. Remember that no one can see you when you are alone!

You can also use your *mental images*, thoughts and sounds. Laughter is a very potent state changer. What is the punch-line of your favourite joke? Who is your favourite comedian? Which funny incident from your past made you fall down laughing? Who could you imagine having a custard pie thrown in their face? The more outrageous the thought, especially when accompanied by larger-than-life internal visual images, the more effective the state change. Try it and see.

Exercise 5:   A break-state anchor

1   Allow yourself to be in the *here and now*. Look at and name several objects in your vicinity. Listen to the sounds in the room. Feel the touch of your feet on the floor, your back against the chair. Ensure that you are in a *neutral* state before moving on to the next step.

2   Think of what you are going to use as a *break-state*. If it is a joke, relive the punch-line whilst vividly picturing the scene. Say it out loud in your mind. If you are using a specific movement or series of steps, imagine doing it *right now*.

3   As you enter and *deepen the state*, choose a word or short phrase as an auditory trigger. Make a picture that typifies the scene. Squeeze one of your other fingers or knuckles. Use a *different* one to the rapport anchor.

4   Now *mentally rehearse* using this trigger. Imagine having just finished a demanding consultation, finding yourself in a negative state. Imagine *using your trigger* and notice how it neutralises your feelings. See how it takes you easily out of what was less than optimal, now ready to move on.

Of course there is no point in having great anchors for these states unless you begin, and then continue, to utilise them on a daily basis. You will find that after a short period of time it will seem as if these states trigger themselves automatically. The anchors will have passed into *unconscious competence,* like driving your car. This is an extremely important point. Initiating your consultations in this way provides an excellent foundation upon which to build a more satisfying patient encounter – for them and for you.

Section Two: getting connected

Initial rapport

Now that you have set up *your* initial states, it is time to invite the patient into your world. At the same time you need to get to know something about their world. So what would it be like if you could deepen your state of rapport, increase your chances of making a more immediate connection, and develop an atmosphere of therapeutic trust? And if you could do this within those very first moments of meeting? By hardly saying a word? Does this seem like a tall order?

As we saw earlier (*see* Chapter 2), a large amount of communication takes place at a non-verbal level, often out of our immediate conscious awareness. You can remember times when you have been out for an intimate meal, can you not? Perhaps at a favourite restaurant? As you think about it now, you can probably remember who you were with, the sounds, smells and tastes, and how you were feeling. And simply by looking around, you could tell which of the other diners were deeply in rapport ... or not!

People who are getting on very well tend to do similar things. Have you noticed how they often seem to be *mirror images* of one another? Their body movements and energy levels *synchronise* easily together. They may lean forwards or backwards slightly, moving at the same time. They tend to breathe at the same rate and depth. You may even hear that their voice qualities are similar, the tone, speed and volume of speech rising and falling in harmony.

And when you are in synchrony with another person's deeper rhythms you begin to communicate in a way that allows them to take in information more readily. This increases the likelihood that the message you send will be the one that they receive. It promotes the development of empathy, trust and comfort between people – just the kind of relationship that we seek with our patients.

Communication experts have found that the ability to establish a deep rapport very quickly is actually a highly learnable skill. So much so that, with a little practice, you will soon find yourself using these skills naturally, and not just in consultations, but also in every other context of your life.

So which particular skills should we focus on in the early consultation stages? The three main areas of rapport are *physiology, voice qualities* and the *words* that we use. We shall concentrate on the first two now, and deal with words more fully in Chapter 5 on building relationships.

Physiology

We have been *matching and mirroring* people's behaviour all our lives. It is a completely natural act, and is one of the predominant methods that we have used in learning, especially during our younger years. We learned to walk, talk and do so many other things automatically in this way, mimicking the behaviours of all those around us – family, friends, peer groups, our heroes, those we respect and look up to. Please take each of the sections that follow and try them out one at a time. Use them first in areas outwith the consultation – at coffee, lunch, casual meetings, more formal meetings, and in public places, such as waiting in line, airport lounges, hotels and restaurants where you can observe from a distance. You will then assimilate the skills even more easily.

Whole body matching and mirroring

This is when you adjust your body position, stance and posture to be close to those of the other person. Make it *similar* rather than an exact replica – a similar degree of head tilt, angle of body in the chair, legs crossed or uncrossed, but not too exact. If their legs are crossed at the knee, cross yours at the ankle. If they are slouching in their chair, lean back just a little. You can often get by with going to half of their position or posture. As you get better, often only a quarter is enough.

As the position of the other person changes you can adjust your own. Just allow a little time, perhaps a few seconds, between their moving and yours. Avoid quick jerky movements which can be distracting, the opposite of what you want. Move from one position to another in the most natural way you can, like a graceful dance with a partner.

Mirroring is simply reflecting back someone's posture and position as if *they* are looking at their own image in a mirror. If they lean to *their* right, you lean to *your* left. They cross left leg over right, you cross right leg over left. This is a very powerful developer of rapport.

Matching, on the other hand, is doing the *same* as someone. If they tilt their head to *their* right, you tilt your head to *your* right. They put their left hand to their left ear, you put your left hand to your chin. Why to your chin? Simply because you don't want to mimic them too precisely. Moving your hand in the general direction is often enough. Although it is perhaps less powerful than mirroring, matching may also be less obtrusive.

Part body matching

You can also establish rapport by matching *part* of the body – upper versus lower, or right versus left. Facial expressions are very easy to mirror back. Because you can't tell what your own facial expression is like (unless you carry a mirror!) you can reflect this back very effectively out of their conscious awareness.

Eye contact time is an interesting part of rapport. Too short or too long a time makes many people feel uncomfortable. Most of us have a *look-to-talk* rule. We have learned over the years to make eye contact regularly when either speaking or listening to the other person. If there is no eye contact then insufficient attention is being given.

However, a significant minority of individuals have a *look-away-to-talk* rule. They give much less eye contact time, and they may often be *inside their own heads* as it were, picturing what you are saying, and making sense of it in their own way. It is not that they are being rude, but simply the way in which they process information. The moral is therefore to match the eye contact time that others give you.

Breathing is something most of us do automatically, without thinking about it. Because we are so unaware of it, *matching* the rate and depth of breathing is one of the quickest and most effective ways to gain an almost instant rapport. However, don't stare at a patient's chest to find out how they are breathing! The clues are usually seen in the rise and fall of the shoulders. A give-away is that people only speak on the out-breath! Be very careful and do not attempt to match anyone with breathing difficulties or severe anxiety. As well as being uncomfortable, this can impact negatively on your own health. Use *cross-matching* instead (see below).

Many people use gestures to mark out time-frames, often to their left or behind them for the past, and to the right or in front for the future (*see* Figure 3.2). You can make use of this by gesturing to their past when talking about problems that they *had*, and gesturing to their future when talking about what they *want* instead. As you become more skilled, you will notice that patients may also use gestures to particular locations in space around them when talking about their beliefs, concerns, ideas and expectations (more on this later).

Whatever you do, do *not* go to the extreme of trying to match repetitive facial tics, small micro-movements or idiosyncratic patient mannerisms. This kind of mimicry will almost certainly be experienced as being disrespectful, thus destroying any rapport that you may have built up.

Caution! Health warning! These physiological rapport skills are extremely power-fully effective. When done well they can give an almost surprising inside view of

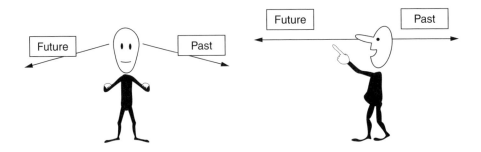

Figure 3.2:   Marking out time frames.

*people's feelings, emotions and internal states of mind and body. Do **not** use them with patients who are seriously unwell. This is especially important for those who have moderate to severe depression, breathing difficulties or major health challenges. The other types of rapport skills, such as cross-matching (see below) and verbal rapport (see Chapter 5 on building relationships), are more appropriate and just as effective.*

Cross-matching

Many doctors are intuitively good at achieving and sustaining rapport with their patients. However, some doctors may be too good for their own good! If you always feel for other people such that you take on their pain, feel run down, tired and stressed out after having seen three depressed patients in a row, and wonder if you are heading for burnout, then you may benefit from *stepping back* a little and using cross-matching. This skill will still allow you to generate good levels of rapport, but it is more protective of your own health and well-being.

Put simply, cross-matching involves using one aspect of your behaviour to match a different aspect of the other person's behaviour – for example, adjusting the tempo of your voice to match their breathing rate, or using head nods or finger movements to match their breathing in and out. I have a swivel chair in my consultation room, and I often match the patient's energy level by slight movements back and forth, speeding up or slowing down accordingly. And no, I have never fallen off, nor have I yet swivelled 360 degrees!

Exercise 6:   Matching and mirroring

Find a work colleague or friendly partner for this short exercise. If possible, get a third person as well so that you can each have a turn at observing.

1   Person 1 can *start talking about a favourite memory* from the past, perhaps a holiday destination or a sporting occasion that they enjoyed, or something else altogether.
2   Person 2 gets into rapport by *matching and mirroring* the physiological variables described above. Choose one or two to begin with, and add some more as you progress. Ask just enough questions to keep the other person involved in describing the memory, *keeping them talking*.
3   Person 3 (if available) takes a detached view, perhaps sitting a little further away. He simply observes and doesn't take part in the conversation.
4   Once in rapport, person 2 can then *start to mismatch* person 1 and see what effect this has – perhaps doing the opposite body movements, or looking away at the 'wrong' time. Do this in a *subtle* manner to start with and notice what happens to rapport. Also *notice how you feel* as you do this. Where in your body do you feel this?
5   Once you have mismatched enough to get the sense of what being out of rapport feels like, spend a minute or so *getting back deeply into rapport*, matching and mirroring again, before finishing your turn.
6   Debrief each position and swap round. Pay particular attention to describing the difference in feelings between being in and out of rapport.

You can use the following additional modifications and notice the different results.

* Find a topic that you *agree* upon. Discuss it whilst one person *mismatches* the other.
* Find a topic that you *dis-agree* on. Discuss it whilst one person *mirrors* the other.

From these exercises you will find that rapport depends not so much upon people agreeing verbally, but more on *matching and mirroring* posture and gesture, etc. It is quite possible to disagree verbally and eloquently whilst still being in total bodily rapport. This is a skill well worth mastering. In fact, when it is done in this way many people find a deeper appreciation of the other person's position, beliefs and ideas without compromising their own. It can lay the foundation for a meeting of minds from which a third way, a new perspective on the situation, can emerge.

Margaret's tale

I remember quite vividly coming back from a course on rapport skills, eager to try out my new learnings. You probably know that feeling. Anyway, Margaret was a woman in her early sixties who had been coming to see me intermittently for several months, with often quite non-specifically vague symptoms, a general 'tiredness all the time, doctor'. Yet her blood profile was normal and she denied any underlying anxiety or depression. She had lost interest in some of her usual pursuits, and wondered what life still held for her, but she wasn't keen about a trial of antidepressant medication or onward consultant referral.

During this particular consultation, after some very general statements, she sighed and sat almost semi-slumped, looking down to her right, breathing slowly, a far-away look in her eyes, saying nothing at all. I resisted the temptation to jump into the opening yawning chasm of silence with words of my own, although I found that difficult! I *mirrored* her posture, *breathed* at the same rate as her and *defocused* my eyes in the same way. After what seemed to be an eternity, yet was probably less than a minute, I began to feel a deep sadness, like a heavy weight over my heart, with a sense of intense blackness. A feeling of profound loss enveloped me. She had not moved, nor had she said any words, during this silent exchange.

I took my courage in both hands and said '*I don't know what's true for your experience at this moment, yet personally I have a feeling of deep grief, a sense of black mourning. Does that make any sense at all?*' Almost immediately she burst into tears, which developed in to wracking childlike sobs which persisted for two or three minutes. My initial thought was 'Oh shit! I am never going to try anything like that ever again!'

The sobs gradually quietened, and Margaret began to speak, haltingly at first, and then in more of a rush. She told me about being abroad in the early 1950s, suffering a mid-trimester miscarriage, her first and only pregnancy, and almost losing her own life as well with the subsequent sepsis. She described the intense feelings of guilt, that she had done something wrong, that she was to blame, and the dawning realisation that she would always be childless, with no family of her own. Had this been some sort of punishment? And there was no mention of it anywhere in her medical record because it had happened abroad.

Subsequently, after this seeming catharsis of previously unprocessed grief, she regained her interests and developed a new purpose for her retirement years. Her visits were infrequent, and when she did consult the issues were usually quite straightforward.

Now this is not to say that matching and mirroring in this way always gets profound results. Yet it can be surprising just how much information is transferred non-verbally. At the very least I have found that it can foster the development of a genuinely empathic encounter.

Voice qualities

You may have already noticed that when you are in rapport with someone there are many aspects of your voice that match, particularly, tone, tempo, timbre and volume.

When matching someone's *tone* of voice you need to pay attention to the pitch. If they speak in a high-pitched voice, then whatever you do, don't strain in a falsetto to match it. Or if their voice is low-pitched, don't speak from the soles of your boots. Pitch is relative, so just slightly increase or decrease your normal pitch in the direction of the other person – a little change means a lot.

The *tempo* or speed of speech is *very* important. For those who speak fast it can be almost agonising waiting for a slow speaker to ... get ... the ... words ... out. Those who normally speak slowly may literally find themselves lost or confused trying to understand a faster speaker. We tend to process information in our minds at the same rate that we speak, so listen to the patient and match their speed.

The *timbre* of speech is the degree of raspiness or clarity of pronunciation. Some people are crystal clear, almost like a newsreader. Others are very gruff and throaty. Some people *emphasise* certain words, while others roll them all together. Just listen to how they say it rather than going for a direct match which may be too much like mimicry.

The *volume* of speech is its degree of loudness. Some people have voices like a soft little mouse, whilst others roar like a lion. The timid little miss who comes to tell you about her problem, head down, speaking so softly, is going to find your normal conversational voice like a painful bellow. The sergeant major, on the other hand, may think that you lack conviction!

Of all of these aspects of voice quality, the two most important ones to match are *tempo* and *volume*. If you get these right, the rest will follow. You only have to start off the consultation in this way, for you will find that, as you continue, you will both move towards a comfortable mid-range.

Exercise 7:   Voice matching

1   Find yourself a willing partner and arrange to *sit back to back*. This will help you to concentrate on vocal cues with less visual distraction.
2   Person 1 says a short sentence in their *normal speaking voice* – for example, their name and address, or something they like to do.
3   Person 2 *repeats* it back, word for word, paying attention to *matching* as many voice qualities as possible.
4   If you have the help of a third person, they can give you feedback and coaching on how to *match even more closely*.
5   When you get it right, the other person is likely to feel a certain *sense of connection*, probably in their chest or abdomen. Notice this feeling. It is your reliable indicator of rapport. After this, swap round.

When you are in rapport there are certain subtle, yet definite signs that let you know you are there. Many people get an *internal feeling*, often in their chest or abdomen. It may be described as a warmth, openness or lightness – a resonance. For some it may be slightly different, although generally most people agree that this is usually the first signal they consistently experience. It is usually accompanied, shortly thereafter, by a moderate *facial flush*. You may often notice this in the other person around the time when they take a *deeper breath* than usual. This is followed by a feeling of *knowingness*, meaning that you have a sense of having known this person for a long time. This is often most marked when you meet a stranger for the first time, connect deeply, and they say the immortal words 'Are you sure we haven't met somewhere before?'. And you both rack your brains, searching for a non-existent memory.

In NLP the whole process of gaining rapport is called *pacing*. It is almost like walking a few steps in the other person's shoes. When you are pacing well you will soon find that if you move your position or posture, or perhaps change your rate of breathing, they will follow suit. This is called *leading*, and it opens up a space of mutual influence, a zone in which both parties can more easily explore not only problems, but also possibilities for solutions.

Jimmy's tale

Jimmy had not long arrived from Glasgow. Registered with one of my partners, he was known to have abused various drugs in the past, although his case records had not yet caught up with his transfer. He had consulted my partner a few days previously and obtained a supply of painkillers for a continuing musculoskeletal chest pain after a fall about three weeks previously. He was back to tell me that they weren't strong enough, and he winced with pain as he dragged himself into my consulting room. He was unshaven and unkempt, with eyes that darted everywhere.

I examined his chest thoroughly, concluding that he had a minor muscular problem that was almost resolved, the prescribed painkillers being appropriate for his needs. I had no sooner informed him of this when he became exceedingly belligerent, his voice raised and his tone harsh.

'Call yourself a f***ing doctor!? These f***ing tablets are NO f***ing use. Give me some f***ing stronger ones, NOW!,' he snarled.

I matched his voice tone, volume and energy, and replied: *'You're RIGHT! I am the f***ing doctor. And these f***ing tablets ARE the right ones for you. Now this consultation is OVER, here's the door!'* He flashed a malevolent look before exiting bemusedly.

I discussed this incident with one of my partners over coffee, wondering if I had gone too far and whether the inevitable letter of complaint would follow. Then I forgot about it until the next week, when I noticed Jimmy was on my morning consultation list. He breezed in, looking quite respectable:

'Sorry to trouble you, doc. I just wondered if I could transfer to your list.'

I was taken aback, and said: *'I'm amazed at your request. I shouted and swore at you last week, told you to get out, yet you want to join my list?'*

'Yes doc,' he replied. *'You speak my language, you understand me. You call a spade a spade. You're like my last GP in Glasgow. He used to swear all the time. We got on great!'*

So I agreed.

Now I wouldn't want you to run away with the idea that I swear at patients all the time. Heaven forbid. However, in this instance, it was an *automatic response* that yielded some interesting results. Jimmy still has major alcohol problems, still tries it on with many people, yet he has tempered his behaviour markedly, at least when with me.

Rapport with children

How do you find yourself connecting with children? Is it easy, or not yet? Although they are not mini-adults, much of what we have covered so far can be adapted to fit all ages, from small pre-verbal children to adolescents. Let us take each of the main sections, *physiology* and *voice*, and explore what we can do.

Physiology

Body movements, facial features, posture and gesture become more and more important the younger a child is. This is because these are their main communication channels. You will know already, if you have children of your own, that in infants, using your own facial movements to *mirror* back exactly what they do allows them to fixate their attention on you. It's amazing how you can then change your expression and they change with you! Even if their faces are screwed up and crying, you can begin to lead them where you want to go by pacing first. Try it out in your next 8-week or 8-month assessment.

In children of all ages it is important to get down to their eye level, and address most of your comments directly to them. Looming large can seem overpowering or even overwhelming. Sometimes it is useful to go *below* their eye level to start off with if they appear timid, and then gradually to 'work your way up'.

Young children under 5 years of age tend to wriggle around a lot. They don't stay still unless they are either petrified or seriously ill. Even if you are not the kind of person who moves around a lot yourself, it's a good idea to wriggle about a bit in your own chair. Since they often sinuously contort their bodies in opposite directions with regard to arms and legs, you can do the same. If you match their facial expressions exactly, at the same time, you will quickly establish rapport – especially looking away and then back again, and exaggerating your head tilts, even if it seems a bit like being a ham actor. Forget the parents – they will be far more appreciative of your efforts to build a relationship with their child.

Many people use objects such as pens, auriscope lights or even toys to fixate and even distract attention. In younger children, making a humming or *zzzsssing* kind of noise as you examine their ears can result in them keeping surprisingly still. And of course the classic, when using your stethoscope, is to wonder out loud just what message *that* tummy or *that* chest has for us today. You can keep children mesmerised for ages while you are waiting to hear the answer. During which time you will have been able to perform the appropriate clinical examination.

Voice

The same rules apply for children as for adults. Match the speed and volume of speech first. However, at the same time, increase the relative pitch of your voice. Not a falsetto, just relatively higher than normal. Imagine that you are making the speech resonance come from the soft palate, at the back of your nose, and you will get the correct effect.

Children can often be ungrammatical in what they say and how they say it. You can match this right back, even if the parents give you an odd look. Younger children, who are starting to speak, are more apt to have two-word utterances. Use the same. Remember to direct most of your comments to the child, even if you are talking to their parents.

Jenny's tale

Jenny, aged three, had had a nasty herpetic mouth infection. She had screamed and bawled when my partner saw her, refusing to allow an examination. Even at the hospital she had become upset whenever anyone appeared to be about to examine her. Now discharged home, her parents had been told to bring her to me for a 'check-up'.

She started crying as soon as she came into the room, burying her head in her mother's bosom, with occasional furtive, frightened glances. I spoke to her parents for a while, watching her out of the corner of my eye. Then she stuck her finger up her nostril and began 'excavating'! Almost simultaneously I did the exact same thing, mirroring her, and said *'I bet I can get my finger further up than you can.'*

After a few goes to see who had 'won', she was smiling and laughing at this rather crude behaviour by an adult. Her parents did look a little disgusted at first, but when I was easily able to examine her mouth and she left in much better spirits, with lots of waving goodbye, they were smiling happily, too. A deep rapport had been re-established.

And the moral of this? Be adventurous. You can always say sorry if it doesn't work out.

Environmental rapport

It is useful to think about how the room in which you consult can be arranged to increase your ability to obtain a more immediate, deep connection. Gone are the days when the patient sat at the other side of a large imposing desk, often in a less grand and lower chair. Most doctors recognise the sense of openness created by adjacent chairs, positioned at an angle of 90 to 120 degrees to each other, allowing patient and doctor to engage in eye contact when necessary, yet with the freedom to look away comfortably.

But are you a left- or right-hand consulter? By that I mean is the patient to your right or your left? Did you choose the position you have, or was it a legacy of room inheritance? We are usually more comfortable with one particular set-up. Yet exploring other positions, although initially uncomfortable, may yield valuable patient information. Often surprisingly so, especially in situations labelled as '*stuck*' or '*here we go again*'. Very occasionally I have sat in the patient's chair with them in mine. The different perspective is not only physical. Mental thought patterns can change, too, with intuitive insights coming to the fore. Not always, however!

Pick a time when you are not consulting, and you have a few spare moments to hand, and go and sit in the patient's chair. Notice how they might see things. To what is your attention drawn? On what do your eyes alight? Are there distracting piles of notes behind your own chair? Are the work surfaces tidy or littered with papers? Is your desk ready for action or are multiple objects shouting for help? If there is a window, who can see in and what can be seen looking out? Is this distracting or not? What about the décor? Are the walls, carpets and furnishings easy on the eye? Or do the threadbare strands jump out? Are the posters on your walls modern or ancient?

Of course, all of this may well be out of your conscious awareness and that of your patient, but at some level it does impact. What first impressions do you want your surroundings to create? There are no rights and wrongs, yet it may be salutary to visit the other consulting rooms in the vicinity. Do they reflect the personality of their owner?

Going by the name of *psychogeography*, it is interesting to note how our room set-up may enhance or detract from the underlying messages that we wish to impart, especially in the realms of rapport. I encourage you to experiment with your room. You can always put it back the same way later, if you want.

Summary thus far

Up to now we seem to have spent a considerable amount of time covering what in reality will take place during the first few moments of the consultation. Yet beginnings are so important that it is really worthwhile striving to get them right. Without the ability to put aside your last task, get into the best possible frame of mind for the next patient, and develop an immediate positive feeling of connection, the ensuing ten minutes or so can be less than satisfactory for both parties.

Rather than practising these skills during the consultation itself, when you might feel self-conscious or uncomfortable, you can split them up into *mini-skills* and try them out elsewhere. Casual conversation, where there is little at stake, is often the best arena. Try out your rapport skills in the public domain. Notice, as an observer, whether other couples or groups are matching and mirroring or not. Watch television chat shows and see if the host has well-refined skills. Listen to their voice qualities and imagine saying the same thing in the same tonality and tempo.

We shall be coming back to and covering other aspects of rapport at the logical levels of capability, beliefs and values and even identity in Chapter 5 on building relationships. The ability to break rapport elegantly will be dealt with in Chapter 7 on closing the session.

Section Three: initiating

Next we need to move on to dealing effectively with patients' opening statements, *backtracking* to establish their *agenda,* and our initial forays into the nuances of non-verbal communication, especially eliciting a *yes-set.*

Opening statements

The patient's opening remarks in response to your question 'How can I help today?' (or however else you get things going) set the scene for the rest of the consultation. Doctors, with perceived pressures of time among other things, are keen to get to the heart of *why* this particular patient has presented with this particular problem *today,* and *what* can be done about it. Sometimes we jump in, catch the ball and run with it for quite some distance before we realise that we are heading the wrong way. Or sometimes we find that we are not even on the same playing field – often at the end of the consultation time, when the patient tells us what the *real* problem is! Very frustrating.

We tend to be very good at interrupting our patients early in the consultation, often to clarify a point or get quickly to the root of an issue. However, we may inadvertently take over the floor while the patient is forced to adopt a more passive role, being shepherded through the next ten minutes or so to our agenda rather than to theirs. And, of course, the evidence suggests that the order in which patients present their problems may not be related to their clinical importance, so we may not even get to the heart of the main issue.

Although patients may have a good idea of just which problems they want to discuss today, what they actually do discuss is tempered by many factors, not least of which are the many non-verbal signals that are exchanged during the first few seconds of meeting. A long prior wait, an overrunning clinic, a filled-to-capacity waiting-room, and a peremptory 'Yes!' while the doctor furtively finishes off the last patient's notes, looking harassed, mean that the difficult-to-broach issue may well be shelved ... yet again.

The real skill in effective openings lies in allowing the patient to have their say, from beginning to end, without interruption. Wait a minute, you may be thinking, that sounds scary, even overwhelming! Yet the vast majority of patients take less than 60 seconds to get their cards on the table, so to speak. And even those who are encouraged to go on, with 'ums', 'ahs' and their non-verbal equivalents, generally dry up before 150 seconds. The uninterrupted whole containing all of the information that is required for the rest of the allotted time markedly minimises the end-of-consultation 'By the way, doc, what I really came for was ...', or variants thereof.

Much has been written about effective listening, yet to my mind without giving practical concrete tips about *how* to do it effectively. We tend to fall into the trap of being distracted inside our own minds, listening to our own thoughts and formulating our own questions. And what is the cost of this? Missing the important pieces of information that are right under our noses. There are several ways to keep our attention focused on the outside. We shall deal with two now, and explore additional ways in Chapter 5 on building relationships.

Many people equate listening with simply sitting doing nothing. However, it is important to convey to the patient that you are listening attentively. This is an active process which is generally signalled through our non-verbal behaviour. We have actually already dealt with all of the behavioural level skills necessary for this to happen now. The process of *matching and mirroring* is the key here.

As the patient makes their opening statement, you can simply pay attention to one or more of the areas addressed above. As they are talking, you can notice their posture, their gestures as they signal both problems and potential solutions, and their breathing rate. You can take the time to gently *match and mirror* in the knowledge that as patients' beliefs, concerns, ideas and expectations are often presented *non-verbally*, you are already picking up on these intuitively, while you also listen to their words. You are, of course, deepening the level of rapport simultaneously so that by the end of the opening statement the patient will feel well heard, and will know that you have an understanding of the situation, developing a genuine empathy.

There is another method that I have found very useful, although it may seem a little odd on first hearing, and that is developing the ability to repeat simultaneously, *inside your own head*, exactly what the patient is saying! Not only does this keep you attentively focused on *them*, in the here and now, thereby minimising your other internal distractions, it is also a great way to deepen rapport. A by-product is that it helps you to become more acutely aware of their voice characteristics, especially volume and tempo, so that when you do start speaking, you are already tuned into their wavelength. You are also more aware of pauses, sighs, coughs, idiosyncratic sounds, and *emphasis on certain words*, thus obtaining far more information about underlying emotional issues than you may have thought possible.

You can easily develop this ability away from the consultation initially. Once again a good place is the television chat show, or a conversation between two other people in which you are a casual listener, or another conversation in which there is no major emotional investment. Simply repeat in your mind, simultaneously with the other person, their exact words. Imagining that you are also now stepping into their shoes as you do this, trying them on for size, will accelerate your skills acquisition. Just a little practice will reap great rewards.

Backtracks, yes-sets and agenda setting

Having listened attentively to the patient's opening statement, ensuring that they have had a full opportunity to divulge their concerns, we need to let them know that we have both heard *and* understood them accurately – hence *backtracking*, the repeating back verbatim of their main concerns. When you do this in a way that fully communicates your understanding, it will elicit the patient's *yes-set*, which is the way in which they show, verbally and non-verbally, their congruent agreement. You can then construct a mutual *agenda* for consideration in the time available.

Backtracking

When people tell you certain things about themselves, the words that they use are not picked purely at random. The words used are personally meaningful in a way that is only truly known by them. By this I mean that although all words have a general, common usage and meaning according to a dictionary, we each have different reference experiences attached to them. For example, words which express values, such as love, integrity, peace, etc., are sufficiently abstract for each of us to read into them our own meanings as manifested by our behaviours. We may each say the same word but *mean* something slightly or even markedly different.

So where are we heading with this? Well, there is a vogue for paraphrasing what people say. That is, we attempt to demonstrate our understanding by repeating back what they say in our own words. However, that is patently *not* what they said, no matter how close we think it is. The words that they use are their own 'hot' words for their condition. Effective *backtracking* is really better done as *parrot-phrasing* rather than as paraphrasing. Say *their* words back to *them*.

For example:

Patient: Well, doctor, I've had these pains in my chest, burning pains like a load of red-hot coals. For months. And I flatulise a lot. Smells terrible, doctor! My husband says it's like rotten fish.
Doctor: Uhu ...
Patient: It's worse in me bed at night. Do you think it's acid?
Doctor: Tell me a bit more first ...
Patient: Well, my mother had acid ... but she didn't flatulise. They said she had a hernia. Do you think I've got the same?
Doctor: Well, let me check if I've got this right. You've had burning pains ... (pauses for nod, i.e. yes-set) ... in your chest ... like red-hot coals ... and you flatulise (said with a straight face) ... like rotten fish ... worst at night ... and you wonder if it's acid ... a hernia ... like your mother ...
Patient: Yes! That's it ... (vigorous head nod).

We can enter the patient's world more effectively by using their words in the way that they use them. As with everything else, though, always stop short of mimicry. The above dialogue also demonstrates *yes-sets*.

Yes-sets

It is extremely useful to calibrate to a patient's *yes* early in the consultation. This gives you a measure of their congruent agreement with your shared management plan later on, or not. If you don't have a full *yes* ... that's right, you've got a no! Or at best a maybe.

Of course you don't have to be like a used-car salesman who's recently been to a sales seminar and has concocted all kinds of weird and wonderful questions to elicit a *yes* from you at every opportunity. You can use *backtracking* very usefully not only to ensure that the patient knows you understand their issue, but also to notice how they look and sound when they *say yes and mean it*.

So what clues are we looking for? Usually their face is symmetrical, there may be some colouring in their cheeks, their head may nod, their eyes focus in a particular direction, and their breathing may change. Sometimes they may make a particular gesture with their hand or arm. Their voice will have a particular tone, emphasis and resonance.

The following exercise will help you to develop your sensory acuity so that you more easily recognise yes, no and maybe. This has applications in all areas of life. I'll let you think about them yourself. All right?

Exercise 8:   Calibrating to yes and no

1   Find yourself a willing partner.
2   Ask your partner questions for which you both know whether the answer is yes or no. Get them to *answer out loud*. Use everyday contexts such as their name, where they live, the car that they drive, family members, etc. As they say yes or no verbally, *calibrate to the non-verbal responses*.
3   Now ask questions that presuppose a yes or no answer. That is, you both know what the answer is. For example, 'Is your name Fred? Do you drive a Subaru?' However, your partner only *thinks the answer* and does not say it out loud. Again *calibrate to the non-verbal responses*.
4   Now ask questions to which you do not know the answer, but which can be answered yes or no. For example, does your partner like a particular pop group, type of food, holiday destination, etc.? They can only *think the answer, responding non-verbally*, without words. Guess the answer from your earlier calibration.

This is a skill that can be used universally. Just imagine applying it in negotiations, business meetings, and buying and selling. In everyday conversations it's easy to do a mini-backtrack and elicit a *yes-set*. Practise it. We shall be covering its applications in the consultation more fully in each of the following chapters.

Agenda setting

Once you have backtracked the opening statement and elicited their yes-set, you may find that the patient has more than one issue, perhaps even several, that they would like to address today. And, of course, especially if they have other chronic ongoing conditions, you may also have specific areas that you want to address, or perhaps even some additional concerns about health promotion. Often we feel that we have to deal with every issue that is presented to us, including those which we feel we *ought* to add in from a medical perspective. After all, isn't that what the archetypal good doctor would do? Very soon you get that overwhelming feeling of too much to do and not enough time in which to do it. This is exactly the moment when *negotiation skills* come in handy.

Good negotiators operate from the underlying presupposition that people are responsible for their own choices in any given situation. Therefore if you feel that you *have to* deal with it all today, at some level you have made that choice, as unpalatable as this may seem. They recognise that there is of course a *positive intention* behind that choice. It may be that you want to provide the best possible service to the patient, or it may be that you are not yet comfortable in your skill of drawing a bottom line today, and it feels easier, at least in the short term, to give in to all of the demands.

I believe that it is important to hold on to the value of rendering best possible service in all situations. However, this means looking at both the short- and the long-term views. We are always having to balance what we can do for this person now within the perspective of those still waiting, the time available, and the consequences to our own physical and mental well-being. This is the arena in which good *agenda setting* comes into its own.

Essentially then, *agenda setting* brings both sets of needs to the table for prioritisation in the light of whatever other constraints are currently prevailing. Some examples will show the way.

A patient brings what appears to be a long written list of problems that they usually go through in minute detail.

'I can see that you have brought your list of what you'd like to discuss today. And I agree that it's important to deal with issues that are troublesome. I also have some things I'd like to check, too, such as your blood pressure. Perhaps you can tell me the main headings on your list. That way we can prioritise, and deal with the most important things in the time we have available today.'

Or:

'What would be the one most important thing on your list, such that if we dealt with it effectively today, you would know that was time well spent?'

A patient who has been slotted in as a 5-minute 'emergency' appointment for an exacerbation of chronic obstructive airways disease also starts to tell you about her chronic constipation and how all the medicines that she has tried haven't worked. And what about a letter to the housing department?

'I'm not sure if our receptionist explained that this is a 5-minute "emergency" appointment. I think we need to deal with your bronchitis right now. Once you're feeling better, we can arrange another appointment with more time to discuss your bowels and housing situation. Is that OK?'

Sometimes we need to balance the patient's perceived priorities with our concerns about what might be more medically important.

'I know that we planned to review your medication for your joints today. However, I wonder if we can start with those "funny indigestion pains" you've been getting whilst walking?'

More usually it is simply a straightforward representing of the patient's agenda, using backtracking and yes-sets to reach agreement.

'What if we find out first whether one of your medicines is causing your upset stomach? Then we can deal with the eczema on your legs. Is that OK?'

So agenda setting involves a bit of give and take, packaging what you have to offer in the time available in an agreeable way. Rather than being all things to all people at all times, negotiating in this way can help you to manage your consultation more effectively for both you and your patient. And the evidence suggests that this is achieved without any appreciable lengthening of the consultation time. I suspect that, for many, these skills taken together may lead to a healthier reorganisation of *how* you consult.

Ending the beginning

So we have now taken a tour through the beginning phase of the consultation. We have seen that not only can the potential pitfalls be avoided, but also we can set ourselves up in a way that allows us to build a platform for the ensuing 10 minutes or so – a platform that can allow our skills to start to flow in an automatic, intuitive way.

We have seen that a good beginning really starts before the patient even comes through the door. It starts with us disconnecting from what has gone before, using our *break-state* anchor if necessary to get us into a more neutral frame of mind, and then ensuring that we are open to receive whoever enters by triggering our rapport anchor which, over time, automatically becomes our second-nature *consulting flow state*. This state of rapport, already present and building, is further enhanced by matching and mirroring the various physiological cues that patients display, knowing that you can, if you so choose, simultaneously match the various voice qualities in order to deepen the connection. All the time you are aware of the importance of the *opening statement*, an uninterrupted divulging of concerns, whilst you continue to build the relationship non-verbally. Then you skilfully *backtrack* as you elicit the *yes-sets* that let you both know of a congruent agreement, a shared understanding. Finally, you conclude this phase by setting the *agenda* that will form the basis of our next steps.

Easy, wasn't it!

To make it even more spontaneous it will certainly be worth your while practising each of the skills in this chapter individually, one by one, starting off in safe environments before moving into consultation time. Then, of course, you can forget about it for a while, at least consciously, before delightfully surprising yourself with the display of your skills acquisition.

CHAPTER 4

Gathering information

Introduction

We now come to the next phase of how to consult more effectively, namely gathering information. This is obviously a vital area, where consultations may run aground on the twin rocks of excessive biological focus and inadequate hypothesis generation. The traditional history-taking model has been at the forefront of this phase for decades, yet has increasingly been found wanting in attempts to explore wider patient perspectives. In the latter part of the twentieth century, however, we began to turn our attention to the individual's *subjective experience* of their illness, focusing on their beliefs, concerns, ideas and expectations. This was not to negate the more traditional methods, but simply to encompass them in the ever-widening net of communication skills development. So what does the twenty-first century hold for us?

We now need to focus more on the *process* of communication, rather than on mere *content*. The content is simply *what* happens as the patient's story unfolds. And it is very easy to get caught up in the story so that we become like rabbits, *transfixed* as if hypnotised by the headlights of the oncoming detail. The process is really one step removed from the content, and deals with *how* it happens. In this way we can find ourselves examining the *structure* of the communication, how it is built, how it hangs together, and how one part sequences into another. Without getting lost in the detail we can uncover some extremely valuable information about just how that particular patient's world is made up. This information is particularly useful for the later phase of explanation and planning (*see* Chapter 6).

As an analogy, it's rather like building a house. The bricks and mortar are the content (the *what*), whereas the blueprint and the scaffolding (the *how to*) are essential for the process to take place, and they are required whether you are building a bungalow or a mansion. Of course, once the house has been built, the blueprint and scaffolding disappear, leaving the finished article. In a similar way, we need to be on the lookout for how patients build their beliefs, ideas and expectations. We need to uncover their unconscious blueprints and scaffolding in such a way that not only do we understand how this unique individual's world fits together, but also we have a set of tools to help them to make the kind of health adjustments that are necessary for their future well-being.

However, gathering information is not simply confined to discussing the presenting problem. We need to find out just what the patient wants *instead*. For too long we have delved deeply into the *why* and wherefores of a problem's existence, in the vain hope that a fuller understanding of the content will in some way bring about an insightful resolution. We need to become more solution focused and more outcome centred. And, of course, as you can imagine, outcomes and solutions have their own structure, their own scaffolding, their own rules for effective attainment.

We shall therefore be exploring some different tools for gathering the necessary information leading to more effective patient outcomes.

Aims of this chapter

This phase of the consultation begins by exploring how patients frame their problems. We tackle the various *unconscious filters* through which their narrative passes as it reaches the light of day. Then we get more specific, exploring beliefs, ideas and expectations through the type of questions that can get to the heart of an issue quickly and effectively. From there we clarify just what direction this particular patient wants to go in today. Of course, we shall be paying even more attention to the non-verbal aspects that are pertinent to this stage.

So what are the specific skill-sets that we shall be exploring?

Section One: habitual patterns
- *Meta-programs*, the unconscious filters through which we process information.

Section Two: questioning language
- The *meta-model*, the engine of NLP.
- The structure of *beliefs and expectations*, and how specifically *meta-model* questions elicit useful information.
- Continuing to notice the *non-verbal communications* accompanying the above.
- The use of *softeners* to allow questioning to be less interrogating and more flowing.

Section Three: what do you want?

* The process of setting *well-formed outcomes*, becoming more solution centred.
* The *miracle question*, using a tool from solution-focused therapy.

Section One: habitual patterns

Meta-programs

Here is another jargon-laden phrase to conjure with! *Meta-programs* are the unconscious, out-of-awareness, habitual filters that we use to frame our communications. They act as information processors, determining *how* we both input and output *what* we actually send to one another in a conversation. Because there is far too much going on, even in a simple interaction, for us to be consciously aware of, these patterns form the mental grooves or habits which automatically provide the structure and framework for what we say and think – sometimes like a stuck record, playing over and over again!

As a simple example, some people are eternal optimists, seeing the world through rose-tinted spectacles. Others are eternal pessimists who see the cloud in every silver lining. Both can experience exactly the same event yet have a different interpretation of it. Is the glass half full or half empty? Some people say that the responses to this question determine the four basic personality types, the other two being the ditherer (half full or half empty, gee it's so hard to decide) or the psychopath (hey, I ordered a pizza!).

Although there are many patterns that could qualify as meta-programs, we shall focus on the ones that are most pertinent and useful to general practice. It is important to state that none of these patterns are right or wrong, or better or worse than any other. You might find yourself siding with one element more than the other. That simply lets you know your own underlying tendencies.

Another brief caveat is that these patterns are context dependent for each individual. A consultation is one context. Choosing a holiday destination is another, as is buying a house or talking about your favourite sport. These patterns may change for each individual as they change situation. They are not personality boxes in which to typecast and imprison people.

In this section we shall consider how to identify the patterns as you allow the history to unfold. We shall make further use of them in Chapter 6 on explanation and planning. As an *aide-mémoire*, you can think of a particular patient who typifies each category. By picturing them in your mind's eye as you go along, you will be creating a memory peg or hook. This will help you to recognise the patterns more easily in other patients when they attend.

For simplicity I have presented both poles of each category. In reality, of course, they fit together as a continuum, some people displaying more and some showing less of each pattern, on different occasions. I repeat, please resist the temptation to put people into boxes.

Towards and away from

People move either *towards* what they want or *away from* what they don't want. *Towards* people have a goal in mind, something that they want to get or attain or achieve. They tend to be good at focusing on their outcomes, although if they are too strongly focused they may not identify what they need to avoid.

The body language of *towards* people tends to include head nods, looking to where they picture the future in the space around them, and even pointing to specific locations.

Here are some patients' examples:

- *'Hi, doc, I'd like an antibiotic for my throat.'*
- *'I wonder if you could write a letter to the housing department for me. With my angina, I'd really like to be closer to the shops.'*
- *'Well, doctor, you see I have this dream. My first grandchild is going to be born in Australia in 4 months' time. I want to be there, hold her, look into her eyes, see the next generation of MacIntyres. I'm absolutely determined'* (patient with pancreatic cancer).

The *away froms*, on the other hand, tend to be good at saying what they *don't want*, what they must avoid, steer clear of, get rid of, etc. They often focus on what has gone or can or will go wrong. They identify obstacles to get round and problems that need solving, but they may often have difficulty defining what they want instead.

The body language of *away from* people tends to include shaking of the head, and pushing-away gestures with the hands, looking in a particular direction as they do so.

- *'I can't help it, doctor, every time I think about going there, I get so worked up I feel sick. I just see myself in a panic, making a fool of myself'* (patient with agoraphobia).
- *'I don't want to be unhappy anymore. I want to be less irritable with the kids. I just want to wake up in the morning and not feel tired and drained'* (patient with depression answering a question about what she really wanted!).
- *'I want to get rid of this unsightly rash!'*

Of course, it is not only individuals that manifest this *meta-program*. Even professions have a bias. For example, medicine as a whole, has an *away from* orientation. We focus on what is wrong, and identify problems to solve, things to cut out or fix. We initially called the field of promoting better health *preventative medicine*, a real *away from*! Of course now it is more appropriately named *health promotion*, moving towards our goal of improving health. Given that medicine tends to attract individuals with a problem-solving, away from bias into the profession, it is little wonder that health promotion hasn't taken off. There's so much illness to get rid of!

Proactive and reactive

People who are *proactive* act as if they are in charge of their world. They are initiators, they know what they want and they want to get there quickly – usually *NOW*, and sometimes even sooner than that! At the extremes they may bulldoze ahead without taking others into consideration. At best they are direct and to the point. You know where you stand with them, like it or not. They follow the Nike advert: *Just Do It!*

They speak in short, crisp sentences, often quite quickly. In linguistic terms they use the *active* voice rather than the *passive* one. Their questions are to the point, and there is no beating about the bush.

Their body language tends to be fairly direct. They may show signs of impatience, such as foot tapping or quick powerful gestures. They sit up in their chair and often have more eye contact.

Some examples:

- *'I want you to refer me to a consultant privately. How quickly can you get that done?'*
- *'Ok, doc, if it's bad news, I want it straight. What's the worst? How long have I got?'* (patient with lung cancer).

People who are *reactive* have a tendency to consider and analyse what they are going to say or do at great length, before eventually getting round to saying it (if at all), because they may be wondering if their timing is right, or indeed whether even more caution or assessment is required, before they finally get round to acting. They speak in longer, more convoluted sentences, just like the last one! They may wait for other people to initiate events before replying or responding. It is as if these *events happen to them*, out of their control, being at the effect end of the cause–effect spectrum.

They use the *passive* voice, include the conditional tense (could, would, may, might) and tend to speak more slowly.

Their body language is often more deliberate, but they may spend longer periods of time sitting in one position making very little movement. They may offer less eye contact because they are *inside themselves,* analysing and thinking about what you are saying.

Examples:

- *'I was just wondering, doctor, um ... what with my seemingly endlessly recurrent sore throats that ... em ... seem to occur out of the blue, whether ... ah ... you might consider the prescription of another antibiotic ... em ... prior to perhaps explaining once again ... um ... about the pros and cons of tonsillectomy?'*
- *'Well, I suppose I need to consider quite carefully the various options you've suggested, doctor. I'm really not that certain what to do, and in this situation I think it's important that people take the necessary time to come to the conclusion that best fits the circumstances.'*

Options and procedures

People who are *options* oriented look for the possibilities and opportunities in a given situation. They are keen to find out what might happen if they explored a different direction. In essence they would like to explore all of the different alternatives before making a choice. They often do not like simply following procedures, as they feel too tied down. At the extreme, however, they may have so much choice that they find it difficult to choose. They may even enjoy breaking the rules!

Linguistically they use words such as *hope, wish, can, will, want, going to, may, could* or *might.* They talk about expanding their options and use *action*-oriented verbs. They are more animated in their language expression and may speak more quickly as they get into the possibilities.

Their body language is open and expansive, with wider gestures sweeping the area in space where they project their future. They may appear more lively, tending to sit forward when talking, almost as if they are physically trying on each choice.

Examples:

- *'What about other treatments for my gallstones, doctor? There's that new-fangled keyhole surgery malarkey. And what about dissolving them?'* (82-year-old woman who was unfit for major surgery!).
- *'I know there are rules about referral, but surely you could just phone the consultant direct? I can be free to see him anytime, anywhere. And anyway, you did say I needed to get something done about it soon'* (patient with a large inguinal hernia).

People who are *procedures* oriented know that there are rules to follow, and usually a *right way* to get things done. They may do things because they *have to,* or *must*, rather than because they want to. They feel *obligated* under the circumstances. They like ways that are tried, tested and reliable. It is as if they don't really have a choice – things just happen to them, and they just have to get on with it, like it or not! Underlying this pattern are the values of safety and security. You *shouldn't* go into the unknown without a plan. They may take a written list with them, and if they are *specifics* oriented, (see later) too, it will be a long one!

They use words such as *have to, must, ought* and *should*, and their negative equivalents. There are few words of choice or possibility. They say things like '*I did this because I had to*' or '*It always happens to me!*'. Of course the archetypical words are '*It's more than my job's worth*'. They may even call you 'sir!'.

Their body language tends to be more stiff and rigid, although they rarely sit to attention. Their gestures are usually more clipped and precise. When speaking about what has happened, they mark out chronological order with small 'chopping' hand gestures.

Examples:

* '*I* hope you won't mind, doctor, but I had *to bring my list. There are four things I* need *to get sorted out today and the wife said I* ought *to make sure I didn't forget anything. The first is ...*'
* '*It* shouldn't *have happened, doctor. If he* hadn't *started shouting at me for no good reason, just 'cause he thought I was late, and I was really on time, just as usual. I suppose I* oughtn't *to have shouted back, but I* couldn't *help it, I didn't have a choice you see*' (recurring domestic upset which followed the same ritual each time!).

Self and others

People who sort by *self* tend to respond to their own inner world of thoughts, feelings and behaviour almost to the exclusion of others. They seem to be *inside* themselves, self-absorbed, attending to their own processes. They may mind-read what other people's intentions are without checking it out for themselves first to see whether they are right. They tend to view each situation as '*what's in it for me?*', and at the extreme they may appear narcissistic. They can leave you with the feeling that they are not paying attention to what you are saying, or worse, that they just don't care. Their interpersonal skills are poorly developed.

There are few linguistic clues other than self-referencing with 'I' statements. Their body language may be aloof, with poor rapport skills. Their eyes may either have a glazed unfocused look, or be directed upwards as they make internal pictures. They may appear quite expressionless or, to use a medical term, schizoid.

This pattern is usually picked up by observation.

People who sort by *other* appear to be *'outside'* most of the time. They are paying more attention to other people and the world around them. They are more likely to ask about your experience first, and if they have the necessary additional skills are usually extremely good at achieving automatic rapport. When developed to the extreme they can usually imagine being in the other person's shoes, feeling their pain or pleasure. Of course the problem is that this is automatic for them – they have yet to develop the choice of 'stepping out'. At the extreme they may have problems with boundary issues.

Again there are few linguistic clues here. You can recognise them imme-diately, though, as they seem to match and mirror you automatically as soon as they come through the door. You move, and they move, too. My personal experience is that many obese patients with emotional difficulties display this pattern. It is as if they don't know where you stop and they begin, physically, mentally and emotionally.

General and specific

This pattern describes how people chunk information. Do they prefer the *big picture*, the overview, or are they more concerned with the specific *details?*

People who are *general* often need to present the big picture first before they can talk about the details. Because they tend to see the situation and the various connections all at once in their mind's eye, they may present informa-tion in a seemingly random or haphazard way. Unless you are processing at the same level, it may seem as if they are jumping from one topic to another, often with tenuous links. Because each topic is interlinked, they may actually start off with one that has a lower priority. For these people it is *doubly important* to elicit their whole agenda at the beginning of the consultation. At the extreme they may remain in the rarefied atmosphere of abstract ideas and be difficult to pin down to concrete statements. They may have difficulties in following through step-by-step procedures.

Linguistically, they use words such as, *generally, usually, the wider perspective, basically, overall, the main thing,* etc.

Their body language tends to be a little more laid back, and they often look upward and outward as if to survey a large projected map. Their gestures are expansive and symmetrical.

Examples:

- *'Well, basically I've been feeling under the weather for a while now. I suppose the main thing is to get my act together somehow, be happier with my lot, that's the general aim'* (patient who was actually very depressed).
- *'You know, doc, just happy. A bit more sun in my life. Things going better for me, not so gloomy'* (same patient being asked for more detail about how specifically *'happy'* would look, sound and feel!).

People who are *specifics* oriented focus on the nitty-gritty, the details. They usually have to *order and sequence* their information in small discrete chunks. Sometimes they present it in excruciating detail, and worse still, if interrupted they either start off at the same place or, heaven forbid, go back to the beginning! (You can tell my preference here.) They may not follow a plan of action unless you have explained all of the steps in detail.

Linguistically they order their information in step-by-step sequences. They may use many adjectives and adverb modifiers to describe the problem and they use words such as *exactly, precisely, before, after, then* and *later*.

Their body language tends to be more precise, although they may become fairly animated when telling their story. They will point to specific places in the space around them, and use gestures such as thumb and forefinger held close together to give an idea of how little things fit together.

Examples:

- *'It was the worst pain I've ever had in my life. It was Sunday morning, 3rd of March if I'm not mistaken. We'd been to church, lovely sermon from the new minister. Well, just as we got home, I noticed a stabbing stitch-like feeling under my rib-cage on the right. It was 12.30. I know that because I glanced at the grandfather clock on the way in. We were going to have roast beef and all the trimmings, you see. But I started to feel queasy just before Alf served it up. Then I got such a spasm I doubled up. On to that nice pink tablecloth Jessie gave me, when was that again, my it was 5 years ago now!'* (patient describing her first attack of biliary colic. She had three more!).

Actually, one example is more than enough for this category!

Some people wonder about the difference between *specific* and *procedures*, as they both have order and sequence. In essence, *specific* people *must* follow the sequence from beginning to end. A hallmark is having to go back to the beginning if interrupted. *Procedures* people have choice points along the way, and can discuss isolated steps without starting all over again. In fact, it is even possible to combine *procedures* and *general*. They then just tell you about how the big picture unfolds in large chunk sequences.

Match and mismatch

This is one of my favourites. People who *match* generally look for how things are *similar*. They look for what things have in common – how this particular problem is similar to what they had last year. When taking on board new information, they like to match it with what they *already* know, so that it makes sense.

People who mainly *match* but who also have a little *mismatch* tend to use comparisons. They tell you how things are *better* or *worse* than last time. For them, changes evolve, usually at a predictable pace, and they hate revolution.

Linguistically they use words such as *same as, similar to, just like the last time, better, worse, more or less* and *gradually improving.*

Their body language is fairly non-descript. It mainly consists of gestures of inclusion, bringing things together. They may speak a little slower, with less tonal variation.

Examples:

* *'Yes, it's my review appointment. Much the same as last time, doc. Maybe a bit more energy. As long as things stay like this I can cope' (patient with lung cancer).*
* *'Do you think it will be the same as the previous op? In and out the same day? Hope it's a better result this time' (patient awaiting operation for recurrent inguinal hernia).*

Mismatchers on the other hand look for how things are *different.* They notice how things don't fit together yet. They focus on what is missing and make sense of things by finding the holes in your argument. This can be quite daunting if they are also *specific* and *away from* people. They will go over everything with a fine-tooth comb looking for mistakes to avoid! Although this might appear challenging, it is simply the way in which they understand the world.

Mismatchers are also, at the extremes, the people who say 'Yes but ...' to everything. Worse still are the *polarity responders*, who always seem to do the opposite of what you say! They are actually great fun and often quite simple to deal with, as we shall see in Chapter 6 on explanation and planning.

Linguistically they use words such as, *new, different, unique, complete turn-around* and *changed.* They tend to *emphasise* certain words, and they have a wider tonal range.

Their body language can be quite interesting. At the extremes they may completely mismatch your posture. If you change, they change as well – to something different! They use gestures of exclusion, pushing away, and separating information out in space around them.

Examples:

- 'Yes, but the LAST doctor I saw suggested that. And THAT didn't work EITHER.'
- 'There's been a COMPLETE turnaround since we saw the marriage guidance counsellor. She gave us some NEW information about how DIFFERENTLY people communicate. You won't believe how things have CHANGED!'.

Internal and external

This category is about what is sometimes called the locus of control or frame of reference. It is about where people place the responsibility for their decisions, actions, judgements and evaluations. Do they rely on an *internal* authority (themselves) or an *external* authority (someone else)?

People who are *internal* weigh up the pros and cons of a situation and *decide for themselves* what they are going to do. They may gather information from outside sources, but at the end of the day they will make their own judgements and take their own actions. Because they have their own internal standards, they may have difficulty in accepting feedback that doesn't match their own opinions or evaluations. At the extreme you cannot convince them to do anything, and they resist when told what to do. You can only present your information in a way that allows them to convince themselves!

Linguistically, they use phrases like '*it just feels right to me, it makes sense*', and they tell you what they have decided. '*I just know that's the right thing to do – I feel it inside*' is typical.

Their body language is characterised by a self-assured posture, although you will notice tension and a pulling away if you give them orders. They will use self-referential gestures, with a palm to the chest when talking about beliefs and values. They may put their hand on their abdomen when talking about gut feelings.

Examples:

- 'I got this information off the Internet. You'll see where I've circled on page three. That's what I want to talk to you about. I'd like you to refer me to the consultant at that hospital.'
- 'I've read through the leaflets you gave me, doctor, and had a good think about it all. I feel the coil best suits my needs at the moment. When can I get that done?'

People who are *external* need direction and feedback from other people. They tend to let other people make the decisions not only about *what* to do but also about *how* to do it. They often find out what to do in a particular situation by asking other people. They are far more likely to comply with authority figures, and at the extreme may blindly do what they are told. Because the motivation to continue doing something is derived externally, they may have to report in more frequently for instructions, feedback or validation of their results. I have found that many of the regular attenders in general practice show this pattern.

Linguistically, they may say things like *'I read it in the papers', 'it was on the news last night'* or *'my friend suggested ...'*.

Examples:

- *'Well, you're the doctor, doctor. You tell me!'* (typical of this pattern).
- *'My mother said I should bring him along and get him checked over. She thinks it might be measles'* (parent of 3-year-old with urticaria).
- *'I know you've told me about the options, and I really appreciate that, but what do you think I should do?'*

Past, present and future

We all organise our time so that we have some way of knowing what has happened, what is happening and what will happen. Some of us tend to live out of one time-frame more exclusively than out of the others. We may evaluate our ongoing behaviour now in terms of how it compares with what happened in the past, or what we would prefer to have happen instead, in the future.

People who are *past* oriented tend to be conservative in their outlook. They may look back with nostalgia to the 'good old days' – unless they are depressed, of course, when it becomes the 'bad old days'. *Depression* is virtually always a past-oriented problem. People may associate with various negative memories, and the feelings produced help to keep them stuck today. When asked, they may say that they have no future or that it looks bleak, or even black. The emotions of guilt and regret are always associated with the past. The typical question that past-oriented people ask is *'Why ... ?'* This may give them plenty of reasons and insight, but little in the way of practically based solutions.

People who are *present* oriented live for *now*. For them, the past and future fade into insignificance. This is all well and good when they are focused on a particular task, utilising all of their incoming sensory information, but not so good when they are engaged in repetitive problem behaviour. For example, most if not all *addictions* fall into this category. At that particular moment they have no access to past memories from which to learn from previous mistakes, and no thought of future untoward consequences of their present action. Their typical question is *'How can I ... (x) ... right now?'*

People who are *future* oriented tend to be imaginative and may be the creators of new ideas, or even entrepreneurs. They may not notice what is going on here and now because they are off on a journey inside their mind's eye. *Anxiety* is a typically future-oriented problem. After all, you can't be anxious about what has already occurred in the past. Anxious people are extremely good at making large, bright, colourful pictures of catastrophes which they want to avoid. The problem is that they then associate into the image and feel the uncomfortable feelings right now. Their typical question starts off '*What if ... (x) ... were to happen?*' They often fail to notice their past resources which they could bring to bear on the situation.

Body language for time-frames is quite interesting. Most people seem to store their *past* on their left, or behind them. They will gesture in this direction while speaking in the past tense. The *future* tends to be straight ahead or off to the right. They will gesture in this direction while using the various future tenses. The *present* is usually experienced as being inside the body or just in front. They will gesture here while speaking about the present time. In some people who are left-handed, the past and future may be reversed.

We shall discuss how to utilise time-frames non-verbally in Chapter 6 on explanation and planning.

Thinkers and feelers

This category relates to whether people *associate* into or *dissociate* from their emotional responses.

People who are *thinkers*, as the name suggests, tend to be somewhat *emotionally distant*. They are the kind of people who can remember past stressful or emotional experiences and appear to be completely detached as they describe them. They tend to keep a cool head in difficult situations, and are unlikely to panic. At the extreme they may be thought of as being out of touch with their feelings – rather a cold fish. They may have difficulty in really empathising with others, and may appear aloof. Because they are sometimes out of touch with their bodily feelings, they may be less good at either reporting or describing symptoms.

There are few linguistic clues here. With regard to body language, they may sit more erect and have a tendency to look upwards and out into the middle distance. They have fewer facial colour shifts when describing emotional situations.

People who are *feelers* often have *strong emotional responses*. They are good at stepping into an experience, reliving the event, and feeling the feelings again. This is fine if it is a happy memory, but not so good if it is a trauma. Sometimes they can get stuck in their feelings and life can seem like a roller-coaster. They may have difficulty in compartmentalising their experiences, and one or two negative events can ruin the whole day. At the extreme they may appear to be hypersensitive and over-react to apparently minor issues. They may over-empathise with others to the extent that they feel their pain. They tend to present in general practice more frequently than their counterparts.

Linguistically there are few specific language patterns. However, their body language can change markedly. You will notice breathing and facial colour shifts. The eyes tend to look down, often to the right. They may display asymmetrical muscle tensions, especially in the face. They will show wide variation in their vocal qualities, with wide-ranging tone and speed. They may appear completely different at the next consultation if there is no major emotional issue present.

However, this category is not so cut and dried. Many people have *choice*, meaning that they may initially go into their feelings when describing an issue, but then distance themselves as necessary. This skill allows them to empathise with others appropriately.

Playing with meta-programs

Of course, none of the above patterns occur in isolation. They can all interact in various ways to produce a veritable array of choices in information processing. *Away from* and *specific* will cause someone to be looking for errors with a fine-tooth comb. *Reactive* and *general* leads to much abstract thinking about an issue without ever getting around to doing anything about it. *Internal* with an *others* orientation is an example of someone who always knows what is best for you, no matter what you think yourself! *Feelings* and *away from* is classic of panic attacks and phobias. They have intense negative feelings about something that they desperately want to avoid.

You can have some fun, and learn more effortlessly, by making up your own combinations and predicting the outcome of the mixture.

The patient from hell

What if you were to combine the following patterns to create the kind of patient you might really want to avoid: *reactive, away from, procedures, mismatch, external, specific, feeler, past oriented, other?*

This would probably be a person who presented you with an extremely large emotional-based problem that only you could solve for them. Of course they would have to go into immense detail about how this has affected not only them but also especially their nearest and dearest, who have been devastated by their inability to help. And of course that has upset them even more. They really must give you blow-by-blow accounts of the past five years' worth of difficulties because you ought to know just exactly what they have tried that hasn't worked. Especially the advice given by trusted others, which they thought about long and hard (you won't believe how long!) before asking someone else, just in case. And of course most of these solutions wouldn't work for them because they knew of other people who had tried exactly the same in the past without success. Rest assured that they would carefully consider what you had to offer before telling you exactly how this would fail before they had even implemented it.

Does this ring any bells?

The doctor from hell

Of course this sort of thing works both ways. What would this particular doctor be like, from a patient's perspective: *reactive, away from, internal, options, mismatch, specific, self, thinker, past oriented?*

This doctor would really know what was best for all of his patients, as he has so much vast previous experience to call upon. And of course there are so many treatment options for each problem these days that it might be difficult to choose exactly which course of action to pursue. Although you could rest assured that he would give it much thought, and come to a very considered conclusion. Of course, some medications could give you very nasty side-effects, and it would be important to explain about these in minute detail. After all, people need to know exactly what they are up against, don't they? And, of course, this doctor would immediately discount any views that his patients had about their illness. Who was the professional here? Wasn't that what he had gone to medical school for? To make diagnoses? To decide on treatment? And these days, people just seemed to burst into tears at a moment's notice, always catching him unawares. Patients just weren't made of the same stuff any more.

Of course these accounts are totally fictional, and stereotypes like the one above just don't exist, do they? However, it is important to get some practice in recognising these patterns. Have a go at the exercise below.

Exercise 9: Recognising meta-program patterns

You can use the following tasks to *hone your skills further.*

1   Look at some of your most recent referral letters. Which patterns do you utilise most yourself in this context?

2   Compare notes with one of your colleagues. Notice where you are similar and where you differ.

3   Look at letters from consultants in different specialities. Are there differences, say, between a neurologist and an orthopaedic consultant?

4   Choose one pattern per consulting session, starting for example with *towards and away from*. Identify which pole your patient leans toward.

5   At partnership (or other) meetings, if there is a difference in opinion, or even an impasse, which meta-programs are involved? What needs to happen in order to facilitate resolution?

6   Which meta-programs would the receptionist from hell have?

You can learn even more about *meta-programs* in Shelle Rose Charvet's excellent book, *Words That Change Minds* (Charvet, 1995). Although it is mainly business oriented, she gives lots of practical examples.

Section Two: questioning language

The meta-model

The *meta-model* was the first set of NLP interventions to result from the modelling of the language patterns of therapists Fritz Perls and Virginia Satir. Richard Bandler has described it as the '*engine that drives NLP*'. You will remember that language is the sixth thing that we do inside our heads (after VAKOG). Words give labels to our sensory experience and are thus two steps removed from 'reality', what is 'out there'. They are descriptive in nature and tell *about* an experience. However, they are *not* the experience itself.

   You can think of words and language as another type of representational system, sometimes called 'auditory digital'. In computer speak, they are how we code 'bits' of incoming sensory information, and as such they are a very useful way to manipulate experiences both for ourselves and for others. We can also think of words as anchors. A particular word, said in a particular way, can bring back a flood of memories, good or bad. Words are important, and with them we can make '*a heaven out of hell, or a hell out of heaven*'.

   In Chapter 2 we discussed the universal filters of *deletion*, *generalisation* and *distortion*. We make sense of all the information that reaches us by paying attention to selected parts only. We operate on these parts using selected rules. This results in our own selected meanings, interpretations and judgements.

From sensory experience we can very quickly rise through levels of abstraction into the realms of beliefs and values.

However, with these processes we can also go off at a tangent, lose touch with the experiences from which they arose and, before we know it, end up in the world of false assumptions, mind-reading, fantasy, projection, delusion, paranoia or worse. People may share the same experience, the same 'territory', yet form completely different maps, beliefs and interpretations. And we tend to judge the actions of others according to our maps, not theirs! This can give rise to many of the problems and issues that we face in medical practice each day.

The *meta-model* is a questioning tool which reconnects the abstractions to the sensory experiences from which they arose, thus allowing the possibility of clarifying and updating our beliefs, expanding out of our boxed-in limitations and gathering specific information for change. It is a 'chunking-down' tool, getting the necessary details which can act as the pivot for doing something different, something new, something 'therapeutic'.

The *meta-model* acts on the universal filters by asking the questions listed in Box 4.1.

Box 4.1:   An outline of the meta-model

Distortions
Challenge and change the meaning

How do you know?
How does *this* cause *that*?
How does *x* mean *y*?
Who says? According to whom?

Generalisations
Expand the limits of the 'box'

What stops you?
What prevents you?
What would happen if you did?
Didn't?
All? Every? Never? Always?
Nobody?

Deletions
Recover the information

Who?
How?   Specifically?
What?   Exactly?
When?   Precisely?
Where?

When using the meta-model it is more productive to challenge distortions first, and then generalisations. Distortions *act on* generalisations, which *act on* deletions in a therapeutic hierarchy. Distortions are the assumptions, beliefs and expectations about *why* someone continues to have a particular problem. What causes it? What does it mean? Why me? Why now? Distortions are what is 'inside the problem box'.

Generalisations are usually beliefs about what people think they can – or more usually can't – do, what they ought to do, should or shouldn't do, what must always or never happen. They are the four sides of the problem box, the rules that keep the boundaries of the problem in place.

Of course, solutions are usually found outside the box (*see* Figure 4.1)!

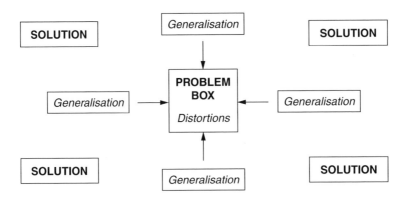

Figure 4.1:   The structure of a problem.

Challenging deletions can often get you too bogged down in detail, and less able to see the wood for the trees. They give less opportunity for effective change. Leave them until last!

We shall be using meta-model questioning throughout the rest of this section, with specific examples, especially in the area of *beliefs and expectations*. You will also find a more detailed map of the *meta-model* to refer to in Appendix 3.

Beliefs and expectations

Having learned just how this particular patient processes information as she tells her narrative of the current presenting issue (*meta-programs*), we now turn our attention to gathering more specific high-quality data about her *perceptions* of her illness. Until recent years there has been a focus on the medical aspects of the diagnosis of disease and its management. Now we are becoming aware that *illness* is actually the wider perspective of ideas, concerns, beliefs and expectations that surround and encompass the kernel of disease. And in many ways this wider perspective can have more effect on a patient's well-being – for good or ill, enhancing or limiting – than the actual medical diagnosis itself.

We shall deal first with the structure of *beliefs*. Just exactly what is a belief? What do they do? Why do we have them? What is their purpose? (And in answering these questions I acknowledge the vast amount of work that Robert Dilts has done in this field over the past 20 years in elucidating the cognitive structure of beliefs.)

Beliefs are guiding principles and generalisations *about* the world at large, what we *think* we can and can't do, who we think we are and who it is possible for us to become. It is as if we have taken all of our life's experiences thus far and formed out of them a kind of rulebook, something to help us navigate a course through what happens to us next. Beliefs are about what is *important* to us. They are the *why* that provides the motivation for what we do.

Think of it in this way. We have certain *values* that we hold closely to ourselves – words such as honesty, integrity, peace, harmony, health, security, protection, determination, making a difference, wealth, etc. Words which may mean different things to different people. These deeply held values are expressed in our behaviours, the things we do every day, knowingly and unknowingly. Beliefs are thus the *operational rules* that connect our values to our daily acts and deeds.

Consider the word *health*. Two people may believe that health is important. One believes that '*Health is a matter of luck. If it's in your genes, there's nothing you can do about it.*' The other believes that '*Health is a matter of doing the right things. No matter what happens, there's always something I can do about it.*' These beliefs will spawn completely different behaviours, thoughts and actions in the face of a health challenge.

And where do beliefs come from? Where do *your* beliefs come from? How do they arise? Most of our core beliefs, the ones that we hold most deeply, and often outwith conscious awareness, arise from *significant emotional events* that we have lived through during the first seven or so years of life – either from single, highly charged events, or based on repetition of events over a period of time. Others we model on the significant people in our lives including parents, family, friends, teachers and other authorities. Whole families have belief systems that have been handed down over generations. Whole cultures have an amazing diversity of health beliefs. We are a product of the times through which we have lived.

To sum up, beliefs are essentially judgements and evaluations that we make *about* our experience. They are *not* scientific truths. That would be factual, agreed knowledge *about* reality (whatever that is!). Beliefs actually help us to operate in that no-man's land where we don't really know for sure what the truth is in the present situation, or what the future really holds. The problem is, of course, that we all too often forget this and mistake what we believe for the indisputable, correct truth. Many wars have been fought over this, both in the external world and daily in our internal thoughts. Perhaps we can consider our beliefs as simply our *best current thinking* at this moment in time.

Belief categories

According to NLP, beliefs fall into three main categories, namely *causation,* *meaning* and *boundaries.* These categories organise and frame our thoughts about the external world (environment), what we do (behaviours), how we think (capabilities), what is important (beliefs *about* beliefs!) and who we are (identity). Of course, these categories are not rigid, and a particular belief may overlap into all three. Indeed, they may also overlap *logical levels* (*see* Chapter 2) to some extent, too. However, the categories do give a good basis not only for understanding the patient's world, but also for how to begin to manoeuvre to let go of beliefs that limit us, and instead open up to new possibilities.

Causation

Many beliefs are of the type that says implicitly or explicitly that one event *causes* another event to happen. For example, many schools of psychotherapy believe that your problems and limitations of today are caused by events that happened in your childhood. *Causation* generally implies a time-frame, with the earlier event being given dominance whether it happened minutes or years before. A subtle element of this type of thinking is that you often appear to be at the mercy of factors outside your control, a *victim* of circumstances, tossed and turned on the stormy seas of life's whims and misfortunes. Life happens *to* you – you are not in charge.

Certain types of words alert you to *causation*. The classic is anything that follows the word 'because'. Other words, such as *forces, makes, creates, drives you to* and *requires*, are typical. Implied causes are more subtle. Listen out for varieties of '*if … then*'. Or simply '*if …*'. In these cases the word *because*, although missed out, is there by implication.

The following are examples of this type of belief. See if you can label the *logical level* at which they occur.

- *'I can't help it. Being fat runs in my family. It's in my genes.'*
- *'I'm sure I caught it off a toilet seat, doctor.'*
- *'Tomatoes cause cancer,' (old wives' tale).*
- *'My mother was depressed when I was little. She didn't give me the attention I needed. No wonder I'm the way I am now.'*
- *'My thoughts are driving me crazy.'*
- *'When he comes home late, it makes me so angry.'*
- *'I sometimes think that this cancer is God's punishment.'*
- *'Her death has made me look at the futility of life.'*
- *'I'm sure I caught my cold when I went out in the rain without a jacket.'*
- *'If you believe you're going to get better, it's just false hope.'*

One of the problems with beliefs, particularly those that limit us, and put us in boxes, is that over time they become removed from the experiences that created them. They become free-floating psychological 'truths' which remain unquestioned for continuing veracity or, worse still, usefulness. It pays dividends to have a mechanism that can *reconnect* a disembodied limiting belief to the type of experience from which it arose. In this way we obtain the means to examine our beliefs and update them accordingly. The *meta-model* is the NLP questioning tool that does this for us. Going '*meta*' involves metaphorically standing back from what we say or do in order to examine the structure from a suitable distance. Then we can ask the most appropriate question.

It is important to elicit a patient's beliefs about their presenting problem or disease in a useful format first. Preliminary questions to elicit *causation* include the following.

- *'What do you think has caused that?'*
- *'Why do you think that has happened?'*
- *'What are your ideas about why this has come about?'*
- *'Because … ?' (as a gentle query with much rapport!).*

These questions will elicit a belief statement just as in the examples of causation quoted above. Then, applying the *meta-model* question for this category is surprisingly simple:

'How specifically does x cause y?'

- 'How specifically does your mother's depression cause you to be the way you are now?'
- 'How specifically do your thoughts drive you crazy?'
- 'How specifically does believing that you're going to get better create false hope?'
- 'How specifically does his coming home late cause you to feel angry?'

The answers to these questions reconnect the belief to the experience or event which gave birth to it. Of course, they need to be asked in a climate of deep rapport, and with the use of *softeners* (see later) as a gentle lead-in. In Chapter 6 on explanation and planning we shall use the answers to *meta-model* questioning to *reframe* limiting beliefs into possibilities for solutions.

Meaning

Regardless of what may have caused this particular problem, issue, disease or disorder, we also have beliefs about what this experience *means* to us. Human beings are meaning-making animals. We are forever interpreting one event in terms of another, making judgements and evaluations. This is a hard-wired function. By equating one thing with another, we are saying that '*this = that*', as they are equivalent in some way.

Conversationally we can be alerted to meaning statements by the word *means* or by variations of the verb *to be*. This often assumes the level of identity, as in 'I am a ...'. You can fill in the blank with anything (see below). Sometimes two statements can be juxtaposed, with the meaning linkage simply presupposed.

Some examples are listed below:

- 'I **am** a cancer victim.'
- 'I **am** an alcoholic.'
- 'I can't stop smoking, I'm so weak-willed.'
- 'I'm just like my mother – she was depressed, too. She never got over it.'
- 'I know that my cancer **is** a punishment.'
- 'Her leaving in that way ... my heart's broken.'
- 'I can't get over this continual worrying. I hate myself so much for it. I'm so stupid.'
- 'Asthma **means** that I have weak lungs.'

- *'I'm sure these crampy stomach pains **mean** I have cancer.'*
- *'I've been getting those chest pains again. More stress I suppose.'*

Before using the *meta-model* question for *meaning*, we need to get the patient's belief statement into the right format. Use questions like the following.

- *'What do you think this might be?'*
- *'What does this mean to you?'*
- *'What might this mean about you? About your relationships?'*
- *'How do you interpret what's happened?'*
- *'How do you make sense of all this?'*

Now we can apply the *meta-model* question for *meaning*:

'How specifically does this mean that?'
or
'How specifically does x = y ?'

- *'How specifically does having asthma mean that you have weak lungs?'*
- *'How specifically does continually worrying mean that you're stupid?'*
- *'How specifically does having cancer mean that you're a victim?'*
- *'How specifically does being unable to stop smoking yet mean that you're weak-willed?'*

Again, remember the importance of rapport. Although these questions appear disarmingly simple, they can often get quickly to core belief issues from which *change* can spontaneously arise.

Boundaries

Boundaries are essentially concerned with *limits*. They are the physical and mental barriers beyond which we may not easily step. They may be about rules that we should or shouldn't follow, or things we can or can't do. They may be rigid barriers, seemingly impossible to cross. They may be semi-permeable and we might or might not be able to make the leap. Think again of the square drawn on the page. The four sides are the boundaries, the limits of its size. Inside is what appears known, perhaps safe, perhaps comfortable. Outside is what seems unknown, perhaps risky, perhaps uncomfortable. Boundary beliefs, then, are often about the limits of what we think is *possible* for us to do now or in the future.

Usually these beliefs are about our capabilities, skills or behaviours. *'Yes, I think I can learn assertiveness skills,' 'No, I can't picture a healthy future.'* However, there can be a somewhat subtle boundary belief issue at the level of identity.

This goes along the following lines: '*Yes, I can see that it's possible, and I agree that I could learn the skills. But it just wouldn't be me! That's just not the way I am. It **doesn't fit** with being me.*' It's almost like saying that we would have to change *who we are* at such a deep level in order to obtain the outcome that we would literally be someone else.

So how do we identify these beliefs linguistically? Possibility and impossibility (i.e. options) use words such as *can, can't, will* and *won't*. Necessity (i.e. rules) uses words such as *should, must, ought, have to* and their negative counterparts. Probability and improbability (i.e. semi-permeability) use words such as *may, might, could, would* and their negative counterparts.

There are certain other words, called *universals*, which also imply boundaries of some kind – for example, *all, none, always, never, everybody* and *nobody*. These imply either so wide a boundary that it is limitless and totally inclusive, or so narrow a boundary that it is totally exclusive.

Examples:

- '*I'm just not the kind of person who takes tablets.*'
- '*I **can't** see how yet another operation is going to help.*'
- '***Everybody** should have the right to see a consultant within two weeks!*'
- '*I really don't think I'm going to make it this time, doc.*'
- '*I'm not sure if these visualisation techniques **could** help my cancer.*'
- '*I **should** be able to fight this stress thing.*'
- '*Sore throats **always** need an antibiotic to cure them.*'
- '*I know I **shouldn't** worry, doctor, but I can't help it. It's just my nature.*'
- '***Nobody** gets better from depression – it's a lifetime thing.*'
- '*I have to get over this agoraphobia.*'

There are two types of *meta-model* question that deal with beliefs of possibility, necessity and probability.

- **'What stops/prevents you ... ?'**
- **'What would happen if you did/didn't ... ?'**

- '*What prevents you being the type of person who can take tablets?*'
- '*What would happen if you did stop worrying? How would that change your nature?*'
- '*What stops you being able to fight this stress thing?*'

Beliefs that contain *universal* words require a different questioning strategy. First repeat back the universal word, and then ask for a counter-example.

- **'All? Every? Never? Always? Have you ever known someone who ... (counter-example)?'**

- *'Always? Have you ever had a sore throat that got better by itself?'*
- *'Nobody? Have you never met anyone who did get better from depression?'*

Of course, all of the questioning techniques used so far are simply intended to open the doorway to the possibility that there might be another way to interpret things, another way to look at the situation. We shall explore more fully in Chapter 6 on explanation and planning how to use *verbal reframes* to expand horizons and change beliefs.

Expectations

Our *expectations* are our beliefs *about* future possibilities or consequences. In fact, expectations really link our beliefs to our capabilities and behaviours so that we can measure the likelihood of success. We may expect that *this* is likely to happen, but *that* definitely will not! The trouble is that our expectations are rather like self-fulfilling prophecies. We may get exactly what we prophesy, but that may not be what we want. Look at Figure 4.2.

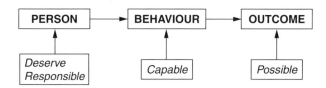

Figure 4.2: Expectations (adapted from Dilts, 1999; *see* bibliography).

In order to achieve what you want (i.e. your outcome), you must first believe that it is possible and attainable. Secondly, you must believe that you have access to the capabilities required for the task, or that you can develop them. Lastly, you must believe that you deserve it, and that you are responsible for achieving that outcome. Three major limiting beliefs can arise from this.

1   *Possibility.* You do not believe that this particular health outcome is possible for you to achieve. You may not even know *what* you want. This leads to a sense of *hopelessness.*
2   *Capability.* This outcome may be possible for *others*, but not for you. You are not capable and cannot see yourself developing the necessary resources. You don't know *how* to go about it. This leads to a sense of *helplessness.*
3   *Worth.* It is possible for you to achieve this outcome. You have, or can develop, the necessary resources. However, you *don't deserve it.* You may

ask yourself *why?* Why me? Or even *who* am I to think that I could possibly achieve this? This leads to a sense of *worthlessness*.

Examples of such limiting beliefs include the following:

- *'I can't see that one little tablet clearing up my indigestion in such a short time'* *(possibility).*
- *'Do you really think I'm fit enough for major heart surgery?' (capability).*
- *'I just feel so guilty about causing the accident. I'll never be able to get over it'* *(worth).*
- *'I know you're doing your best, doc, but to be honest, I think it's curtains now'* *(possibility).*
- *'I know I should just tell him to stop abusing me in that way. I just don't know how to do that without him flying off the handle again' (capability).*
- *'This redundancy thing has knocked me for six. I can't bring myself to apply for anything. I can't stand the thought of being turned down again. I feel like I'm on the scrapheap' (worth).*

Have you begun to notice that patients in consultations may have explicit expectations, which they voice, or implicit ones, which they may keep to themselves? Sometimes the implicit ones are buried deeper, out of conscious awareness, and help is needed to bring them to the surface. The following questions are useful.

- *'What were your thoughts about what we could do for this?'*
- *'When you said that, did you have some idea of the direction you wanted to go in with this?'*
- *'If this were solved to your satisfaction, what would need to have happened?'*
- *'And is there anything that might prevent you (us) from resolving this?'*

We can apply the three criteria for *expectations* (*possibility, capability* and *worth*) to any health outcome, and we might find deficiencies in one or more areas.

Take the problem of depression. Have you noticed that in some cases patients report that the future looks bleak, or worse still that they cannot see a future at all? One of the first interventions is therefore to build a sensory-rich picture of what life could be like if they were no longer depressed. What would they be doing *instead*? What would they look like and sound like? How would they walk and talk? In this way we can build a detailed sense of *possibility*. Next, what skills or capabilities or resources do they *already have* in their life that could be brought to bear on the situation. What skills might they need to develop first? What external resources might help? Antidepressants, for example? Counselling? Finally, what is their current level of self-worth, self-esteem or sense of deservedness? What degree of responsibility do they personally take in deciding to act now? What small task could they succeed in, the act of succeeding thereby sowing the seeds for future, larger gains? Who will they be once they have recovered?

Of course, these three areas are interactive and recursive in nature. Starting with any one can begin to allow previously unlooked-for changes to occur in the other two areas. Thus there is a synergistic coming together of beliefs in a way that can dramatically increase the chances of fulfilling, or even exceeding, expectations. We shall deal with this further in the section on setting outcomes (*see* page 99).

Physiology of beliefs and expectations

So far we have been dealing with the verbal structure of beliefs and expectations. Yet did you know that they also have non-verbal components? Beliefs and their relative strength for an individual can frequently be clearly seen in posture and gestures. We often say that some beliefs are '*closely held*'. What does that mean? For core beliefs, especially about identity, a patient may bring one or both hands up to their chest. Other beliefs that are more loosely held are literally at arm's length!

When talking about *causation*, some people will literally describe with their hands how one thing impacts upon another, often in a linear way. Beliefs about *meaning*, where one thing is expressed in terms of another, may involve both hands coming together close to the mid-line. *Boundary* beliefs, on the other hand, may give rise to the type of gesture that is appropriate to coming up against a wall or other barrier, with the palms in front, pushing away, or even gesturing over a projected imaginary obstacle. Beliefs about *expectations* often start off with a self-gesture, quickly followed by a movement in the direction where they project their future, either in front or to the side.

For those who seem to gesture less, *you will find the same clues in their direction of gaze*, which is usually quite different for each type of belief. Often, when speaking about a closely held core belief, you will notice a deeper breath, frequently followed by a facial flush and a change of voice tonality. Beliefs are *not* merely intellectual – they also have a visceral, body-based *felt* response. There is a great deal of truth behind the words '*embodied beliefs*'.

When pacing and leading a patient's belief statements, you can deepen your level of rapport by gesturing and looking to the same area of their projections as you speak. We will deal with ways of *placing the information* that you have to offer to help to expand and enhance health beliefs by non-verbal means in Chapter 6 on explanation and planning.

Softeners

No, this is not a fabric conditioner to keep your clothes nice and soft! However, what would it be like if you could take the edge off the sharpness of the interrogatives, wrapping them up in a more gently enquiring package? Too often we may have the thought '*Expectations! Great idea to ask about. I'll try it with the next patient.*' And when they arrive we ask '*What is it that you expect from this consultation today?*', uttered in the way that your average robot might intone in its best professional bedside manner! You can imagine the replies, if you have not yet already heard them.

Softeners, then, are sentence fragments that you can use at the beginning of a question, allowing you to get to the roots of a particular issue more sensitively. Here are some examples.

*   '*I was wondering ...*'
*   '*It's interesting that ...*'
*   '*Understandably ...*'
*   '*Obviously ...*'
*   '*Would you mind if ...*'
*   '*Now what if you could ...*'
*   '*I was just thinking ...*'
*   '*I had a patient once ...*'
*   '*As you think about it now ...*'
*   '*I'm curious about ...*'
*   '*Now I don't know if ...*'

The great thing about all of these sentence fragments is that they can be used in *any* conversation – consultations as well as business meetings, with family or friends, at dinner parties, on the golf course, etc. For now I'll start you off with some practice using them and you can generate some more yourself. Aim to write out another 20 or so softeners.

*   '*Would you mind if I asked you some questions about just how low you've been feeling recently?*'
*   '*I was just wondering, what would happen if you did stop worrying. How would that change your nature?*'
*   '*That's an interesting thing to say. How does having cancer mean you're a victim?*'
*   '*Now I don't know if you're the kind of person who could stop smoking now or in a few days time?*'
*   '*As you think about it, how had your mother's depression caused you to be the way you are now?*'

- *'I had a patient once ... a bit like you ... made redundant too ... said it really knocked his self-confidence ... and I wondered how you were feeling?'*

Do you remember the 20 examples you were going to do?

As you think about it now, you probably have your own favourites to add to this list. What I'm especially curious about is just how you're going to begin using these softeners now. Obviously you may have to start with just one or two at a time. And I don't know if you're the kind of person who schedules this for your next set of consultations, or the one after that. You see I had a colleague who was learning this once, and the interesting thing about him was that, after merely reading this material, he found himself automatically using it, without thinking. And he said to me 'Would you mind if I told everybody else just how easy it is simply to do this now?' And I said 'Of course not. Be my guest.'

Section Three: what do you want?

Outcome setting

Thus far we have noted exactly which filter patterns a patient uses to process information, started to find out a little more about how they structure their beliefs about what has been happening, and begun to delve into their expectations of future possibilities and consequences. We have seen that expectations are the glue that connects our beliefs about what we think we are capable of doing to the actions that form the next steps – what we think we want or don't want, what we hope will happen, or what we dread might actually come to pass. In NLP terms, these are our outcomes.

Outcomes have sometimes been called *dreams with deadlines*. How many times have you told yourself that you are definitely going to do something, yet you never get around to it? How many times have you daydreamed about how things could be different, yet they still remain the same? We hear this kind of talk all the time. I'll start on my diet tomorrow (as you eat squidgy chocolate dessert today). I'm really going to give up smoking (it's just that it's not the right time, maybe next month). Yes, I know I should take a bit more exercise, and I'm trying hard to see where I can fit it in. Actually we are successfully getting our outcomes met all the time. They just don't happen to be the ones we consciously want. There's that old saying *'Failing to plan is planning to fail.'* Whatever happens, at some level we are creating the results we already have. So are they the results you want?

Please don't run away with the idea that outcomes are big fancy important things that we need to deliberate on at length. They might be, of course. Yet many outcomes are quite mundane. If you regularly get to work on time, then that's a product of outcome setting. If you are thirsty, decide to have a drink of your favourite beverage, and do so, that's a result of outcome setting, too. If you are peckish and make a sandwich, that's another. You are reading this book right now, so what is it that you want from it? Knowledge, new skills, entertainment, or something different? Our outcomes are powered by our internal drives, which may be as basic as thirst or hunger, or you may value learning, or pushing the limits to known frontiers. Perhaps you are even working on the cure for cancer.

Patients have outcomes, too – for example, surviving their fight with cancer, getting that antibiotic for their throat, hoping that the operation will be successful, worrying that the needle will hurt, being concerned about not being able to cope with their mother's Alzheimer's, wanting this depression to lift, praying to God that wee Johnnie will pull through, or hopeful that the infertility treatment will work.

And of course these are brought to bear in the context of your consultation room, perhaps conflicting with your desire to finish on time, or you are already running late and are in survival mode. Yet you know that the antibiotic is not needed, that the operation is only palliative, that they're losing the fight – and the needle may well hurt! Both patients and doctors have outcomes that they want to have met. The real question is how to *dovetail them together*. So how do we set things up in a way that can give us and our patients greater leverage in meeting our health outcomes?

Outcomes have a *structure*. There are ways to formulate them so as to maximise the chances of getting what you want, and also what your patient wants. Bear in mind, however, that sometimes no matter how much you may want something, no matter how perfect the plan, no matter how often you visualise it, or how many affirmations you repeat, there is still no firm guarantee that it will come to pass.

Yet, like me, you will probably have had times in your past when you thought you couldn't do something. It was impossible, too hard, you weren't skilled enough, you knew you would fail – but you succeeded anyway! You surpassed all of your expectations. You delightfully surprised yourself. Somehow you rose to the occasion and the rest is history, as you look back now in satisfaction. NLP is very much an outcome-oriented technology. The principles of outcome setting that can be applied in any context are described below.

As you engage with these principles, please look at them from your perspective as a doctor *and* from that of your patient. Bear in mind that this process can be used to help you to set and attain any outcome – personal or professional, family or pleasure.

Stated in positives

As you look at some of the outcomes described above, you will see that some of them are phrased in a way that expresses a problem to *move away from*, and others describe a solution to *move towards*. Negatives (i.e. away froms) do not compute operationally. They can make intellectual sense at one level, but you cannot take the action of not doing something. Whatever you do, don't think of a pink elephant right now. I repeat, don't do it! Don't picture a pink elephant. Don't hear it trumpeting in your mind's ear. What happened? Of course you thought about one. As one NLP trainer put it, '*You can't think about what you don't want to think about without thinking about it first. Think about that!*'

Yet we do this all the time. We say things like '*This won't hurt*', '*Don't worry*', '*Mustn't be late*', '*You have to stop worrying*', '*I hope I don't miss lunch*', '*Don't stop your medication*', '*Do you need anything for pain?*', '*I hope you won't get side-effects*', '*Please don't tell me it's cancer doctor*', '*I just don't want to be depressed any more*', '*Have you got anything for not sleeping?*', '*I must lose weight*', '*I really have to stop smoking*', '*I want to get rid of x, y or z.*'

So one of the very first steps in outcome setting, and indeed for any communication, is to *say it the way you want it*. Take any statements that are phrased in the negative and turn them around to their positive counterpart. Find out what will be *different*. Keep the following question in mind and ask it.

'What do you want instead?'

Of course, feel free to use the softeners that you have already learned.

* '*Understandably you don't want to worry. So if you weren't worrying,* **what would you be doing instead?**'
* '*So I was wondering, if you weren't depressed,* **what would be different about you? What would you be doing instead? What is it that you really want for yourself?**'
* '*Are you comfortable enough?*' (instead of '*any pain?*').
* '*I plan to finish on time.*'
* '*Stay calm.*'
* '*So what weight do you want to be?*'
* '*Keep the medication going until you finish the course.*'
* '*I want to have healthier lungs and easily walk up the stairs in my house.*'

You can start practising saying things the way you want them to come out. Of course it's OK, and often quite useful, to pace your patient and start with the negative first. This shows that you understand and it deepens the rapport. Then gently enquire about how specifically *they want things to be different*.

Started and maintained by you

This is an extremely important point. Ultimately we are only in control of ourselves, our own thoughts, feelings and behaviours. And the converse is also true. We are not responsible for another person's behaviours, feelings or actions. Sure, we can *influence* them in some way to take action, but we can't do it for them. So if your outcome depends on another person changing, then you're not really in control.

For example, how many times have you heard the anxious, depressed wife of an alcoholic say '*If only he would stop drinking, then everything would be all right*'. This puts the responsibility for her outcome on to someone else's shoulders, leaving her at the mercy of his whims – a victim's choice. One question that I have found useful in these circumstances is '*If he did stop drinking, and everything was all right,* **what would be different about you then?**' Mostly the answers are concerned with peace of mind, freedom to do other things, or perhaps safety and security. These are the real outcomes here, and the trick is to develop those outcomes *regardless of whether he continues drinking or not*. If we chunk up to the larger benefits of the initial outcome, we can often open up a solution space and have other choices to get these needs met.

The questions to ask in this section are as follows.

- **'What would having that do for you?'**
- **'What resources do you have to accomplish this?'**

These may be the personal resources that you or your patient already have, or ones that you can develop, or external resources that you can make use of. This includes prescriptions for medication, minor or major operative procedures, or referral to a consultant, practice nurse, counsellor, etc. The only common denominator is that the resource is available and the patient plays their part in taking responsibility to follow through with action. You may prescribe an effective remedy, yet the patient may decide not to comply with it. Seemingly, the commonest reason for transplant failure is organ rejection due to failure to take immunosuppressive medication!

Of course, one of our own personal resources is our ability to influence other people appropriately, perhaps by having a 'win-win' outcome, getting both sets of needs met satisfactorily. By imagining how it would be if you placed yourself in their shoes, their circumstances, you can examine the consequences from their viewpoint. You can ask yourself the following questions.

- *'What do I need to do to ensure that they want to help me to achieve my outcome?'*
- *'What are the most persuasive elements from their perspective?'*

These questions can be most helpful in the type of situation encountered by the wife of the alcoholic. Although she cannot stop drinking *for* him, she may be able to change her own behaviour in a way that helps to influence him in the right direction.

Sensory-based evidence

One of the problems with setting outcomes is being *too vague* about what you want. You may know the general direction in which you want to go but not yet have the specific details – a skeleton that needs to be fleshed out. Sometimes patients who are depressed may be superb at going into minor detail about what is wrong. It's as if they have a map of Ordnance Survey proportions of their problems – about what has *not yet worked*. By contrast, if you ask them what they want instead, you will often be met with either peculiar or resigned looks, followed eventually by 'Well, *happy I suppose*'. That's like having a world atlas, pointing to your country of origin and saying 'Well, *anywhere around here will do*'.

In order to get where we want to go, we need to build a detailed sensory-rich map of the destination. If you got what you wanted, what would you be seeing, hearing, feeling, smelling and tasting? Imagine how it would be if you had *already* achieved your goal. Step inside and wrap it all around you. What is different in your sensory experience now? Successful people in all walks of life have at least one thing in common. They are clear and specific about what they want.

Therefore the questions for this section are as follows.

- **'How will you know when you have your outcome?'**
- **'What will you be seeing, hearing, feeling, smelling and tasting?'**
- **'If someone else saw you achieving your outcome, what would they be noticing?'**

You can build up this sensory-rich picture gradually. Often it is useful to get an outside perspective, too, imagining the outcome through a friend's eyes, or as if someone had video-taped your success. This part of outcome setting can initially appear rather 'canned'. However, when we get to the section on the *miracle question* you will see how it can flow. In the mean time, here are some examples:

- *'I'll look at the scales, see 70 kg, feel my clothes looser, and hear friends saying I look great.'*
- *'I'll be able to walk upstairs to go to the toilet, and keep my inhalers in my pocket!'*
- *'I'll be back doing the things I enjoy, swimming and cycling, with that satisfying feeling of pleasantly tired muscles.'*
- *'Happiness means taking the time to enjoy doing my gardening again. Even the smell of the compost!'*

There is one thing that stands out for me time and time again with patients who have cancer. Maybe you have had this experience, too. And that is how some of them, who appear to be at death's door, can somehow keep themselves alive in order to fulfil something of great importance to them – like awaiting the birth of a first grandchild several months away, planning and taking that holiday of a lifetime, or the big family reunion in summer (yet it's still January). Anecdotal, I know, yet *what if* they were invoking the same sort of outcome process that we are going through right now?

Consider the consequences and by-products of achieving an outcome

Surprisingly, some people really want to stay much the same, without changing. They may *say* that they definitely want to do such and such, but for a variety of reasons they don't. Sometimes things just don't appear to work out. Sometimes there are glorious failures, often accompanied by the words '*See how hard I tried*', or a variation on the theme. Sometimes the problem box, which is in their known world, is a more comfortable and safe place to be than the unknown, potentially unsafe world of the solution. Better the devil you know. Now I am not suggesting that this phenomenon, which is often called *secondary gain*, is necessarily a conscious choice. That would be manipulation. For the most part it is out of conscious awareness. Basically it means that the outcome as it stands offers less than the current situation.

I have a patient who has had agoraphobia for more than 30 years. She has successfully defeated any therapist who has been foolish enough to think that they can cure her! It would seem that we have an unwritten agreement. Every now and again she makes a small improvement, tells me what a wonderful doctor I am, and gives me unsolicited small gifts (usually tins of biscuits, and for Christmas a small bottle of brandy – not my tipple!). In return I am supportive and don't push her too hard beyond her limits. She has an occasional relapse to keep me on my toes and stop any complacency, usually when there has been a family fall-out. Yet in the past two years she has actually made considerable progress, and she recently made a 130-mile round trip for a day out shopping with a friend! Her over-riding concerns are safety, security and control. I have been careful to preserve these feelings as I encourage her to *do small tasks* (the big trip was her idea, and I cautioned her against it – reverse psychology!). I see her for ten minutes every two months or so.

Every outcome we have – large or small, important or non-important – has certain potential benefits and consequences for ourselves and the significant other people in our lives. Take the patient with chronic back pain, on invalidity benefit, perhaps with a disability allowance or even receiving assistance with transport. If his medical condition improved significantly he might actually be worse off financially or even emotionally. So in setting a realistic, achievable health outcome we need some questions to help us to cover all of the angles. We don't necessarily need to ask them out loud, but it pays to keep them in mind.

- *'What will happen if you get this outcome?'*
- *'What will happen if you don't get it?'*
- *'What WON'T happen if you get it?'*
- *'What WON'T happen if you DON'T get it?'*

These questions are all about gain and loss. What would you gain/lose if you achieved your outcome? What would you gain/lose if you didn't achieve your outcome? Take my agoraphobic patient, for instance. If she got completely well, she would gain the freedom to do what she wanted whenever she wanted. However, she could lose the attention of family and friends, and the degree of control that she has at present. If she didn't get completely well, she could use minor relapses as a way of getting what she wanted from her family. Overall, her loss would be the restriction of the boundaries of her world, keeping her a prisoner in a cell of her own making. Now I hasten to add that none of these were 'conscious' choices, yet becoming and remaining aware of them has certainly helped me to manage the situation more effectively.

You can use these questions for *any* outcome. Suppose that you were deciding on the merits of prescribing an antibiotic for a sore throat. The gains of doing this might be along the lines of perceived patient satisfaction and a quick consultation, especially if you were running late. The loss would be that you had educated them that they needed an antibiotic each time, thus increasing your future workload. If you didn't prescribe, you would gain the chance to use your developing influencing skills to expand and update their health beliefs, allowing them more scope to manage self-limiting illness themselves, thereby freeing up future appointments. The loss might be that it took longer, and left them disgruntled, perhaps making future appointments with a partner more likely. We shall return to this later in Chapter 6 on explanation and planning.

Ecology concerns

An ecology check ensures that the outcome you want *fits* with your life, your personality, your family, friends and even your work. If a patient took on board your advice about exercise for improving health to the extent that he spent 3 hours a day at a gym, to the detriment of his family and his job, that probably would not be ecological!

Some patients actually need treatment because what they are doing to themselves in order to achieve an outcome is not ecological. It is like having two parts of yourself embroiled in internal warfare. One of my patients had a problem with binge eating that was seriously affecting her self-esteem, to the extent that she was becoming increasingly depressed. In terms of her *meta-programs*, she was almost completely *other* oriented. Everyone else's needs came first. She could not enforce her boundaries and she found it very difficult to say no. It turned out that the only thing she really did that was truly for herself was to gorge herself – short-term relief and longer-term pain. Her real outcome was 'asserting myself respectfully', and developing these skills was one of the interventions that led to an increased sense of congruency and well-being.

Ecology is continually being checked at each stage of setting outcomes. However, some specific questions include the following.

- **'How will this outcome fit with the rest of you? Your family? Your friends? Your business? Your job?'**
- **'What will be different as a result of your having this?'**
- **'Is it worth the cost to you?'**
- **'Does it fit with your sense of self?'**

An ecology check essentially looks for *incongruency*. If you don't have a yes (remember yes-sets?), then you have got a no. Beware of responses that start with:

- 'Yes, but ...'
- 'On the one hand ... yet on the other ...'
- 'Well part of me wants to, but another part ...'

Non-verbally, look for any body language that indicates no whilst giving verbal assent, such as one hand gesturing and the other staying still, a pulling away of the body, a simultaneous shake of the head, a facial grimace, an intake of breath, or a change in voice tone halfway through a sentence.

Ecology also helps to fit smaller outcomes into larger frames. By fitting what a patient wants into the larger frame of their health beliefs and expectations, we can help them to get more *leverage* to actually achieve their outcomes. This sense of fit and dovetailing with the other things that are of value to them helps to provide both commitment and motivation for success. We shall look further at how to do this effectively while dealing with any incongruency in Chapter 6 on explanation and planning.

Here is a useful *aide-mémoire*, adapted from Ian McDermott, for setting outcomes. You could photocopy it on to card and make sure that it is visible on your desk!

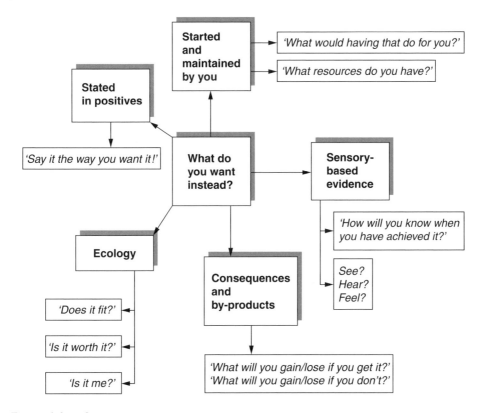

Figure 4.3:   Outcomes.

The miracle question

Sometimes in the past, when I asked a patient about what they really wanted for themselves – their health outcome – I was somewhat stymied by two types of response. First, there were those who either kept on answering with what they want to move away from (i.e. the negative), and secondly, there were those whose thinking remained high in the stratosphere of large, vague chunks and who never got down to the detail.

An example of this is the depressed individual who states '*All I want is to be happy*'. I wondered for some time about what to do, until I stumbled on the work of Steve de Shazer and brief solution-focused therapy.

De Shazer is a fan of *noticing differences* and putting them to work. He says that too many people keep right on doing the same familiar things and then wonder why their problem still remains. He also claims that by helping the patient to focus on what would be different about a potential solution, that resolution can occur without ever really crossing swords with the problem. Although this is not strictly an NLP approach, I have found it very useful in combination with other NLP strategies. De Shazer asks the following *miracle question:*

> **'Imagine that you went to bed tonight and whilst you were asleep a miracle occurred, such that when you awoke your problem had gone. You don't know how or why, because you were asleep. You only know it's gone. Tell me what would be different now?'**

I'll give you an example in the following dialogue. The patient is a 33-year-old housewife who has felt down and depressed for several months. She has three children aged 10, 8 and 5 years. She has been struggling to tell me what she wants because she is not really clear about it herself.

Patient: *Well, I just don't know. That's a hard question. I don't see an easy answer to it (shrugs, sighs and looks at the floor).*

Doctor: *OK, I can see it's not easy. And I know you really want to feel better, don't you? (pacing and leading) (patient nods yes). Would you mind if I asked you a question … a crazy kind of question … that some people find really helpful (gesturing to her)?*

Patient: *(looks up quizzically with a slight smile) Uh-huh … (nods).*

Doctor: *OK then … here goes … just imagine you go to bed tonight … (she nods) … and when you're sleeping … a miracle occurs … the kind of miracle that when you awake in the morning … your problem's completely gone … resolved.*

Patient: *Gone? Like you mean I'm better?*

Doctor: *Yeah … the kind of miracle that means you don't know how … you don't know why … you're just better … (she laughs) … tell me … what's different about you then?*

Patient: *(takes big long breath) … Well … I just wouldn't be depressed any more.*

Doctor: *You're not depressed any more … (pacing) … so what's different now?*

Patient: *Well, I'm just not irritable any more … I don't feel down.*

Doctor: *OK ... you're not irritable ... not down ... what are you feeling like instead?*
Patient: *I'd feel happier ... I'd actually want to get up and do something ... rather than dragging myself out of bed ... (smiles).*
Doctor: *So how do you know you're happier ... what lets you know?*
Patient: *(quizzical look) ... I'd feel it in my shoulders ... that old cliché ... a burden lifted.*
Doctor: *A burden lifted (paces) ... and you go downstairs ... and the kids at breakfast ... how would they know you're better ... **without you telling them**?*
Patient: *Well, I wouldn't be shouting at them for a start! (laughs).*
Doctor: *No shouting (smiles and paces) ... so what would you sound like instead ... what's your voice like ... ?*
Patient: *(tilts head to left) ... much softer ... much gentler ... some laughs ... God, I haven't sounded like that for months!!*
Doctor: *Good ... good ... and if you were to see yourself through their eyes ... how would you look different?*
Patient: *Look different? (she's pacing me now!!) (breathes in, sits up straighter and looks ahead). Well, I'm smiling ... there's a twinkle in my eyes ... my hair's combed ... and I'm just getting on with things.*
Doctor: *Getting on with things ... ?*
Patient: *Yeah ... you know ... tidying up ... getting them ready for school ... having a clean living room again!*
Doctor: *And your husband ... how would he know ... without telling ... you're better now?*
Patient: *(huge grin) ... He'd think all his Christmases had come at once ... !!*
Doctor: *(laughing) ... Whoa ... we'd better stop there ... can't have you getting better **that** quickly! (initiating polarity response with a wink).*

This short interlude took place within a ten-minute consultation. And no, the patient wasn't *magically cured* in one brief session. However, it was the beginning of putting some details together about what she wanted for herself, beginning to reconnect her with previous resources, and adding a bit of gentle humour to lighten the process.

The beauty of this approach to setting outcomes is that it is very conversational, almost casual. I have used it in a host of situations, from physical disease to psychiatric and psychological presentations, relationship issues and social problems. All of the criteria for a well-formed outcome can come into play. As well as experiencing a potential solution at first hand, you can also step into the shoes of the significant other people in the patient's life, seeing it from their perspective, or you can help them to step out of themselves, like a fly-on-the-wall onlooker, observing from a safe distance. You can change time-frames as they imagine going further into the future beyond the time when they have changed, looking back on a successful outcome, all the while deepening the fertile soil for healthy change.

If you are interested in an in-depth coverage of Steve de Shazer's approach, consult the Bibliography at the end of this book.

Gathering the information together

We are now almost at the end of this chapter on gathering information – and there has been a lot of information to gather! Picking up from the end of the last chapter, having established today's agenda of issues, we have moved on at quite a pace. Initially we have remained focused on the process as it continues to unfold, noticing the particular *meta-programs* as they arise. Are they moving *towards or away from*, and are they *general* or *specific*, *matching* or *mismatching*? Just exactly *how* are they filtering information? And with just a little attention, you will find yourself beginning almost effortlessly to pick up both the verbal and non-verbal cues.

And *how specifically* will you begin to notice yourself not only eliciting the patient's beliefs about what has caused this particular issue, what it may mean, and the boundaries, but also framing them in such a way that you can recapture the experiences from which they were born? And *how precisely* will you start using the *meta-model*, noticing those beliefs that are enhancing and those that are limiting? Wondering about their expectations. Is it really possible that you are now developing the capabilities, even more responsibly, for delving into issues of self-worth and deservedness? What if you were becoming the kind of doctor who had *automatically* formed a closely held strong belief about your ability to notice significant non-verbal responses? How would that enhance what you already do? Just like my colleague who said to me '*always remember the softeners*'.

So as you pause at this chapter's end ... what outcomes have already been forming in your mind for you and your patients? If you were to *imagine* incorporating all of these behaviours into your mental and physical vocabulary ... in what way would your patients be benefiting? How would they know that you were *doing things differently*? Would it be something they saw, heard or felt? You might be wondering just which of your current resources are already available to help, and which ones you can easily add. It is worthwhile considering just how much more effective you are becoming as a result, especially when you measure the cost in terms of failing to be the best you can be. And when you *really* ... and I mean *really* ... think about it deeply, there's *really* nothing better ... than *going beyond expectations*.

See you in the next chapter ...

CHAPTER 5

Building the relationship

Introduction

This chapter is concerned with the type of relationship-building skills that can be used in every phase of the consultation – beginning, middle and end. We have already encountered the early rapport skills used in the initiating phase, but it is now time to build substantially on these, adding more depth and breadth, really getting to the heart of all good therapeutic relationships – in other words, sowing and cultivating the seeds of *trust*. Although it is possible to establish a fairly instant rapport on first meeting, trust – especially deep trust – takes time to develop fully, and is not without some risk, yet is ultimately one of the most rewarding experiences that general practice offers, perhaps the *most* rewarding.

Trust is essentially a two-way process, and it needs a high level of commitment by both parties. Some people trust too readily and may be let down often. Some have been battle scarred and may never trust again. I recently had some personal experiences that threw all of this into sharp relief.

I don't know if you've ever had the experience of one of your patients committing suicide. Not that long ago, one of mine, a man in his early sixties, hung himself. He had been moderately depressed for several months, with various precipitating factors, his wife having died several years earlier. I had received an intimation from a relative that the patient had been having suicidal thoughts. I broached this subject with him in some depth on two occasions, and he assured me that he was not having such thoughts. Although he had been on treatment for some time, he claimed that he was now improving in response to an increase in medication. I went off on holiday and returned to the news of his death. His relatives, including his children and grandchildren whom I had personally looked after for a number of years, blamed me for failing to prevent the suicide. Rather than speak to me about it, they abruptly left my list. All trust had evaporated.

Only yesterday, a woman in her late sixties came to see me. She had returned from the oncology clinic with the news that her metastatic breast carcinoma had progressed at an accelerated rate. There were no other treatment options and, as she put it, *'I know I'm at the end of the line, doctor'*. We discussed her concerns for the future, and I asked her if there was anything else she needed. She replied *'Nothing at the moment. I know I can trust you, doctor. I've got faith in you. You'll look after me just as you did for Jimmy. He was so peaceful at the end.'* Jimmy had been one of my first patients when I had joined the practice 12 years previously. Already terminally ill with metastatic bowel cancer, he had initially experienced a lot of problems with pain control, which we had surmounted by various means. He died as he had wished, in his bed with a fine malt whisky!

There are many powerful emotions that we may feel during the course of our everyday consulting – some good, some not so good and some decidedly negative. In the course of traditional medical training, we may have been taught about the necessity of being objective in our diagnosing and treating, of standing back, sheltering behind a mask of impassivity as we hand down our judgements and pronouncements on life and death. Such detachment has a protective function, yet at the same time may actually alienate us from the very people whom we are trying to help. This chapter, then, is all about developing the skills and resources that can *build relationships through good times and bad*, and that can help us to engage and deal more effectively with the current presentation of illness whilst fostering a climate of mutual trust and understanding.

Aims of this chapter

There are a variety of different perspectives that we can take as we explore continuing building of relationships. We have already discussed rapport at environmental and behavioural levels, and we can add to this further by looking at the other *logical levels*. We need to tune in more to the emotional current of both things that are said and those that are left unsaid. We need to be able to step inside the other person's experience and try it on for size, developing our skills of *empathy*, but in a balanced way, without going overboard and losing ourselves. At the same time we can also experience a process that will help to resolve some of the thornier issues in difficult relationships. Once again we shall visit our *consulting flow state*, adding some other states to the mix to prevent burnout, while remaining relaxed yet attentive. We shall explore *congruent* and *incongruent* communication, both for our patients and for ourselves – always, of course, with an eye to picking up the non-verbal nuances.

The specific areas that we shall cover are:

Section One: deepening rapport

- Developing *rapport* at the levels of capability, beliefs and values, and identity.
- The three *perceptual positions* and their uses; developing *empathy*.
- The *meta-mirror* for resolving relationship difficulties.

Section Two: revisiting states

- Adding the *peripheral vision state* for relaxed consulting.
- Identifying signals for *congruence* and *incongruence*.

Section Three: more on structure

- Paying attention to other useful non-verbal clues in passing; *eye-accessing cues*.
- Using *meta-comments* and signposting.

In this way you will begin to achieve the goal of integrating your developing relationship skills with the ongoing tasks of history taking, hypothesising, diagnosing and treating.

Section One: Deepening rapport

Logical levels of rapport

You will recall how, in Chapter 3 on initiating the session, we dealt with rapport on the levels of environment and behaviour, looking in particular at the physiological clues, and how to match and mirror. Having accomplished that fundamental level, we shall now consider the other levels of capability, beliefs and values, and identity.

Capability

At this level we are seeking to develop our ability to match the thinking patterns and strategies as patients deliver their stories. We have already considered one area, namely meta-programs. However, even more basic than that are *predicates*, which are the visual, auditory and kinaesthetic words used in the telling of the tale. These are called *representational* systems, because they represent our senses. As you listen to people talking, you will notice how they may describe similar events in different systems.

Some people may '**see** *what you mean*', while others find that it '**sounds** *right*', or maybe even '*that doesn't **feel** right*'. Sometimes, though, '*it all makes complete* **sense**'. The last of these is called an *unspecified* word, which is one that does not immediately give away the representational system that is being used. Of course, occasionally olfactory and gustatory language is used, such as '*a **bitter** pill to swallow*' or even '*a **fishy**-smelling discharge!*'

Box 5.1 contains a list of some of the more common words.

Box 5.1:   Commonly used predicates

Unspecified	*Visual*	*Auditory*	*Kinaesthetic*
Sense	See	Hear	Feel
Experience	Dawn	Talk	Hold
Consider	Look	Sound	Touch
Decide	Show	Whine	Grasp
Change	Reveal	Croak	Hard
Know	Hazy	Chatter	Contact
Realise	Fuzzy	Tell	Stiff
Convince	Colourful	Call	Firm
Plan	Clear	Listen	Slip
Process	Appear	Ring	Solid

Of course, these words are often used in short phrases which give a clearer picture of just exactly what is on a patient's mind – or not!

Box 5.2:   Commonly used short phrases

Unspecified	*Visual*	*Auditory*	*Kinaesthetic*
If memory serves me right	We don't see eye to eye on this	She turned a deaf ear	It's like a pressure building up
We need to make a decision	The future looks pretty bleak	That sounds frightening	It cut me like a knife
Do you know the answer?	It's like a black hole in my past	He's got a high-pitched shriek	When will you be in touch?
What do you think about the diagnosis?	There's a shadow on my X-ray	Doesn't ring any bells with me	I can't stand it any more

---

We all use these words routinely, although often without awareness. They give an *insight* into how we are processing information at that particular moment in time. Again, beware of the trap of putting someone in a box – for example, 'He's a visual, she's an auditory, he's a kinaesthetic', etc. By matching back the representational system that the patient is using, you can *tune in* more effectively to their thinking style. They will feel that you have *grasped* their situation and come to an *understanding* of their problem. Practise this in your next series of consultations.

Sometimes it is useful to be able to *translate* between each of the representational systems. Look at the list in Box 5.3. Use the translations given below and notice the responses that you get.

Box 5.3:   Translations between different representational systems

Unspecified	*Visual*	*Auditory*	*Kinaesthetic*
I don't understand ...	I can't see what you're saying ...	Sounds double Dutch to me ...	It just doesn't fit ...
I think ...	The way I see it is ...	I've sounded it out and ...	I've got a feeling that ...
That's confusing ...	It's a bit hazy to me ...	Like a lot of voices singing off key ...	I just can't get hold of that ...
I understand ...	I can picture that ...	Loud and clear ...	I get your drift ...
I was wondering ...	I was daydreaming ...	I was just telling myself ...	I was going through the motions and ...

Beliefs and values

Beliefs and values are an area in which you can begin to develop a very deep level of rapport. They are important to people and need to be respected, even if you do not agree with them. Many beliefs and values that surround health are not entirely logical or rational from a medical perspective. However, for a patient they are the literal 'truth'. Because they are in a sense embodied, to wantonly disregard or refute someone's beliefs is rather like slapping them in the face. You may not have physically touched them, yet your words may have sounded the death knell for that particular consultation, or even for that relationship.

It pays great dividends to *always* (yes always!) pace a person's belief or value before going on to help them to expand their thinking around that issue. Pacing is *not* agreement. It is simply acknowledging that for this particular patient, at this particular time, this is how they see the world. In effect you are establishing a *yes-set*, which makes it more likely that they will be open to your further interventions. Even if you strongly disagree with them, the fact that you have respectfully listened to and acknowledged their position makes it far easier to *'agree to disagree'*. It is sometimes amazing how expressing differences in this way can not only foster mutual understanding, but can also markedly strengthen your relationship.

We have already covered a great deal of material about beliefs, values and expectations in the last chapter, all of which continues to be pertinent. The very act of asking questions (with softeners!) in this area shows that you are concerned with the patient's unique view of the world. When someone is interested in you in that way, you will feel that your deeper concerns are also being broached and met.

Think back to a time when this happened for you. Can you remember when someone asked you about something that was important to you, close to your heart? Maybe one of your special interests? And they listened non-judgementally, encouraging you to go on, interested in what you were saying. What did that feel like? What kind of connection did they make with you? How do you think about them now? What would it be like to be having that kind of connection, now, in reverse, with your patients?

An important part of rapport at this level is handing over your information in a way that fits with the patient's worldview. By nesting your material within their existing framework, you are immeasurably increasing the chances of it being acted upon. After all, not to do so would create cognitive dissonance! We shall cover how to do this both verbally and non-verbally in Chapter 6 on explanation and planning.

Identity and beyond

Gaining rapport at this level is an extension of the previous level to include those *core* beliefs and values about self. This is not simply respecting the unique individual in front of you – it is also about accepting their worth as a human being, no matter what has happened. In a sense this is a place where judgement stops and acceptance starts. Now let us be clear, this is not about condoning what may have happened in the past. It is about separating what someone does (their *behaviour*) from who they are (their *identity*).

One of my patients was addicted to heroin. Initially I found myself being very judgemental, and at the same time feeling guilty about it. It was clear that this patient was still abusing the system, had no real intentions of stopping using heroin after his methadone course had finished, and was obviously involved in illegal activities in the locality. On one occasion I pondered over what I knew about him – his background in Glasgow, his stay in a young offenders' institution, physical and possible sexual abuse as a child, and never having had a job. I tried to imagine what life would have been like in his shoes, and shuddered at the thought. Although I could never really fully appreciate his circumstances, not being him, I did start to wonder whether I would really have been all that different if I had had his life.

Curiously, though, I also began to get a feel for just how skilled he really was. He had formidable negotiation skills, not only of the heavy-handed intimidating type, but also an occasionally very disarming persuasion style. He was financing a habit that sometimes cost £100–200 per day, and he planned his acquisition of this amount meticulously, usually by stealing and fencing goods. In that way he was a hell of a lot more successful in raising money than some health services managers I knew! His skills were somewhat unicontextual, yet akin to those required in a successful small business. (I am not condoning, just stating!)

Once I saw him in this light I actually found it much easier to be tougher on his behaviour while at the same time affirming his undoubted skills. This bemused him somewhat, and consultations became both easier and harder. Easier in the sense that I actually looked forward to some of them, and I enjoyed the *reframing* of the problems he posed as skills that he could use in a different arena. Harder in the sense that no matter what I did, his future was in his hands – his choice. Sadly there was no happy ending, and he is presently ensconsed in prison, presumably still feeding his habit.

Identity also covers *roles*. People are not simply who or what they present. We all have differing roles in life: *mother, father, son, daughter, breadwinner, victim, doctor, lawyer, bricklayer, waitress, black sheep, shift worker,* etc. Often concerns about an illness that may on the surface seem trivial have their roots in a perceived threat to identity. Knowing a little more about what our patients do for a living, how they define their boundaries and how they see their role can help us to tailor-make a better solution.

And, of course, there is also information that is *beyond identity*. This can be information about immediate family and circumstances, and the type of wider social connections that we all have, which may enhance or constrain how we deal with illness. Knowing this information builds rapport by helping to contextualise our remarks and potential solutions. In a wider sense, *beyond identity* also encompasses our religious and spiritual beliefs and values. Caring for a terminally ill committed Christian who, in the terms of one of my patients, is *'going to glory'* is quite different to an atheist who believes *'It all ends here, doctor'*. And of course there are all the other rich varieties of faiths that abound. Again, no matter what the belief, we can build relationships even in this delicate area by demonstrating respect and a non-judgemental stance. In this way we may encounter the deepest levels of rapport, which may be one of the most fulfilling parts of our practice.

Exercise 10:   Developing more rapport

1   Notice which *predicates* your patients use during today's consultations. Match them when you are asking for more information. What happens?
2   Watch a chat show on television. Look for body *matching and mirroring*. Notice the *predicates* used by host and guest. Do they match?
3   Listen to a radio programme. Pay attention to the types of predicates used. Which ones predominate? Are they really more *'auditory'* on the radio?
4   Watch a politician being interviewed. Which predicates do they use? Is it true that they use far more *'unspecified'* words?
5   Go back to the chat show. Does the host ask questions that develop rapport on all of the logical levels? What about the radio programme? And the interview with the politician?
6   Think of someone you do not get on with. Which *logical level* are you mismatching on? If you wanted to improve your relationship, what could you do to match at that level? What difference does that make?

Perceptual positions

Perceptual positions are a way of gaining a greater *perspective* on a situation. They are a way of broadening your outlook so that potential solutions arise from a more balanced place of wisdom rather than a one-dimensional view. There are three positions, namely *first* (self), *second* (other) and *third* (observer).

First position is your *own view* of the situation – your own reality, as seen and experienced through your own senses, standing in your own shoes. You think in terms of what is important to you, and what you want to achieve. You use 'I' language, referring to you personally – for example, *I feel, I think, I know, I decide*.

This is the position for standing up for yourself, and making your needs known in a given situation. You set your own outcomes from this position and do a final ecology check from here. Developing this position leads to assertive behaviour and skills mastery, especially if you know your values and what is important to you.

However, too much first position, without ever visiting the other two, leads to imbalance. You may appear arrogant and aggressive, striving for your outcomes at the expense of family, friends, patients and colleagues. At times you may feel so strongly about something that you may be on the verge of being overcome by your emotions. You know what is best for people, regardless of what they think themselves. You may come across as overbearing or even patronising!

Second position, on the other hand, is like *stepping into someone else's shoes* and experiencing the situation as if you are them. Essentially you are imagining the view from their perspective, thinking in the way that they might think. Whilst no one can literally think another's thoughts, this position is fundamental to the development of empathic communication and deep rapport. You become attuned to the other person's feelings and you also develop an intellectual understanding of how their world fits together.

Second position is particularly useful when you can't understand where the other person is coming from, especially if their behaviour seems odd or not easily explainable. By putting yourself more frequently into this position, you will convey a sense of reassurance and a seeking of mutual understanding.

However, I have noticed that many general practitioners often step into this position and fail to come out! It is rather like a black hole. I believe that this is one of the major causes of excessive stress and burnout. By over-identifying with other people's needs and emotions you may leave little time for your own. Feeling someone else's pain, albeit briefly, can be a useful source of information. However, getting stuck and being unable to clamber out is a recipe for personal misery. It can even lead to loss of self-esteem. I applaud the intention of doing one's best for patients, yet this is better accomplished from a more balanced viewpoint. Your own health deserves a place and a voice at the table, too.

Third position is the ability to take a *step back*, get some distance, and experience the situation as if you are a detached observer, a 'fly on the wall'. You imagine seeing both yourself and the other person *over there*, beyond arm's reach. You are likely to have little emotion in this position, which makes it a good one for *re-viewing* difficult situations. It allows you to think about what is going on and perhaps to notice things that you might otherwise have missed.

This is a very useful position to use when planning, especially when there are multiple other viewpoints to co-ordinate. People who are good at handling aggression from others in a controlled unemotional way often do this from this position. They lessen any intense feelings of anger that they may have felt in first position and take things less personally.

However, excessive use of *third position* can give you a rather austere image of being detached, unemotional and, at the extreme, unapproachable. Whilst you may have a great deal of objectivity and may be very analytical, you may come across as a *'cold fish'*. Sometimes this position can mask a deeper sense of loneliness and isolation.

I have written about these positions as if from a doctor's perspective. However, I'm sure you can identify patients who seem to live permanently in one of these positions. Of course, you could always do that as an exercise!

Empathy

I suspect you can now appreciate that the skill of developing empathy is essentially about learning to take an effective *second position*. This is a key skill in building a solid doctor–patient relationship. Although many may have believed that you either have this ability naturally, or not, in fact like most things it is a highly learnable skill and one that, whether you know it consciously or not, you have already begun to master.

Empathic communication is expressed both non-verbally and verbally. We have already discussed at some length, in Chapter 3 on initiating the session, the various non-verbal skills that allow you to establish rapport more easily. Matching, mirroring, pacing and leading are all ways in which you can express sensitivity and genuine interest and reflect your developing understanding of a patient's unique situation. By adding *second position* skills, imagining for a time that you are in their shoes, feeling their feelings and thinking their thoughts, you can more deeply communicate this desire to appreciate their current predicament. In and of itself, this genuine empathy can be deeply therapeutic.

Whilst you can convey this in myriad ways in your body language, it is also useful to complete the loop at a more conscious level by verbally expressing your thoughts and feelings about how a patient presents their current concerns. We can do this by using *I–You* statements. These connect your *first position* understanding of the patient's *second position* predicament. In this way you can also check out whether you have been accurate in your observations or simply mind reading, off at a tangent from reality.

You can make the statements in the language of all of the senses:

- *'**I** can see that your mother's illness has upset **you** markedly.'*
- *'**I** can hear in your voice that **you** are still grieving deeply.'*
- *'**I** can feel how angry **you** are about the cancer's return.'*

- *'**I** can understand how **you** think you might never get over this.'*
- *'**I** can sense how difficult it has been for **you** looking after your sister.'*
- *'**I** can see that **you** are not coping with the situation at home.'*
- *'**I** can hear your concern about how **you** will tell him the bad news.'*

Whether or not you have ever had the personal experience of your patient's difficulty is immaterial. Empathy is a second position understanding, your ability to see and experience the situation from their perspective. If *you* were *them*, this is how you understand their response on their terms. This is quite different from *sympathy*, whose structure involves thinking *about them* from your own *first position* perspective, staying outside their position, failing to even dip your toe into their understanding.

Tony's tantrums

Tony, aged 12 years, was becoming the bane of his mother's life. Remarried after a messy divorce, she had twins who were 7 years younger, and an ex-husband whose new wife had produced a baby boy, all of which amounted to major hassle in Tony's household. His step-dad was well meaning but ineffectual. Tony wanted things and he generally wanted them now. He fluctuated from being tearful, sullen and depressed to spiralling out of control, shouting, bawling, kicking and now punching. Today he sat in one chair, looking down at the floor, while his mother sat in the other, tearful, at the end of her tether bewailing the fact that she couldn't get through to him. She had even been doing his homework because she didn't want any hassle from the school. Something had to be done. Threats of children's homes, a social worker and a dozen more maternal strategies had failed to do the trick.

From a third position perspective it was easy to see how they both pushed each other's buttons. Typically in this sort of situation, doing more of the same, only louder and harder, simply perpetuates the problem. In fact, the attempted solution often becomes the problem! From second position, Tony's mother felt a complete lack of control, and being manipulated in this way was more than she could bear. Second-positioning Tony was more complex. He was actually quite heady with power. A single look, a couple of words and he could set her off. Very exhilarating! Yet also very frightening as he lost control of being in control. And underneath it all was a need to be loved, needed, and to have a place in both families, rather than being the outsider he rapidly saw himself becoming.

The solution? Well there are no easy *'one step and they were free'* solutions in this type of scenario. However, getting mum to imagine being Tony was a big help. She could feel his sense of helplessness and at times confusion, and she could acknowledge that her triggered response was making things worse. As a fly on the wall she replayed the latest incident. Then she imagined what would happen if she simply walked away instead, before 'flying off the handle'. This very simple act, together with following through with small rewards at fixed intervals in return for improved behaviour, took things from simmering to a place on the back burner – not perfect, but they coped better.

The meta-mirror

Have you ever wished for a way of sorting out difficult relationships? Do you have consultations with some patients that could be regularly classed as dysfunctional? Are there certain *'heartsinks'* who appear on your list and make you feel bad well before they have even stepped through the door? How about your colleagues? Your family? Your friends? What would it be like if you could go through a process by *yourself* that would help to improve or even resolve these issues, without requiring the bodily presence of the other person? Interested?

I learned the following process from UK trainer Ian McDermott. Originally conceptualised by Robert Dilts, I have modified it further. It utilises the *perceptual positions* model to help to explore and resolve relationship issues. In certain 'difficult' relationships, we often treat ourselves in the *same way* that the other person has done. Not only might we feel metaphorically beaten up by *them*, but we also beat *ourselves* up in our own mind in the same way. We should have said this instead, done that, or thought differently. It is as if our 'inner self', what NLP calls *meta-position*, treats us in the same way as the external other. And it often does so very critically. No wonder that we may feel caught between a rock and a hard place!

This process works best if you lay out four positions on the floor, or use chairs, and physically move between them, as shown in Figure 5.1.

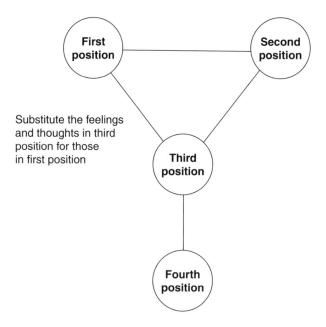

Figure 5.1: Perceptual positions for meta-mirror.

Exercise 11: The meta-mirror

You may wish to have someone lead you through this. First of all *choose a relationship* that you wish to explore. Save the more difficult issues until you can go through the process easily! Think of a recurring issue with regard to this person. Think of *a specific instance* that typifies the relationship. Next imagine that you are going to *relive it*, yet this time with a different perspective, open to learning something new. Now follow the guidelines below.

1 Step into first position

Imagine the other person across from you in your mind's eye. See how they stand/sit/walk/talk/breathe/move.

Look at their eyes, direction of gaze, tilt of head, and whether they are looking towards or away from you. Notice their posture and their gestures.

Listen to their voice. Is it fast/slow/loud/soft/deep/shrill?

Listen to the words. Which ones are *emphasised?*

What are you thinking and feeling in this relationship? What makes it difficult? *How* does that feel in your body? Name the feeling. *Where* in your body do you feel it? In your chest? In your abdomen?

Do you feel challenged? Threatened? Angry? Sad? Anxious? Something else?

Notice which logical level this pertains to.
- Environment? Your room, work, clothes, other colleagues, etc.
- Behaviours? Is it about what you are doing?
- Capabilities? Are your skills being challenged? Is your competency being challenged?
- Beliefs and values? Are some cherished beliefs, attitudes or rules being challenged?
- Identity? Are you being challenged for who you are? Your role?

From here, does he or she look congruent or incongruent?

Now step out, go neutral, and shake it all off!

2 Second position

Step into the shoes of *the other person.* Try them on for size and fit. Use *their* posture and *their* gestures. If they are taller than you, imagine being taller. If they are heavier, imagine that, too. Imagine the situation from this point of view as you look back across at the *'you'* in first position.

How does that *'you'* walk/talk/sit/stand/breathe, etc.? (Go through the questions in 1 above.)

As the other person, what are you thinking and feeling about *'you'* over there?

Name the feeling. Where do you feel it in your body?

Which of the logical levels is challenging you?

Does he or she (the *'you'* in first position) look congruent or incongruent?

Now step out, go neutral, and shake it all off!

3 Third position

Step into third position and view the relationship *dispassionately.*

Who is triggering *what* in this situation?

How do they reinforce one another?

What can you learn from this viewpoint?

Now turn your attention to the first position 'you'.

How is he or she coping with this situation? How do you feel about that? What advice would you give to that 'you'?

What should 'you' in first position do more of? What should you do less of?

Now step out, go neutral, and shake it all off!

4 Fourth position

Step into a fourth position, *disconnected from the other three.*

Allow any residual emotions to go back to the positions where they belong.

Now think about how the *third position* 'you' is relating to the *first position* 'you'.

Was *third position* angry, sad, wishing that 'you' would be more aggressive, less aggressive, more assertive, less assertive, proactive, reactive, etc.?

What is the *predominant reaction* of third position?

5 Stay in fourth position

From here, mentally *swap round* your first position and third position reactions spatially.

For example, if you were non-assertive in first position and assertive in third position, swap these over. If you were upset in first position and calm in third position, swap these over.

6 Return to first position

This time, *take the new way of thinking and feeling* from third position into this, a *revised and updated* first position.

Experience the *new feelings* as you look across at the other person in second position.

What has changed now? *What* is different?

How do they look/sound/breathe/move etc. now? (revisit the original questions if you wish).

How does this allow you to act differently?

How are you actually doing things differently? *How* are you resourceful now?

Now step out, break state, and shake the feelings off!

7 Revisit second position

Step into second position once again, experiencing the 'other' person. See
how the '*new you*' in first position has changed.
Revisit the original questions if you wish.
How is the relationship *different now?*

8 Come home

Return to the *updated first position* and finish in the here and now.

Congratulations, you have finished. This may seem like one of the longest and
most complex exercises we have done so far! However, it takes longer to write
it out than it does *just to simply do it.* I have been able to use it in its entirety
with patients who have had relationship issues, to good effect. I have also used
portions of it during an ordinary consultation when I have sensed that the
patient needed a slightly different perspective. This can be done in casual conversation without the need to move about spatially. Most people understand the
concept of '*walking in someone else's shoes*' or '*taking a fly-on-the-wall view*'. Only
one person so far got '*swatted*' (No, that is a joke!).

Taking the time to gain a thorough understanding of this process will pay
dividends for all of your relationships.

Section Two: revisiting states

You will probably recall the *consulting flow state* that you set earlier. Have you
been using the trigger frequently? Have you experimented with adding any
other states? How has that enhanced what you already do? We are now going
to add the state of *peripheral vision.* But first a little prelude.

Often when we are consulting it is easy to go into *tunnel vision*, to become
focused or fixated on one thing to the exclusion of all else. This is usually pre-
ceded by times when things haven't been going so well. Perhaps you're running
late, or maybe you've had a series of difficult or involved consultations. No
matter what the cause is, you can probably recognise the signs and the feelings
that go with an *unproductive* state. Tunnel vision is closely linked to a sympathetic,
adrenaline-mediated arousal state. This can occur with focused concentration
and extreme motivation when everything else is blocked out, even fears and
phobias. These are *high-intensity* states, and you can't live in them for long
without something giving way – usually your health!

Peripheral vision, which is the opposite of tunnel vision, is a far more relaxing yet information-friendly state. It is closely linked to the parasympathetic nervous system, and it mediates a relaxed attentiveness. It is a state which is sometimes called *uptime*, as it facilitates the ability to focus one's attention on the *outside* world, the other person, being more acutely aware of what is going on. Compare this with *downtime*, which is going inside oneself, paying attention to one's own internal experience at the expense of the outside world.

In *peripheral vision* you are much more aware of movement, often even subtle movements which are at the heart of non-verbal communication, and which are otherwise more easily missed. Internal dialogue fades into the distance, yet you are *more* aware of the variations in other people's vocal qualities. Best of all, however, because of the parasympathetic connection, you have a sense of easy relaxation which can prevent burnout. It is an excellent addition to your *consulting flow state.*

So does this seem like a useful state for you to acquire? Do you want it? And if the answer is *yes*, how do you access it? Well, do the following exercise, which is adapted from *Training Trances* (Overdurf and Silverthorn, 1994).

Exercise 12:   Peripheral vision

1   Find yourself a place where you will be *undisturbed* for about 10 minutes.
2   Allow yourself to *sit comfortably*. Without moving your head, allow your *eyes to look up* above eye level. Fix them *on a spot* high up, and continue to breathe easily for one to two minutes as you keep your *attention on it.*
3   Still looking at the spot, *widen your gaze* to include the front left wall and the front right wall of the room. Imagine that you can *'soften' your eyes* as you do this.
4   Now, keeping your awareness of the spot, and the front walls, *widen your gaze even further*. Imagine that you are drawing back along the side walls *simultaneously*, almost as if you are *looking out of the very corners of your eyes* while still being aware of the spot.
5   Pretend that you can extend this awareness *even behind you*, seeing all around you.
6   Bring your eyes down to normal eye level only as quickly as you *maintain this state*.

> 7   Practise this a few times, and then *anchor it to* your trigger so that it blends with *consulting flow*.
>
> Once you have mastered this you can *do the same thing with sound.* Simply imagine that at the same time you are entering peripheral vision, you can hear the sounds in the front, left and right, along the side, and then all around you.

This is usually a state which is easily experienced. However, if you're not there yet, *do the following.* As you look ahead, bring both of your index fingers up in front of you, level with your eyes, with your arms extended. Keep looking straight ahead as you *slowwwly* extend them in an arc towards your ears. Keep your fingers in vision and once they are at the periphery, wiggle them so that you keep paying attention to them as you look ahead. This will also quickly condition the state.

Practise getting into this state before you consult, and 'top it up' in between patients. I know of one GP who actually has a purple dot high up on the opposite wall, above the patient's head. This means that his state is continuously being triggered, to good effect.

Other useful states

Whilst there are many states to be found in Appendix 1 which you can practise with, there is one particular state which deserves special mention. Have you ever had the experience of making an *intuitive diagnosis* (one which was correct, of course!)? You know, when a patient is halfway through their story, and you get an intuition about a diagnosis which doesn't necessarily fit the facts of the history as told, but which is borne out in retrospect.

I remember one patient quite clearly. I had seen him at his home when on call one weekend. He was in his fifties, and had had some left flank pain that was a little odd. Some five years earlier he had suffered a myocardial infarct, but he had been well since then. He had had no urinary symptoms, and his abdomen and peripheral pulses seemed to be fine. I got it into my head that he had an impending aortic aneurysm rupture, despite the lack of clinical signs. I am not usually given to flights of diagnostic fancy, but for some reason I had a strong feeling about it. I remember the vascular surgery resident being loath to admit him, but he did so. He phoned me back later to confirm the leak and the patient's subsequent recovery from surgery.

We have all experienced situations similar to this, and you can probably remember one or two right now. They are quite different to the ones that we agonise about before sending the patient to hospital 'just in case'. There is a different feeling associated with them, a different *inner voice* of intuition. It seemed to me that at these times our diagnostic antennae are turned way up high, and we are picking up information, perhaps non-verbally, that usually evades our everyday awareness. It is there but we're not conscious of it. It dawned on me some time ago that this would be a useful state to tap into more frequently.

You can do this in the same way that you have already elicited and anchored previous states to your trigger. Simply *recall* a memory of this type of intuitive diagnosis. One where you made the right diagnosis helps immensely, of course! *Remember* the experience as vividly as you can, and *step inside it*, wrapping it completely around you. Pay attention to the *feelings* in your body and *intensify them*. Listen to the qualities of your inner voice and *amplify* it. Run the memory two or three times, and as the feeling reaches a peak, *anchor it* together with *consulting flow*.

And the results? Well, you won't be surprised to hear that I'm not yet a magically perfect diagnostician! However, I more often find myself with intuitive thoughts about what is going on in the consultation. Rather than simply mind reading, though, I *check these thoughts out* with the patient, along the lines of *'I've had a strange thought come into my mind. Do you mind if I ask you a question that may seem a little odd?'*. This covers all the bases and lets me off the hook if I'm way off target. Try it and see.

Congruent or not?

In a nutshell, congruence occurs when our verbal and non-verbal communication matches up. We are in synchrony, all our parts are singing from the same hymn sheet – we are aligned, committed. Think of a time when you decided to do something, without reservation, and you then did it. You went for it. This is *congruence*. Think of a time when you were in two minds. Will you or won't you? Should you or should you not? You didn't want to, but you felt you had to. You said yes but you wanted to say no. This is *incongruence*, a different feeling altogether.

You remember *yes-sets*, don't you? Congruent communication is an unequivocal verbal and non-verbal 'yes'. A *reverse yes-set* is when you get an unequivocal, congruent 'no'. For example:

- *'You don't have chest pain, do you?'* 'No.'
- *'It's not a nice day today.'* 'No.'
- *'So you're sure you're not depressed?'* 'Definitely not!'

Both *yes-sets* and *reverse yes-sets* convey congruent *agreement. Incongruence* is the bit in the middle – neither a full yes nor a full no. Maybe, perhaps, yes ... but, no ... but.

Congruence and incongruence are not necessarily good or bad things in and of themselves. They are simply a means of telling ourselves whether or not we are heading in the right direction – a kind of ecology check. Whilst congruence is a signal which lets us know that we are fully committed to a particular outcome, a particular direction, incongruence lets us know that something is not yet right. Both signals are valuable. By becoming more familiar with our own signals for congruence and incongruence, we become more sensitive to the signals that our patients send out.

Exercise 13:   Your congruence signal

1   Identify a time when you were *congruent*, you wanted something and were *committed* to it. You were *determined* to do something and you did. It could be something small, an everyday experience like deciding to have lunch, watch a particular television programme, etc., or it could be something bigger, like deciding to go to a special holiday location, buy that car, etc.

2   *Step back into the memory*, reliving the experience now, seeing the pictures, hearing the sounds and feeling the feelings. *Pay special attention to* the tone of your internal voice and the location and type of *feeling* in your body as you are feeling committed.

3   Now choose two other memories of congruence and do the same thing. They can be different times, places or events, but what they have in common is *that feeling of congruence*. Again note what you see, hear and feel.

4   As you think of those three memories, what do they have in common? Where is the *feeling located* in your body? What is the tone of your inner voice? What are the qualities of the inner picture?

5   When you have identified what the qualities have in common, try to replicate them *without going back to the memory*. If you can do this, then your conscious mind can manufacture the signal. So choose a signal that you cannot replicate consciously without going back to the memory. When you have this, you have found *your congruence signal*.

Whilst congruence signals can vary from person to person, there may be some similarities. Many people feel an expansive openness or warmth in their chest.

Others feel it in their solar plexus. Your internal voice may sound strong and vibrant, coming from your throat or chest. Sometimes congruence is a matter of degree. The stronger the signal, the more congruent you are.

Now repeat the exercise to *find your incongruence signal*. Think of three times when you have been in two minds about something. Will you or won't you? Should you or shouldn't you? Remember a time when someone gave you a present and you opened it in front of them. You thought it was awful, yet at the same time you felt that you had to thank them profusely for it! *How did that feel?* Or think of a time when someone asked you to do them a favour, such as work late. You didn't really want to, but you said yes anyway. *How did that feel?* Or remember a social situation in which you felt unsure of yourself.

Find the signal that is reliably present, a signal that you can't consciously manufacture. For some it is a tight feeling in their stomach area – the tighter the feeling the greater the incongruence. For others it is like hearing two internal voices. Which one do you listen to? The more incongruent they are, the louder they get.

Get to know these signals well. They can be your friends in many situations. They may prevent you from making rash decisions or pursuing courses of action that may not work out. Have you ever said to yourself after an unfortunate ending to an event *'You know, I had a feeling beforehand that this might not work out'*. Next time, pay attention to it!

Using these signals with patients

When we are in a situation with another person who is behaving incongruently, we might find ourselves becoming a little confused, uncomfortable, at odds, or even feeling our own signal of incongruence. When we are deeply in rapport with someone, yet we have this feeling, we need to ask the question *'Does this signal belong to me or am I picking it up from this person?'*

Incongruence is the 'but' in the 'Yes, but ...'. This can be expressed both verbally and non-verbally. Listed below are some patients' examples:

- *'I can **see** what to do ... it just doesn't **feel** right'* (incongruence in representational systems).
- *'Yes ... I'm OK'* (said with a sigh in a monotone).
- *'Something **tells** me this might not work out.'*
- *'Yes I'll try that ... **but** ...'*
- *'Well, if you're sure that's the answer, doctor'* (said with a slight shake of the head).

- *'Yes, I have been taking my medication, doctor'* (simultaneously looks across quickly left and right).
- *'On the **one hand** what you're saying makes sense ... on the **other hand** I can't picture myself doing it ...'*
- *'No, there's nothing else ...'* (hands fiddling restlessly).
- *'I **want** to ...'* (the 'but' is left unsaid).
- *'OK, I'll do that ...'* (said with a shake of the head, left fist clenching, right fist opening).
- *'I'll try that ... but I'm not sure it'll work.'*

The clearer you are about your own signals for congruence and incongruence, the more easily you will begin to pick up patients' signs. Whether you see and hear them clearly or not, your feelings will alert you. Of course, there are several ways that you can start to address this, such as the following.

1   Notice it but do not comment on it. Store it for later use.
2   Use 'But ...'. Whenever you hear an incomplete sentence, lean forward with a quizzical look and ask *'But ... ?'*. This needs plenty of rapport!
3   Ask a question. *'I'm curious ... when you said you'll do that ... I wondered if you had some unspoken reservations?'*
    'I was wondering ... when you said you were OK ... did you really mean that?'
4   Ask about the part of them that disagrees. *'I can't help thinking that, at some level, part of you doesn't agree with what you've just said?'*
    Or *'... part of you doesn't agree with something I've said?'*.
5   Go after the complete representation. *'What were you seeing/hearing/feeling as you said that?'* This brings to the surface issues that may have been out of conscious awareness.
6   Reverse the words on either side of the 'but'. For example, *'I'll try it ... but I'm not sure that it'll work'* becomes *'You're not sure that it'll work ... but you'll try it'*. This reversal can act as a very powerful intervention in its own right. Experiment with it whenever you hear a 'but'.
7   Play back to the patient both parts of the incongruence at the same time.
    'So you're sure you agree to that' (shaking your head 'no' at the same time).
    'So you have been taking your medication regularly' (simultaneously shaking head 'no').
    'You're right ... you probably won't find that easy' (smiling and nodding 'yes').
    You definitely need to practise with this one. It requires more skill and more rapport.

If you are interested in other examples of how to deal with incongruence thera-peutically, I suggest that you read *Provocative Therapy* (Farrelly and Brandsma, 1974).

Incongruence is often a message that something is missing and more resources are required. You can think about what is needed using the various *logical levels*.

- *Environment.* You may simply need more information, such as patient information leaflets, self-help groups, opening times of various facilities, crèche facilities, etc.
- *Behaviour.* You may not know what to do. Perhaps some specific advice is needed about diet, exercise, etc.
- *Capability.* You may know what to do *but* you don't yet have the skill, the 'how to' – perhaps learning how to relax, how to assert yourself respectfully, how to use your inhaler or nebuliser, etc.
- *Beliefs and values.* You may have the skill *but* not believe that this is a priority. Taking exercise may be good for your health *but* you don't have time to fit it in. You want to stop smoking *but* you don't have other ways to calm yourself. This level often requires good negotiation skills for resolution.
- *Identity.* You may believe that it is important *but* it doesn't fit with your sense of self. Exercise helps to prevent heart disease *but* I'm just not a sporty person. Relaxation time is important *but* who else is going to get the job done? Again, good negotiation skills are needed.

Simultaneous and sequential incongruence

Wow! That's a bit of a mouthful. What does it mean? Well, up until now we have been mostly dealing with *simultaneous incongruence*. This is when you are in two minds, and it is occurring *now!* You can see this quite easily when body language is at variance with the spoken word. As the person is saying one thing verbally, non-verbally they are 'saying' the other. Whenever we receive this kind of double message, we tend to believe the non-verbal component. It seems to carry more weight. We have all had the experience of feeling 'not quite right' about someone. The words they said seemed all right but...we had a gut feeling, or an intuition that things weren't adding up. It seems that emotions, beliefs and values are more likely to 'leak' in our body language.

We can be in two minds linguistically, too. We might say that we want to do this ... but ... we also want to do that. This is the classic *'on the one hand ... **but** ... on the other hand'*. Think of the previous sentences as having two halves separated by a 'but'. The non-verbal communication for the first half of the sentence may be entirely congruent with the spoken word. And the non-verbal communication for the second half may be congruent with *its* words. We have the beginnings of a *sequential incongruence*. The two halves are congruent in and of themselves, yet they are *incongruent* when they are juxtaposed. Now you may think that I am making a semantic mountain out of a linguistic molehill. And to all intents and purposes, this type of sequential incongruence can be handled in the same way as simultaneous incongruence.

However, there are certain conditions where the degree of sequential incongruity is rather larger. For example, consider someone who is a binge drinker. For a great deal of the time they are sober, on the straight and narrow. Then something happens and they go on a 'bender'. Once that is over we hear the immortal words 'I don't know what came over me – I just wasn't myself', often followed by a great deal of guilt or remorse about their actions. Then there are promises to all and sundry about keeping off the booze, staying dry – which may happen for a short period, or maybe even for quite some length of time, before the next 'relapse'. This, then, is a true sequential incongruence.

I have a patient who used to be a binge eater and was sometimes bulimic. She would be fine for days, and then, as she put it, '*I would go into the kitchen to do something, then "come to myself", having raided the fridge, with the remains of food all over the table'*. She had no real recollection of starting to binge. One minute she was fine, and a few minutes later she had binged. She said it was '*like going through a trapdoor'*. Afterwards she would be overcome with guilt and make herself vomit.

Sequential incongruence, then, is like having one 'part' of you in charge for some or even most of the time, and then another 'part' taking over and engaging the action. It's almost as if both 'parts' have their own sets of beliefs and values. They may be quite dissociated from each other. In a sense, the part that comes to the doctor to request treatment is not the part that requires it. The sober part comes into the consulting room for help, while the bingeing part remains in the pub! Many addictions and compulsions fall into this category. Being a chocoholic or a smoker who can't give up are mild to moderate examples of sequential incongruence. An extreme variation of this is multiple personality disorder.

The treatment for sequential incongruence of a major degree is beyond the scope of this current book. However, viewing, thinking about and understanding the situation in this way can help to forge a better relationship, and may even be therapeutic in its own right.

Congruence and the GP

So far we have considered congruent and incongruent communication from the patient's perspective, but what about viewing it from our own perspective? Do our words and actions match up? Do our verbal and non-verbal messages align? What would it be like to be on the receiving end of our own communication?

- *'Tell me all about it'* (head turned away, looking at the computer screen).
- *'Anything else?'* (closing notes and putting them in the out tray).
- *'This won't hurt'* (accompanying facial grimace).
- *'I'm sure you're going to be OK'* (eyes down to right).
- *'Take your time'* (said quickly, with foot tapping).
- *'Are you happy with that, then?'* (accessing next patient's records on the computer).
- *'Of course I don't mind'* (said with a sigh, looking away).

For all of the above mini-scenarios it is useful to *imagine saying the words and doing the non-verbals simultaneously.* Notice how that feels in your body. Uncomfortable, isn't it?

We also *mark out messages* within messages by changing our vocal qualities, *emphasising some words* rather than others. Sometimes this *marking out* can be *easy* to detect, and sometimes it is not *so easy!* You get the drift? Marking out, or embedding of language, happens all the time in every conversation, usually well outside our normal awareness. Yet sometimes the message that is conveyed is not what we intended. Sometimes it is the very opposite!

- *'I'm sure you'll be fine'* (said with a rising inflection on 'fine', like a question).
- *'This won't ... **hurt a lot**'* (said with a downward inflection, like a command).
- *'I don't think that ... **this is a serious problem.**'*
- *'I don't think you need to ... **worry unduly** about this.'*
- *'Of course, everything that's said is in confidence'* (said with a rising inflection on 'confidence').
- *'Well ... I'm sure that ... there are still ... lots of treatment options left ... it's not that ... **you're finished** ... not like ... **there's nothing more we can do**'* (said h..h..hesitatingly).

Once again, imagine saying these phrases out loud in your mind. Place the emphasis as suggested, and notice how that changes the meaning of the statement. Some of them perhaps sound apocryphal, but are they really? Start listening out for embedded language in everyday conversations. As well as voice qualities, people can also mark things out using their eyes, or by means of gestures. In Chapter 6 on explanation and planning we shall deal with how to use embedded language to your patient's advantage – that is, to mark out in beneficial ways.

More on non-verbal communication

More, I hear you say? Haven't we covered enough already? Aren't you going a little overboard? It is very important not to under-emphasise the value of paying attention to body language, posture, gesture, eye movements and voice qualities. So much of what we are really thinking is conveyed in this way. And so much of what patients feel unable to say out loud in a consultation is expressed non-verbally – for us to notice, pick up on and utilise, or not. It includes information about emotions and affect, beliefs and values, comfort and discomfort, liking and disliking, relating and not relating. When verbal and non-verbal communication conflict, the non-verbal message *virtually always* wins out. In fact, some illnesses, such as depression, are often only diagnosed after the non-verbal cues have been decoded.

Patients rate doctors very highly on their ability to receive and decode these cues. The better the doctor can do this, the more satisfied the patient will be. And not only that. The result is a greater level of trust, and increased compliance with medication and action plans, together with a diminution of psychological and even physical problems. The prize is well worth attaining.

Much of this chapter has reinforced the importance of non-verbal messages and given many examples of their usage. One of the areas that we have yet to focus on in any depth concerns the eyes.

Eye-accessing cues

It often seems that our eyes move randomly when we speak. Have you ever noticed, though, that if you ask someone a question and they have to 'go inside' to think about it, their eyes may move to a specific location – up, down, left or right? It seems that these types of eye movements help us to access our stored information and memories in a particular way. The originators of NLP noticed this and studied the connection between eye movements and representational system predicates. They asked themselves '*Do eyes move to a particular location when people are thinking in pictures, sounds, words and feelings?*' This gave birth to the much vaunted and talked about NLP eye-accessing cues.

Now what follows is not necessarily the 'truth', but merely a useful generalisation. Whilst it is not true for all people at all times, it can be a very helpful aid for determining *how* someone is thinking about a particular experience. When answering a question, if someone looks up they are usually visualising. *Up and to their left* is remembering a past image or memory. *Up and to their right* is constructing a picture, perhaps of a future possibility. *Straight ahead and defocused* is often visualising as if watching a video. *Across to their left* is remembering sounds from the past, *and across to their right* is constructing what something might sound like. *Down to their right* usually accesses feelings, *and down to their left* is internal dialogue. You can verify this for yourself by watching television interviews.

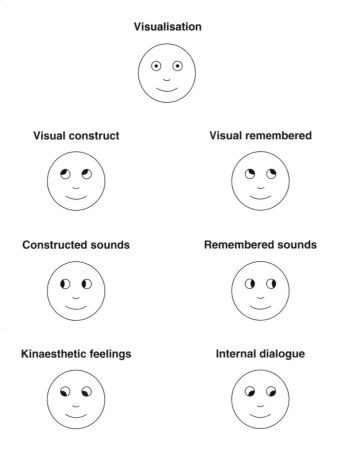

Note: Looking *at* the other person.

Figure 5.2:   Eye-accessing cues.

The eye patterns as seen in Figure 5.2 above are the most common ones. Some left-handers and a few-right handers may have the cues reversed. This is simply normal for them. By seeing whether patients access down to their *right* when responding to questions about *feelings,* you can assume that the rest of the cues are as above. If they access down to their left instead, then the other cues are likely to be reversed as well.

So this looks rather complicated. What is its practical use? Well, first, eye-accessing cues – they give you a clue as to *how* someone may be thinking. If you ask a question to which the answer is *'I don't know'*, and they look up to their left, you can assume that they are making a picture of which they are not yet consciously aware. You can follow up with *'If you did know ... how would you picture that?'*. This subtly paces their ongoing experience and also deepens rapport.

Perhaps you have asked a question about what is making them feel so down, and they shake their head and look down to their left. You can follow up with *'Could it be something that you're saying to yourself?'*

Or perhaps in response to a general question, they sigh and look down to their right. You could ask *'How do you feel about that?'*. By pacing the patient's current experience in this way, it can almost seem as if you are mind reading. Most people will get the feeling that you really understand them at a deep level.

What I believe is even more important than the eye access itself is *where the eyes go to immediately after that.* Think of it in this way. The eye access is like finding the relevant file on a computer. It can be stored in a variety of areas in a variety of ways. However, once accessed it needs to be projected on screen to be read. In the same way, it is as if we project our memories, imaginations and experiences into the space around us.

Ask a colleague to think of someone they like, and then clear their mind. Now ask them to think of someone they don't like. If you watch closely, you will notice that they seem to project the images out in front of them to *different locations*. In fact, you can next ask them to think of one of the images without telling you which one it is. Based on where their eyes go, you can then tell them which one they are thinking about. No, not mind reading, just *calibration* skills.

In a way this makes *complete sense*. It seems that our minds code information differently depending on the category to which it belongs. It would be of little use if 'like' and 'dislike' were stored in the same place, as this would lead to quite a confusing mix-up! In the same way, we have codings for things like past, present, future, large problems, small problems, resolved issues, things that we used to do, fears, phobias, compulsions, revulsions, attractions, good decisions, bad decisions, resolved grief, unresolved grief, convincers, strong beliefs, doubts, hopes, expectations and a myriad other things! They all have a *structure.*

Think of a current problem that you have. How does that compare with one that has already been resolved previously, a problem that you used to have? Even if you can't see it clearly in your mind's eye, imagine that you could. Imagine that you could reach out and touch each one with a hand. How are they located differently in space?

As you now begin to notice more clearly where people look immediately after accessing, you will see what I mean. And what are the benefits of this? Well, by noticing where people store these things you can easily gesture to the area of projection and thus pace their ongoing experience when talking to them. It can also give you a handle on whether a problem is still a current issue or whether it has resolved, as the projected location will have changed!

Other eye patterns

There are a few other things worth mentioning about eyes. In Chapter 3 on initiating the session we have already discussed *eye contact time* and *look-to-talk* rules. Blinking is something that we do all the time. Some people blink more when they are thinking, especially if they are having to deal with a lot of information at once. Sometimes the blink rate can slow right down. This may be indicative of an open-eyed trance state, especially after a long monologue!

Some people may look down to their left after every question. What they may be doing is repeating the question to themselves on the inside prior to answering it. Such people are highly auditory digital (words mean a lot). Some people may go visual each time because they have to picture what you are saying first, before going to retrieve the information requested. This is sometimes called their *lead system* – the representational system through which everything else is processed first.

Certain eye cues may be avoided altogether. A person can systematically block out visual auditory or kinaesthetic information processing. This might be as a result of previous emotional trauma.

Sometimes a person may go visual in order to access feelings. This is called a *synesthesia*, whereby they are accessing a *mixture of representational systems simultaneously*. This is fine if it is a pleasant memory, but not so good if it is not. Phobias have this structure – that is, a visual image accompanied by intensely negative feelings.

Occasionally there may be no access at all, and the person just looks straight ahead. Whilst they may have 'gone blank', it can also be because the requested information is close to the surface and needs no thinking about at all, as retrieval is easy.

Sometimes your question may cause the patient to go on an *internal search*. It is as if they are travelling back through time, through their memory banks, searching for something connected to the present situation. It may appear that they have 'gone inside', spaced out a little, with their eyes defocused or perhaps staring into the distance. Just give them time to do this internal processing without interruption. The information that they bring back with them may be very important to the present situation.

Because past problems can seem to run our everyday lives, it is possible to take a negative feeling anchor and ride it back into the past to the original causative event. This will give you an opportunity to re-address it in the here and now with specific NLP techniques.

Accessing-cues matrix

Box 5.4 contains a matrix of the various types of accessing cues in the NLP communication categories model. These are the main non-verbal patterns that accompany certain types of communication. Whilst it is not set in tablets of stone, this matrix is a useful *aide-mémoire*.

Box 5.4:   Matrix of the different types of accessing cues in the NLP communication categories model

Pattern	Visual	Auditory	Kinaesthetic	Auditory digital
Eye movements	Up right or left. Defocused	Across the midline	Down, usually right	Down, usually left
Posture and gestures	Straight, erect more tense. Thinner body. Jerkier movements	'Telephone posture'. Head tilted. Rhythmic movements	Either more rounded or athletic. More flowing movements	Arms folded. Head up, erect
Breathing	High up in chest. More shallow	Mid-chest, even breathing	Low into abdomen. Deeper breathing	Tighter, more restricted
Voice	Speaks rapidly. Higher pitched	Melodic, rhythmic, medium pace	Lower, deeper, may be slower	Monotone, tends to 'bit off' words
Predicates	See, look, view, appear, regard	Hear, listen, sounds, cries, speak, tell	Grasp, concrete, firm, handle, feel	Decide, understand, motivate consider

Meta-comments

What is a meta-comment? How would you know if you came across one un-expectedly? Are they friendly or not? What do you think about the previous three sentences? A meta-comment is a comment *about* a comment. *Meta-* means to stand back, to view from a distance, from a different level. Meta-comments can be statements that describe what has happened, verbally and non-verbally, and thus connect us to another level of processing that is more useful, or, more frequently, they can be used to describe the *process* of what is going to happen. As such they are useful at any stage of the consultation, as they give it *structure*. Some examples will allow you to see the different usages.

Comments about verbal and non-verbal behaviour:

- *'When you said that you didn't like what he said, your voice trembled and you looked down. What were you feeling then?'*
- *'How do you feel about feeling angry with him?'* (to widow whose husband had died suddenly).
- *'When you spoke about the chemotherapy you seemed very distant. What else was going through your mind?'* (this patient thought that she was going to die).
- *'When I asked if you felt depressed, you said no, yet at the same time you nodded your head and I wondered if you were going to cry. How are you really feeling?'* (depressed yet stoical patient).

Sharing thoughts:

- *'Let me tell you what's going through my mind about your symptoms ...'* (to patient with somatisation of depression).
- *'I have several thoughts about what we could do about this ... tell me what you think of them ...'*
- *'Sometimes when people have a panic attack, they think they're going to die. Is that what you were thinking?'* (panic attack that happened 'out of the blue').
- *'Sometimes it's difficult to work out if irritable bowel is made worse by diet or stress. What were your thoughts?'* (introducing the possibility of stress as a cause).

Comments about consultation structure:

- *'I think we've got enough information now. The next step is to examine your chest, if that's OK'* (possible asthma case).
- *'What I'd like to do is start by hearing what you've got to say, then we can move on to what we can do about it.'*

- *'At this stage we need to get on with some investigations. Can I send you to the nurse for some blood tests?'*

Providing a rationale:

- *'I'm going to ask you some questions that may seem a bit odd ... is that OK?'* (NLP therapy!).
- *'It's important that we get the right sequence and order of how things happened. Some of the questions are a bit tedious, but we need all the details'* (alleged abuse case).
- *'Sometimes the discomfort you've been having can come from the womb. That's why we need to do an internal examination, to check it all out.'*
- *'There are three important things about managing your diabetes better. The first is ...'*

In this way *meta-comments* can help to build the relationship further by involving the patient, including them in what is going on. By reducing uncertainty and *signposting* what is going to happen next, they can be helped to feel more comfortable, less anxious and more reassured. This is a two-way process. The more comfortable the patient is with what is happening in the consultation, the easier you will feel inside. That in itself will increase rapport.

Summary

In this chapter we have seen that continuing to build an effective therapeutic relationship requires the kind of skills that can be used in each consultation phase. These skills are recursive and loop back into each other in a mutually enhancing way. The deeper reaches of *rapport* need further development at the levels of *capability, beliefs and values, and identity and beyond*. This is enriched even more by a balanced use of *first, second and third perceptual positions*, giving the freedom to engage in a mutually satisfying empathic encounter. The *meta-mirror* can help us to see relationships from a different angle, and it may transform relationships that were previously thought of as stuck – a liberating experience.

Of course, it is still important to take care of our own state of mind and body, ensuring that we stay out of the dark tunnel and step into *peripheral vision* instead, preventing high-intensity burnout yet still being able to pick up the salient, subtle parts of the ongoing communication. Noticing the discrepancies that lead to *incongruence* and having the questioning skills to elucidate further its causes, whether these are *simultaneous* or *sequential*. We now have an eye for reading non-verbal communication accurately, giving our patients a greater sense of being understood on all levels. And by using *meta-comments* at various stages we can provide the type of structure and signposting that lets them know that they are intimately involved in the process.

Good relationships are fundamental to general practice. They are the life-blood of a long and satisfying career. There is nothing quite like looking after several generations of a family and being able to relate to each of them in their own different way. Your time spent in putting this chapter into practice will be well rewarded.

CHAPTER 6

Explanation and planning

Introduction

In general, though of course this doesn't include you, doctors are very poor at providing adequate explanation and planning for their patients. We may have developed excellent information gathering and diagnostic skills, yet somehow we often fail to get our message across in a way that not only makes sense to but also is acted upon appropriately by our patients. One of the problems that comes up time and time again is that patients often want information about diagnosis, causation and prognosis, whereas we are often more concerned about treatment and drug therapy.

To use a football metaphor, patients are keen to find out the score! They have come with a set of *symptoms* for which they believe there is a prior *cause*. They may have a particular *outcome* in mind, although they may be unsure about which *resources* they require. To cap it all, they want to know about short- and longer-term *effects* – their prognosis.

So why is it that half of all patients who are prescribed medication may only take it sporadically or not at all? Why are patients not committed to following 'doctor's orders'? What prevents them from understanding the messages that we put across? What stops them asking for the information that they really want?

Would it be too simple and easy to say that *doctors* may be the main answer to all of these questions? Could we be the obstacle that prevents adequate information transfer? And if so, how? And what is more, what can we do about it?

Well, in yet another nutshell, we need to learn how to relate explanations to our previously elicited information about patients' beliefs, ideas and expectations. We need to channel what we want to get across through their processing filters, their communicating style and their language. Not ours, *theirs!* We need to package what we want to say so that it fits them like a glove. By using what we have already found out about how our patients process information, we can deliver our message so that they really own it, are committed to it and will act upon it! Just like the Japanese martial art of Aikido, we can align with our patients' energy and redirect it towards the most appropriate, mutually agreed, dovetailed outcome.

Yet at the same time, a patient's beliefs about their illness may leave them woefully impoverished. These very beliefs may act as a straitjacket, constraining them and preventing them from having health-enhancing choices. Some old wives' tales may be relatively harmless, but some pseudoscientific information gleaned from the Internet and inappropriately used may not be. We are bombarded with information about health from every aspect of the media, from advertising to soaps to medical dramas. Some of this may be helpful, but some is not so.

It is not much use channelling information through a patient's limiting belief set. That may simply lead to a dead end. So part of explanation and planning involves helping people to update, expand or even change their beliefs. Sometimes that is all that is required – no 'treatment' as such. More often we are re-laying a more adequate foundation on which to add new material. A more balanced viewpoint. Opening up to new choices. Whatever else we do we must always (Always? Yes, always!) take our patient's illness framework as the starting point for any intervention.

Aims of this chapter

This is the time when we begin to pull together the various threads of the previous chapters. We have sown and cultivated many seeds, and it is now time to begin the harvest. Much of the information contained in this chapter will build on and utilise material covered in Chapter 4 on gathering information.

It is important that, having elicited valuable information about beliefs and expectations, we structure our explanations in a way that allows us to help our patients to get out of their self-imposed straitjackets. Initially, then, we shall focus our attention on *verbal reframing* skills. This is the 'how to' for expanding thinking about limiting beliefs, updating our maps and opening up to new possibilities. Then we shall move on to revisit *meta-programs* and more specifically, how to use the language of each category to get our message across in a way that best fits the patient. We shall look at new material about how people actually *convince* themselves to do something, and how to language that effectively. We must also *chunk* our information at the right level and be open to *negotiation* on the various points. A handy metaphor is often useful when explaining complex issues. As always, the use of non-verbal communication will remain paramount throughout.

The following specific areas will be covered.

Section One: changing beliefs

- *Verbal reframing*: context and meaning reframes; 14 ways to re-language limiting beliefs.

Section Two: utilising information filters

- Using *meta-programs* to get the message across, including *convincer* patterns.

Section Three: chunking and negotiation

- Chunking information at the right level: *induction, deduction and metaphor.*
- *Negotiation* framework: finding out what is behind any objections; how to dovetail outcomes together.

Section Four: language application

- Using the *Milton model*: artfully vague language for change.
- The *SCORE model*: covering what patients really want to know about their illness.
- *Non-verbal communication.* Using posture, gestures and embedded language to get the message across.

We shall start the ball rolling by looking at how to expand our thinking about health beliefs so that instead of being stuck in a limiting mind set, we open ourselves to more choice in our specific situations.

Section One: changing beliefs

Verbal reframing

What is a frame? A frame is simply the boundaries that we put round an experience so that we can make sense out of it and give it meaning. We are meaning-making animals, always interpreting our experience through the frames of our beliefs and values. *Reframing* involves changing the boundary surrounding an issue in some way so that the *meaning changes*, too. We literally perceive things differently, and this can allow our behaviours to change as well. Have you ever seen an old picture that was brightened up immeasurably by putting a new frame round it? Or have you laughed heartily at the punch-line of a joke, reframes being the basis of all humour? Or have you used creative thinking to solve a problem?

There are two main ways in which reframing can be used:

1 context reframing
2 content reframing.

Context reframing

The meaning of a behaviour depends on the context in which it is placed. Change the context and you change the meaning. This works particularly well in the area of comparisons. For example:

- *'I am too x ...'*
- *'She is too y ...'.*

The question to ask yourself is *'In which **other** context would this behaviour actually be valuable?'*

For example:

- *'I worry dreadfully'* becomes *'You'd make a great downside planner in the insurance world.'*
- *'He's so nit-picking'* becomes *'He'd be great as a proofreader.'*
- *'My daughter won't do as she's told'* becomes *'You can be sure she won't be easily led when she's out with her boyfriend.'*
- *'I'm very weak-willed'* becomes *'You're probably very good at allowing yourself to partake in the pleasures of life.'*

So put the behaviour in a context where it proves to be a resource instead. Every, yes every, behaviour can be useful somewhere, at some time, with someone else. Change the context and you change the meaning.

Content reframing

When you react negatively to someone or some event, you can stay within the same context yet change the meaning of your *reaction*. The event stays the same, but your perception of it changes. The linguistic form is:

- *'x means y'*
- *'x equals y'.*

The question to ask yourself is *'What **else** could this mean instead in **this** context?'*
For example:

- *'He's very stubborn, doctor'* becomes *'He's persistent in going for what he wants.'*
- *'I feel guilty about what I said'* becomes *'That means you're already learning what you could say differently.'*
- *'I'm a cancer victim'* becomes *'That means you're just not yet aware of the other available treatment choices.'*
- *'I'm a born worrier'* becomes *'You're an expert at predicting what's not yet right.'*

As you can see, although they are presented as two main categories, there is a great deal of overlap. Each of the above examples could be reframed via context *or* content reframing. All that matters is that in some way you change the meaning so that it is perceived in a more health-enhancing way.

Of course we all engage in reframing all the time. Optimism and pessimism are two opposite reframing patterns. They each take the same event and give it either a good or bad meaning. Which type of person feels better to be around? Generally the optimist. However, there is a caveat here. Positively reframing every single occurrence can make you appear glib and uncaring! Still, that might be better than always being the person to point out the downside of every situation, although devil's advocacy does have its place unless taken to the extreme.

It is worth mentioning here that neurophysiologists have discovered that our thoughts affect the chemical balance of our body. Optimistic thoughts can boost our immune system, making our killer T-cells and antibody production more effective. Increased levels of serotonin enhance our mood. The message is that *positive reframes are actually good for our health.* (But maybe there is a downside to feeling good all the time. After all, who wants to live in a fools' paradise? But then again, if you were fooled into it, you wouldn't know ... .)

Verbal reframing patterns

Whilst there are two main categories of reframes, NLP has explored the subject of reframing extensively and come up with many more patterns that fit the framework. We are going to explore 14 such patterns here. We shall use three examples of limiting beliefs that can adversely affect health. By running them through each pattern we shall attempt to sow the seeds of change, encouraging a more enhancing meaning, and perhaps even allowing new behaviours to surface.

In order to run these patterns effectively, it is important that the belief statement is organised in a particular way. You will no doubt recall from Chapter 4 on gathering information that two types of belief are *causation* and *meaning*. Linguistically these are arranged as an *equation* in the following ways:

- '*x causes y*'
- '*x means y*'
- '*x = y*'.

By asking the question '*How specifically does ... ?*', these statements can be refined even further. At this stage you will have the belief statement in the correct format to run the ensuing patterns. What follows, then, is a description of the pattern together with its effect on each of the three beliefs. Notice how (or if!) this changes your experience of the situation or not. Ask yourself what else would need to happen for change to occur.

The limiting beliefs we shall experiment with are as follows.

1 '*I can't stop smoking ... I'm too weak-willed*' (i.e. x = y).
2 '*Having cancer means I'm a victim*' (i.e. I am subject to the effect of something outside my control).
3 '*Depression runs in my family*' (i.e. it's caused by genetic inheritance).

As you look at the reframing diagram in this section it will help you to visualise how the reframes fit together.
Warning: remember to use rapport and softeners when reframing!

Redefine

To redefine is to *substitute* a new word for one of the words used in the belief statement. The word may mean something similar, yet at the same time it may begin to lead in a slightly different direction. It can be used to 'soften' an otherwise harsh statement and create an opening for further change. Redefining can be used on *both* sides of the belief equation. Ask yourself '*What other meaning could this have?*'

1 '*You're not yet strong-willed enough to do something different with your hands.*'
2 '*Some aberrant cells in your body make you feel that you are not wholly in charge yet.*'
3 '*Is thinking negative thoughts something that you want to pass on to your children?*'

Notice how the original limiting belief, when restated, begins to be modified. The goal is not necessarily to have an instant belief change, although you do have permission to accept that if it happens. What we are looking for is a small movement in a more positive direction.

Consequence

By believing in a particular way, we open ourselves up to the future con-sequences of that belief, whether they are positive or negative. Sometimes it is useful to take the belief out into the future and notice what might happen if you don't change now. Ask yourself *'What will happen if they continue to believe this?'*

1   *'How much weaker might your will get if you don't act now?'*
2   *'This kind of belief may only prevent you from grasping the choices that are available to you.'*
3   *'If you continue to believe that, what are the consequences for all of your descendants?'*

Intention

When you do something, it implies some prior intent on your part. There is something that you want to get satisfied through doing it. Sometimes this is called the *secondary gain* in the situation. It directs attention to the purpose of the belief. So you might ask yourself *'Why are they saying this? What is the secondary gain? What are they trying to get?'*.

1   *'It's not that you're weak-willed, it's just that you need something else to give you the relaxation that you get from smoking.'*
2   *'I know that you're not responsible forgetting cancer. However, you are responsible for making the best choice of what to do next.'*
3   *'You're absolutely right. It's important to sort out just how much of depression is genetic and how much is due to factors over which you have a much larger degree of control.'*

Counter-example

Many people believe that beliefs are all or nothing, in the sense that one good counter-example will blow the belief apart. Scientific method seems to work on this principle. The theorem holds until one example disproves it. This category can give a very powerful reframe. However, the caveat is that for the reframe to be successful, it is usually best to help the patient to find a counter-example in their *own* experience. The main strategy is to invert one or both sides of the belief statement and ask *'What would happen if that weren't true?'*

Mathematically and linguistically:

$$If\ x = y,\ what\ if$$
$$x = (-y),$$
$$(-x) = y,$$
$$(-x) = (-y).$$

Where (–) implies the opposite of the belief.

1   *'Do you know anyone who gave up smoking yet was weak-willed?'* $((-x) = y)$.
   'Do you know someone who was strong-willed and couldn't give up?' $(x = (-y))$
   (removes 'will' from the situation).
2   *'Do you know someone who had cancer and was proactive, choosing for themselves
   to do different things?'* $(x = (-y))$.
   'So it will be all right for you to be a victim of successful treatment?' $((-x) = y)$.
3   *'Do you know anyone who was the only one in his or her family to be depressed?'*
   $(x = (-y))$.
   'Do you know someone who wasn't depressed, yet other family members were?'
   $((-x) = y)$ (these examples test the 'all genetic' part of the belief).

Bear in mind that you may have to ask several counter-example questions to
achieve a major belief shift. Also I'm curious, and wondering, are you still
remembering to use softeners?

Apply to self

This is one of my favourite patterns. All that you do is reflexively apply the belief
back on itself. This evaluates the belief according to its own criteria. Do it to
either side of the equation or both together. It's both confusing and fun to do.
Don't think about it, just do it.

1   *'You're right! That's a wishy-washy weak-willed belief to believe ...'*
   'Why can't you stop this weak (week)?' (phonological ambiguity).
2   *'That belief has sure spread like cancer.'*
   'How many other people are victims of that belief?'
3   *'Now that's a depressing thought!'*
   'Maybe your family should run ... away ... from depression.'

If you can do these on the spur of the moment, patients will often laugh, making
it difficult for them to hold on to the limiting belief. Also, because it's unexpected, out of the blue, you can get a major shift.

Another outcome

This challenges the relevancy of the belief by switching to a completely different outcome. The issue is not this but *that!* Simply ask yourself *'What is another outcome?'*

1 *'The issue is not about stopping smoking … it's about what you would do with your hands instead.'*
2 *'The issue isn't about whether or not you're a victim … it's more about what other choices you'd like to make.'*
3 *'It's immaterial if part of depression is genetic … the real question is how to go about thinking the kind of thoughts that enhance your life.'*

Chunking down

When you chunk down, you break the belief up into smaller pieces. This makes it easier to change the relationship that the belief defines. It is almost like saying that if you focus on and change one smaller part, the larger part will also change. *Meta-model* questions that you can ask the patient and yourself are *'Who or what specifically? What are examples or parts of this?'*.

1 *'How much will-power is needed to cut down by one cigarette per day?'*
2 *'How specifically do some aberrant cells cause you to feel like a victim?'*
3 *'Who specifically in your family was depressed yet recovered?'*

Chunking up

If you take an element of the belief and generalise it, then you will be chunking up. This is all about finding out what higher level or larger category the belief belongs to, and then using this as a lever for change. Ask yourself *'What's important to them about this? How can I exaggerate this, taking it to the limit?'*

1 *'What is really important to you about will-power?'*
2 *'So, because a small part of you contains some aberrant cells, that automatically means it will take control?'*
3 *'What is important to you about depression and your family?'*

Whilst you are not necessarily giving the patient another belief to think about, you are causing them to think about the existing belief in a way that gives both you and them new information. You can then apply the other patterns to that answer.

Hierarchy of criteria

Criteria are the values that are important to someone in a particular situation. And of course some values are more important to you than others. We can use a value that is higher up the ladder, so to speak, as leverage on the lower one. So ask yourself *'Which criteria could be more important in this situation? How can I apply it to the current belief?'*

1   *'Don't you think it's more important to prevent lung cancer and heart disease than to worry about will-power?'* (Giving something worse to move away from).
2   *'Don't you think it's more important to do something for yourself right now and take back control in your life?'*
3   *'Don't you think it's more important to be a role model for your kids and show them how to deal with this effectively?'*

Change frame size

You can re-evaluate a belief by changing the context to include time-frames (longer or shorter), people (larger or smaller numbers), changing perspective like a video camera, panning across to focus on something they have not yet considered. This is a example of context reframing. One strategy is to chunk up to a universal quantifier: *'All? Every? Always? Never?'*

1   *'You've never, ever had any will-power to do anything at all? Is there anything else you couldn't stop doing, yet did?'* (also looks for a counter-example).
2   *'So everybody with cancer is a victim? Always? Forever? Have you ever heard of people who have been a victim to the cure?'* (turns the belief round to encompass the thought of cure).
3   *'So everyone with depression who has a family will always pass it on? Did you know that the cure for depression runs in some families? How do you know you're not one of them?'* (loosens up the belief by junko-pseudo-logic).

Sometimes, in order to loosen up a limiting belief, it is useful to throw in everything, including the kitchen sink! Especially if you say it with a big smile on your face. You can always retract it after the change has occurred.

Meta-frame

A meta-frame establishes a belief *about* the belief. You will recall that *meta-* means standing back, looking from a distance, commenting on the process of what is happening. Essentially you are asking yourself *'How is it possible that they could believe that? And what could they believe instead that they don't yet know about?'*

1   *'You only believe that because you think that will-power is required for stopping smoking. You don't yet know what the other options are.'*
2   *'You have that belief because you haven't yet had the opportunity to meet some of my cancer patients who are choosing to make the most of life, here and now.'*
3   *'You only believe that because of your limited experience with very few families. For most people the genetic component is actually quite small in comparison to thinking negative thoughts.'*

Model of the world

This asks if the belief is true in everyone's world. If our beliefs are one way of perceiving the world, how would someone else, with a different set of beliefs, view the same situation? The questions to ask are *'Is this true for everyone? Who would see it differently?'*

1   *'Some people believe that effectively stopping smoking is nothing to do with will-power. It's about finding out what need smoking fulfils in you, and satisfying it another way.'*
2   *'I have a patient who used his cancer to re-evaluate what was most important in life. He's now doing what he really enjoys and his cancer is in remission.'*
3   *'I can show you a dozen patients right now who were depressed because of how they perceived their life circumstances. All of them have improved with various types of treatment.'*

Reality strategy

How do you know what's really real? No, that's not a philosophical question! We all have a mental strategy that lets us know the difference between what actually happened and something that we made up on the spur of the moment which didn't actually happen. People who don't have a good strategy for this are called schizophrenic! Because a belief is a cognitive perception *about* reality, it can be re-evaluated and updated. Ask yourself *'How do they represent this belief? How do they know if it's true? How do they know if it's not true?'*.

1   *'How do you know that will-power has anything to do with stopping smoking? How would you know if that weren't true?'* (Confusing, huh?).
2   *'How do you know that having cancer means you're a victim? How would you know if that weren't true?'*
3   *'How do you know that depression runs in families? How would you know if that weren't true?'*

Analogy/metaphor

Of course, Milton Erickson would start off by saying *'That reminds me of a story …'*. Often it is very powerful to say one thing in terms of another. You can convey so much meaning in this way. You don't need a long involved tale plus a hypnotic trance. Usually a simple everyday situation is all that is required. It often works better if it's something your patient is interested in. An analogy is usually a short pithy statement. A metaphor can be more complex and obscure.

1   *'How much will-power do you need to fully turn off a tap that drips 20 to 30 times a day?'*
2   *'Don't let your white blood cells hear that! They're already scavenging away, kicking the ass of cancer cells before eating them up!'*
3   *'A GP friend of mine had a patient who had a longstanding family business that was on the verge of going bust. He decided to sell out to a supermarket company who wanted his land to redevelop. He and his family are now comfortably well off. He said "Sometimes you've got to forget the old ways and grab the chance of doing something new."'*

The main trick with using the verbal reframing patterns in this way is simply to quickly generate them and throw them out, with rapport of course! Then you can notice the response that you get, calibrating as to whether it has made a change or not. When patients make changes there is a noticeable physiological shift – often a deeper breath, a facial flush, an obvious yes-set, or a change in eye accessing. Your developing skills in this area will allow you to expand patient choice significantly in the context of explaining about their current symptoms and planning for the future.

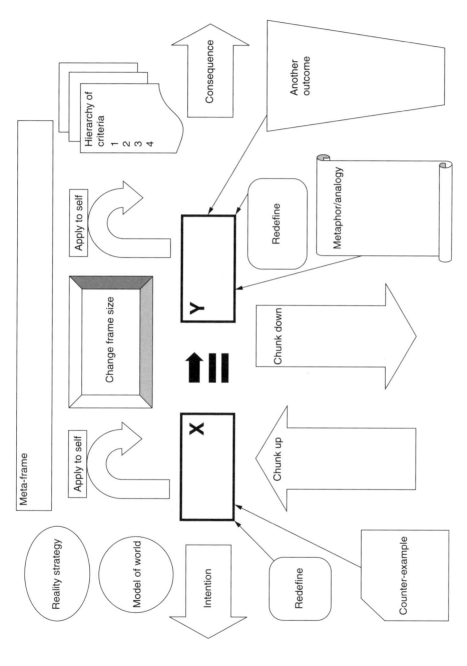

Figure 6.1:   Reframing patterns (adapted from Robert Dilts).

Exercise 14:   Verbal reframes

1   *Look back* over the section on beliefs in Chapter 4 on gathering informa-
    tion. *Choose three limiting belief statements* to work with. Alternatively,
    choose three everyday limiting beliefs that you have come across in
    practice. Yours and those of patients!

2   Systematically *work through each* of the 14 verbal reframe patterns.
    Notice which are easy for you, and which are less so. *Use the template*
    to help you.

3   *Imagine delivering these reframes* to particular patients who automatic-
    ally come to mind for each pattern.

4   Continue to note down examples of limiting beliefs that arise during
    consultations. When you have a few minutes, run them through the
    template.

5   Notice especially those reframes that help patients to *make significant
    shifts*. Who else could you *use them* with?

Section Two: utilising information filters

We need to get our message across in a way that respects the patient's framework of illness and at the same time ensures commitment to our agreed action
plans. Too often we fail to pace our patient's present state adequately in our
desire to lead them in what we believe to be a more healthy direction. We fail to
accommodate their beliefs, expectations, need for appropriate information and
need for shared understanding. We often fail to talk their language, using our
own language of medical jargon instead. How can we address these potential
shortcomings?

In Chapter 4 on gathering information we spent some time working out how
patients actually filter and process the information that they give us. We looked
specifically at meta-programs – how people unconsciously and automatically
structure their communications. In Chapter 5 on building the relationship we
covered sensory predicates – the visual, auditory, kinaesthetic and unspecified
words through which they tell their story. What if we were to use that *very same*
information to package our recommendations so that they could be more easily
acted upon? What do you think the effect would be of inputting our messages
in the identical channels they have used for outputting? Do you think that this
would be *'speaking the patient's language'*, at the level of both process *and* content?

In this section we are going to revisit meta-programs, and we are going to examine more closely the types of influencing words that pertain to each category. We are going to fit these together in various combinations so that we can get the message across clearly, succinctly and understandably. We shall fit them together in the way that a comfortable glove snugly envelops an entering hand.

For each category we shall list the most useful words and give some examples of how they can be used.

Towards and away from

Obviously you want to prevent misunderstandings, steer clear of faux pas and use words that head you in the direction that you want to go, achieving your aims. How is that previous sentence for using the appropriate language to move away from what you don't want, towards what you do want? In general it is a good idea to chain these two together by finishing where you want to be.

Towards words and phrases include the following: get, attain, move towards, the benefits of this are, the advantages of doing this, here's what you get, this is the destination, we're heading this way, this is what we want instead, moving on now, the solution is, as you get better, etc.

Away from words and phrases include the following: steer clear of, the problem is, prevent, overcome, avoid, we need to get rid of, tell me what's wrong, that's not right, the disadvantages are, you don't want to get worse, don't worry, etc.

Probably more people are motivated to move away from than towards. Some people need to have a fairly stark picture of what might go wrong before they are galvanised to do something about it. Even then you still need to finish on what you want instead. Remember that the rule for avoiding difficulties is to link the *away from* to the *towards*, and to get the benefits.

So let us now turn our attention to some examples (*towards and away, T and A*).

- '*If you want your throat to get completely better* (T), *finish the whole course of antibiotics* (T).'
- '*If you don't want your lungs to deteriorate* (A), *use your inhalers on a daily basis* (T).'
- '*It's important to prevent the major complications of hypertension* (A). *That's why you must ensure that you comply with this treatment* (T).'
- '*Picture a pair of lungs ravaged by cancer* (A). *That's what we want to avoid* (A). *Stopping smoking now* (A) *will allow your lungs to remain healthy* (T), *ensuring you're fit to play with your grandchildren in the years to come* (T).'

- *'Up until now you had seen yourself in a panic (A). How would you look if you're cool, calm, collected, with things turned out the way you wanted (T)?'*

Of course, *'If you fail to learn these patterns (A), your ability to communicate effectively will suffer (A). Your patients will thank you (T), for time well spent practising (T).'*

Proactive and reactive

There are many reasons, some of which we've covered, and some of which we've yet to, that once you've fully analysed them, considered them from different perspectives, you'll understand that it's important to get down to it, take the initiative, get galvanised, and just do it now! When someone is reactive you can pace that and then chain it to proactive mode.

Proactive words and phrases include the following: just do it, step on it, take the initiative, get going, take it away, get a move on, right now, this minute, immediately, hurry up, NOWWWW!

Reactive words and phrases include the following: think about it, consider carefully, don't make any hasty decisions, there are many reasons, you might like to dwell on it a bit longer, cogitate, reflect on.

Most people are somewhat in the middle of this category. The extremes will be quite apparent. It is often important to include a mixture of both types, (proactive and reactive, Pr and R) finishing with proactive.

Examples include the following.

- *'You're right. It's bad news. We need to take action right now (Pr).'*
- *'Now that you've had some time to think about the choices I suggested (R), what steps do you want to take now (Pr)?'*
- *'Let's think about it a bit more – after all, your blood pressure is not really that high, and if we were to start medication, that's not a decision to take lightly. What are your thoughts (R)?'*
- *'You need to go to hospital. Now! Where's your phone (Pr)?'*

Options and procedures

There are lots of ways in which you can learn this material easily. And the possibilities for how you might use it are endless. Often it's best to learn by following a tried and trusted procedure, step by step, that is proven to increase your factual retention over time. However, you could just break the rules and do it your way!

Options phrases include the following: lots of ways, endless possibilities, any way you want, here's an alternative, other options, break the rules, break the mould, the choices are, you can ... etc.

Procedures phrases include the following: first we ... then ..., there are three things we need to ..., going by the book, we ought to follow the guidelines, tried and trusted procedure, always done it this way, etc.

People tend to be more one way or the other on this one, rather than in the middle. I believe this is also the pattern that separates out those who like and follow guidelines and protocols (procedures, P) from those who don't. Options (O) people will not want their choices to be constrained. If they are *away from* and *mismatch* as well, the guidelines may be consigned to the bucket without being read!

Examples include the following.

- *'Essentially there are three main types of medication to control your blood pressure. The books say we should use this one first (P).'*
- *'There are a number of options. Firstly we could do nothing. Or start you off on medication. Then if it persists, refer you to the consultant (O and P equally).'*
- *'Here's an alternative. What if you take this for a month and then see where we go from there (O)?'*

As you might expect, medicine is very much a procedural-based profession, and rightly so. Especially surgery. Let's face it, over the years we have had to adopt treatments and approaches that offer the safety and security of being well tried and tested. Yet the innovations that multiply year after year are the product of options thinking. They answer the question *'How do you make improvements to existing procedures, and what new alternatives might be better?'* The two types of thinking work hand in hand.

Self and other

This is one of the small number of patterns for which there are few linguistic clues. *Other*, in the external world, tends to get automatic rapport. They can obviously be influenced by the depth of rapport that you attain with them. Words themselves are less important than the degree of trust that is engendered. They will take it *all* on board.

You will recall that *self* tends to be in their own world, with poor rapport skills. They need to have communication focused more strictly on the *content*. You must ensure that you get your facts right with this one. If you don't, they will take you to task. Be sure that you know what they deem to be important, and filter what you say through this. They may be rude at times, but they don't mean it personally. That's just the way they are. Anton Meyer, the surgeon in the television programme *Holby City*, has this pattern.

General and specific

I hope you've got the big picture so far. Essentially, the main idea is the concept of developing a broad-based communication style to fit all comers. More specifically, though, you must match exactly the detailed patterns that people present. With minute precision!

General words and phrases include the following: big picture, main idea, generally, the concept is, here are the principles, basically, overall strategy, mostly, the wider frame, plus any other 'fluff' words you can think of that convey no detail whatsoever. Listen to politicians!

Specific words and phrases include the following: the devil is in the details, exactly, precisely, here is a complete list of ..., let's go through this one by one, painstakingly, examine the small print, minutiae, proofread, etc.

Most people tend to be *general* oriented (G), with far fewer being *specific* only (S), thank God! Often when outlining what you want to happen, it is helpful to give an overall view of the big picture before getting stuck into the details. This also works well for talks, presentations and seminars.

Examples include the following.

- *'Overall, I think the best approach is to check your blood pressure a few times in the next month or so and see where we go from there (G).'*
- *'This inhaler works specifically on the muscle that surrounds the bronchi, the tubes in the lungs. It acts on one part of the chemical reaction which controls how dilated they are. Two puffs four times daily spread out evenly is the norm (S). Any questions?'*
- *'Here, take this leaflet. It'll tell you all you need to know (G).'*
- *'Once you've been on the antidepressants a little while, you'll start to feel much better (G). They work by increasing the amount of serotonin, the happy chemical, in your brain (S).'*

Problems can arise when someone who is mainly *general* is negotiating with someone *specific*. The *general* person will feel overwhelmed by too much detail, and may tune out, come over all glassy-eyed, and eventually be led kicking and screaming from the room. The *specific* person may find the whole thing so vague that they press for more and more details. At worst they may think that the *general* person is a flake and is withholding sensitive information. Paranoia and accusations of hidden agendas may spring forth. We shall deal with this further in Section Three on *chunking and negotiation*.

I'm sure you've got the hang of all this by now. Match specifically the patterns as you read them.

Match and mismatch

This is another of my favourites. If you want to, you can have a lot of fun with mismatchers who are polarity responders. Or not, if you don't. Want to, that is! You may have found so far that this book gives you some totally new and different ways to improve your consultation skills. Yet it also builds on the same firm foundations that you have already laid down over many years.

Match words and phrases: same as, like, similar to, as before, exactly the same as, in the same way as, identical to, unchanging, like last time, etc.

Match with some mismatch words and phrases: better, worse, evolving, gradually improving, there's been some progression, fading away now, moving along nicely, much the same except, etc.

Mismatch words and phrases: completely different, unrecognisable, a turn-around in my thinking, unique response, never happened to anyone else, revolutionary new treatment, etc.

Probably three or four people out of five mainly match with a little mismatch thrown in (M). One out of five is a mismatcher (Mis), with one out of ten at most being polarity responders (Polar). Remember that mismatchers who are more extreme may give you a typical 'yes, but ...' response. The true polarity responders tend to think, say and do the complete opposite.

Examples include the following.

- *'Let's use the same antibiotic that got you well last time (M).'*
- *'Let's ring the changes and go for something new that you've never had before (Mis).'*
- *'Given that you're improving, let's stay on the same track, shall we (M)?'*
- *'I don't suppose you're the kind of person who could ...* **stop smoking now!** *(Polar).'*
- *'You got over a similar problem to this in the past (M). What if we approach this one in the same way (M)?'*
- *'This is a revolutionary new approach to cancer treatment (Mis).'*
- *'I would tell you to lose weight, but I don't suppose you could ...* **do that now I mean!** *(Polar).'*
- *'You probably won't believe me when I say ... you're going to* **get better quickly** *(Polar).'*
- *'Take the medicine now. Or don't ...* **take it now!** *Only you can decide to* **take it now** *... or not, if you don't want to ...* **take it, that is!** *(Polar).'*

The last pattern is a more advanced one, which easily confuses a polarity responder, giving them the illusion of choice to take the medication. And even if they don't (take it, that is), it's great fun to use. I guarantee you won't get caught! At the end of the day it is important to use any tactic you can to get the patient to comply with treatment in their best interests, so long as it is not unethical.

Internal and external

The experts in the field of communication say that matching your pattern to fit the patient gets the best results. A friend of mine who does this all the time says that it really works for her in all areas of life. That's my firsthand experience, too. Of course, only you can decide whether or not learning these skills is important enough for you to want to become really proficient. You will probably find your own reasons for choosing to do so.

I really enjoy this pattern.

Medicine often calls this internal and external locus of control. We may spend a lot of time getting the internals to take on board what we want them to do, while the externals to make their own decisions. Much better still is to filter what you want to have happen through their own natural pattern. It's far less time consuming, and much more satisfying.

Internal phrases: only you can decide, mull it over and let me know what you think, what do you think about ...?, try it out, here's the information for you to decide, here are the options for you to consider, etc.

External phrases: the experts say, it was in the *BMJ*, most people think that ..., I would strongly recommend, this is tried and trusted, the stamp of approval, I have it on good authority, I have a patient just like you and he said ..., etc.

Studies show that people tend to fall on either side of the centre on this one, with fewer displaying a little of both. You need to decide, though, based on the patient's responses. You may be mainly internal, yet like to have an external check from time to time, ensuring that you are in the same ballpark as the rest. After all, it is your ball! Or you may be mainly external, with an internal check, like the lemming who wonders if jumping off the cliff is really such a good idea after all.

Examples include the following:

- *'The experts say that this drug combination eradicates* Helicobacter *95% of the time (External).'*
- *'It's important to take the whole course of medication. But only you can make the choice to do that now (External with internal check).'*

- *'Here's the leaflet to look at. When you've decided what kind of contraception suits you best, let me know your choice* (Internal).'
- *'I have a patient just like you. He had similar side-effects. He said they wore off after the first 2 weeks. You're at day 12 now, aren't you?* (External).'
- *'If you decide to go for the operation, you can be assured that the consultant is held in high regard for his expertise in the procedure* (Internal with external check).'

By now you may be finding yourself becoming more and more expert in these patterns. You could always check it out with a colleague, though, to ensure that you are headed in the right direction.

Past, present and future

Think of a problem that *currently* limits you in some way. How do you experience that? Make a mental note of what you see, hear and feel. Now experience it as if it were something that *you used to do*. How has it changed? Now experience it as if it had been a problem that *you had had*, and resolved, a long time ago. How is it changed now? Changing *verb tenses* in this way, from present to imperfect to past to past perfect, changes how you internally represent an experience and how you feel about it. Which feels better, thinking of the problem happening now, or as something that had happened, way back then, in the completed past?

Now think of a time when *you had had* a particular resource, such as confidence or something similar. Think of a specific time. What was it that *you were* experiencing then, as confidence? How *are you* representing that in your mind's eye? As you think about it *now*, how does it feel in your body? Where and when *will* it be useful to feel this feeling again, in the future? What will it be like, looking back, *having* successfully felt it again?

We have taken a resource from the past, and by using various verb tenses we have not only brought it into the present, but we have also imagined having it in the future. And not only that, we have gone even further into the future, after the successful completion of the event, and looked back on that success, all the way back to now. And all through the skilful use of language. The rule then is to *use language to put problems into the past, and to bring resources into the present and future.*

Here's how *NOT* to do it. This example takes a problem from the past, experiences it in the present, and installs it in the future.

> *When you had felt anxious and panicky back then, what was it like? How do you feel when you feel that way? What's coming up in the future that might*

make you feel the same again? What would it be like if it happened again?
AAARRRRGGGGGHHH!!

You can use the *backtrack frame* to subtly move an experience into the completed past and open up a solution space. For example:

> *So let me backtrack … up until now **you were** feeling anxious and panicky … **you'd had** a sick feeling in your stomach … your heart **had been** fluttering … you'd felt shaky … is that **what had happened** back then? OK … so I was wondering … how would you rather be feeling instead?*

Use your verb tenses wisely, and they may come in very handy, as we shall see later.

Thinkers and feelers

This is another category for which there are few specific linguistic clues. Thinkers tend to be dissociated from their experiences and are good at thinking *about* things. You can pace them by giving a fairly dry description of what you want to have happen, as if you are watching it on a black-and-white video somewhere in the distance. You can also use more unspecific words such as *consider, decide, understand, cogitate, perceive*, etc.

Feelers tend to be right in the middle of whatever they are experiencing – associated, for good or bad. For neutral or positive emotional states you can use all of the sensory specific words possible, building a richly textured experience and asking them how they feel about it. However, for negative states you want to *do the reverse* to pull them out of it. Use unspecific words mainly, but also get them to look up and think in pictures. This will dissociate them from the experience somewhat. In particular, use pictures that are distanced, and more black and white, like still-frame photographs.

For example:

> *That wasn't a particularly nice experience you **had** back then. As you tell me about it, imagine that someone **had** followed you around with a video camera that only uses **black-and-white film**. Pretend that we're **watching it from the outside**, and describe what had happened to **that you** back then.*

You can learn to use the language of association and dissociation, both verbally and non-verbally, to explain future plans and expectations appropriately.

Convincer channel and mode

This is an additional meta-program pattern that is one of the most useful ones for really getting your message across so that it is both understood *and* acted upon. This is the type of information that helps someone to start the process of becoming convinced. Because if you're not convinced, then you're unlikely to act.

So how would you know, personally, that the information presented in this book is going to *trans-form* your consulting skills? Is it that you would *see* yourself utilising these skills on a daily basis and know that it *looks right?* Would it be after you *hear* the words of the various language patterns effortlessly flowing out of your mouth, and know that it *sounds* just right? Is it that you have that certain *feeling* inside, the one that lets you know that what you're doing really feels *right?* Or, having *read* through the material so far, do you know that it just logically *makes sense?*

And is it that you're convinced *automatically*, right now? Or are you the sort of person who needs to demonstrate your capability two, three or *several times* first? Perhaps you'll know after a *period of time*, maybe a week, or a month or two? Or are you the kind of person who will *consistently* not take my word for it, but only really find out for yourself by trying it out on your own terms?

This really is a vital area for getting information across in a way that convinces the patient to act on it now. How does it work? Well, people will primarily filter what you say so that it *looks right, sounds right, feels right* or *makes complete sense.* If they can't see what you're saying, if it doesn't sound right, if they don't feel good about doing it, and if it doesn't make sense to them, then guess what? You're right, they won't act. Usually the signal strength from one of these input channels is stronger than that of all the rest. This is their *primary filter.* Occasionally they will run a strategy that incorporates two or more channels to a differing degree.

So how do you utilise this? As far as I can see, the simplest way to cover all of the bases is to *draw a diagram* and while the patient pictures it, you can tell them what to do, ensuring that it feels right to them and makes complete sense. Visual methods of conveying information seem to work best. And you can also ask questions. Does that look right to you? Does it sound right? How do you feel about that? Does it make sense? You can easily gauge their yes-sets to ascertain whether they are congruent about it.

Some people seem to make up their minds *automatically*, one way or the other, on one pass. Most people need a degree of *repetition* – two, three or more – before they are convinced. Advertisers know this fact well and make great use of it. For others, a *period of time* is the main factor. They may have to do something for a week or a month before they are convinced. Some people are *never* completely convinced, and they need to re-evaluate each time. They are the most challenging ones to deal with and they may appear sceptical. Treat them in the same way as an *internal*: '*Only you can decide ...*'.

So for each patient to whom you are handing over information, you can assume that they will automatically take as long as they need to think it over enough times before deciding for themselves to take action.

Meta-programs in action

Now is the time to put the influencing language of meta-programs together in various combinations to best fit the unique individual in the consulting-room chair. I shall label the first few examples, and you can determine the rest yourself.

- '*Only you can decide* (Int) *if you want to steer clear of bronchitis and lung cancer* (A). *If you do, throw your cigarettes in the bucket* (T) *and taste fresh air again* (T).'
- '*The experts say* (Ext) *that to prevent strokes and heart disease* (A) *it's important to take this tablet every day* (T). *You know it makes sense* (Convincer).'
- '*I think it's important for you to fully consider just what the consequences might be of failing to take this medication regularly* (Ext, Reactive, Away). *Then, having done that, decide for yourself to ACT NOW, take it every day* (Int, Pro, Toward).'
- '*I don't suppose you're the kind of person who'll agree to that. Or are you* (Polarity)? *I can tell you what the experts say, but you probably won't act on their advice* (Ext, Polarity).'
- '*What was the medicine that helped last time* (M, Past)? *We'll use exactly the same one again so that you can get better quickly, probably within 72 hours* (M, Future).'
- '*There are three things that are important about diabetes. The first is ...*'
- '*Here's your prescription. See you in a month or so.*'
- '*The fact of the matter is that this medicine will probably suit you better. Statistically speaking it's the logical next step.*'
- '*I don't know if you can see yourself doing that next time you meet her. How would you know that it was right for you?*'
- '*Unless you want the sounds of tight, wheezy breathing rasping loudly in your ear, you know it makes sense to use your inhalers daily.*'

These are a few examples. You can use them to build your own ways of saying things so that they fit with your personality. It's important to feel comfortable rather than think that you need a prepared script. After just a little practice you are likely to find yourself using them instinctively in the right place at the right time.

Section Three: chunking and negotiation

Induction, deduction and metaphor

Chunking is a jargon word from computer terminology. It is all about how much information can be organised and grouped together. Chunk sizes can be small or large. Think of your telephone number. It may have anywhere between six and nine digits, depending on where you live. This is quite handy because research has determined that most people can remember $7 \pm$ (plus or minus) 2 bits of information. On good days we can remember nine bits of information. On not so good days, we can remember five. When we are stressed or overwhelmed the number can decrease further.

We can format each chunk to contain a little or a lot of information. Each chunk of your telephone number contains a single digit. However, you can remember much larger numbers by altering the size of a chunk. For example, 7301492365871 is easier to remember when chunked as 730 1492 365 871. How we learn, understand and apply information depends on our chunking skills.

Chunks can be thought of in terms of a hierarchy of categories. An atom, a molecule, a cell, an organ and a human being are all examples of *nested chunks*, one encompassing the next. The complexity increases as we chunk up, and it decreases as we chunk down. Most people have a preferred chunk size that they like to deal with. You will recall from the *general and specific meta-program* that some people like the more rarefied atmosphere of the big picture, while others prefer the minutiae of the details. Large chunks and small chunks.

Some people like to build the larger chunks from the smaller ones first. Moving from small to large in this way is called *synthesis* or *inductive thinking* – understanding the parts and then the whole. When chunking up in this way, you can take two apparently disparate things and see what they have in common.

Others prefer to go from large to small. This is called *analysis* or *deductive thinking* – understanding the whole and then the parts. Chunking down involves taking a category and finding an example that fits within that, then finding an example of that, and so on, getting smaller and smaller. So in general practice it is important to chunk the information to suit the patient.

Chunking up

You can chunk up by asking yourself the following questions.

- *'Of what is this a part?'*
- *'Of what is this an example?'*
- *'What is the benefit of this outcome/approach/treatment?'*
- *'What intention lies behind this behaviour?'*

These questions step you up into the next category or level and open up a wider solution space with more potential choices about what to do.

Some patient examples include the following.

- *'For many people, smoking actually helps them to stay relaxed.'*
- *'Chemotherapy is an example of one approach to helping to get rid of cancer cells.'*
- *'Beta-blockers are drugs that help to get more oxygen to the heart muscle.'*

Chunking down

You can chunk down by asking the following questions.

- *'What is a part of this?'*
- *'What is an example of this?'*
- *'What is a first step towards the outcome/approach/treatment?'*
- *'What other behaviours could also fulfil the intention?'*

These questions lead to more specificity and precision in choices. They can help you to become really clear about which actions to take.

Patient examples include the following.

- *'Have you thought of switching to a lower-tar brand, or even cigars?'*
- *'Chemotherapy comes in all shapes and sizes. Let me tell you about treatment pulses.'*
- *'The beta-blocker we shall use is called metoprolol.'*

Chunking across

This is when you move laterally to a different class of objects or behaviours and make a connection to the original one. First of all you chunk up at least one level to get a broader, more *abstract* category. Then you pick a different member of that new category to chunk down with (*see* Table 6.1).

For example, many people smoke as a means of relaxation. This is the higher, more abstract category. So you then ask the question *'What else can give me the same effect in a different way?'* Well, taking a long diaphragmatic breath, in and out, activates the parasympathetic nervous system and leads to relaxation. Try it and see. Learning the skill of meditation can do likewise.

Table 6.1:   Chunking skills

	Smoking	*Chemotherapy*	*Beta-blockers*
Chunk up	Relaxation	Kill cancer cells	Increase oxygen supply to heart
Chunk down	Cigarettes	Pulses	Metoprolol
	Cigars	Vincristine	Atenolol
Chunk across	Deep breath	Radiotherapy	Calcium antagonists
	Meditation	Surgery	Nitrates

Chunking across laterally is also the way to construct *metaphors, similes* and *analogies*. Many surgical procedures are explained in terms of plumbing analogies. The fight against cancer is a war metaphor, with ammunition, big guns and wholesale killing. More subtle metaphors for handing over information include the *'My friend John ...'* type of story. For example, *'I had a patient once, just like you, and he ...'*.

Even more subtle are *isomorphic metaphors.* This is when you initially map out the main processes causing the patient's problem, together with a proposed solution. You then work out the critical relationships with regard to how parts of the problem could connect to the solution. Then mapping across laterally, you can develop a story-line with different characters, yet preserving the key relationships. Tell the story in an enthralling, entrancing way that gets the patient's full attention. This installs the solution, out of conscious awareness. *Isomorphic metaphors* are an art in and of themselves and are beyond the scope of this book. If you are interested in the subject, read *Therapeutic Metaphors* (Gordon, 1978).

Negotiation

Negotiation skills are required in all areas of medical practice, not just when dealing with patients. Negotiations are joint searches towards agreed solutions whereby both parties fulfil their outcomes. Getting your outcome met at the expense of the other person, a win–lose situation, is called *manipulation*. Dovetailing outcomes to obtain a win–win solution, with both parties getting what they want, is influencing with *integrity*. Of course, not everything may be negotiable, so it is important to have clear, palatable alternatives.

In essence, negotiations are really an exercise in chunking skills – up, down and across. All negotiations (yes, all of them!) require both parties to chunk up as high as is necessary to get *agreement* on common areas – the generalities. The next step is to chunk back down to the specific details only as quickly as that agreement is maintained. In this way the details are seen within the perspective of the larger, higher-level frame that has already been agreed upon. Any subsequent area of specific disagreement can be chunked up again until agreement is reached. Chunking across can open up new avenues to be explored.

You will recall that the people who have most trouble with negotiations are those with a *general* preference negotiating with a *specific*. When this was explained to one of my colleagues who was *general*, he went back to a partnership meeting and said to the partner with whom he had had difficulties, '*We disagree because you're just a little chunker*'. You can probably guess the outcome there!

You can use chunking skills questions to sort this out. The *general* person needs to be asked the following questions.

* '*Can you give me a specific example?*'
* '*How would you know if the outcome was right?*' (get sensory-specific answers).
* '*What specifically needs to happen in order to get your outcome?*'

The *specific* person needs to be able to chunk up. Use questions like the following.

* '*What's important about that?*'
* '*What's your purpose in saying that?*'
* '*If you got your outcome, what will having that achieve for you? What is the main benefit?*'

The other important skills in any negotiation are as follows:

* being and remaining in a *resourceful state* yourself
* being able to build and maintain *rapport*
* the ability to set an *outcome* (the therapeutic options) and know the *evidence* (the steps) for its achievement
* being able to step into *first, second and third positions*, taking on board the patient's views
* eliciting *beliefs and expectations*, reactions and concerns
* using *softeners* to introduce *meta-model* questions
* using *backtracking* to restate key points in the patient's words
* calibrating to *yes-sets* and degrees of *congruence*
* using *ecology frames* to discuss potential consequences, benefits and advantages

- utilising *meta-programs* to put the message across to best fit the unique individual.

These are all skills that we have covered previously. *You already know how to negotiate!* Below are some examples of different parts of the process being used with patients.

A patient who smoked was being asked about what smoking did for him, by repeating the question *'And what's important about that?'* for each higher level of chunking.

- *'It gives me something to do with my hands when I'm uptight.'*
- *'It calms me down.'*
- *'It relaxes me more.'*
- *'It allows me to think straight.'*
- *'It gives me time for me'* (identity level statement).

We could then explore other ways of getting 'time for me' that involved doing something different behaviourally, yet which preserved the underlying positive intention. You can use this approach with any behaviour that a patient does 'too much of'.

Some other examples of these types of skills in action include the following.

- *'Here are my ideas about what to do ... what are your thoughts about that?'*
- *'You said that you wanted to be referred ... what's important to you about that?'*
- *'I was wondering ... when you feel like you need a drink ... what does that drink do for you?'*
- *'Those are the three choices as I see them ... which is your preference?'*
- *'What would have to happen for you to be able to easily stop smoking now?'*
- *'You seem really keen to pursue that course of action ... what's the main benefit of that to you?'*
- *'I'm not sure that we really agree on this ... what do you think?'*
- *'And if you were to stop drinking ... how might you achieve that?'*

Negotiation skills help you to relate your explanations better to your patient's framework of beliefs and expectations surrounding their illness. By chunking up, you find out what is really important to them. You draw them into the consultation by allowing them to share the decision-making process. You allow them to touch core issues safely, and to feel more deeply understood. By chunking back down with the specific details of an agreed management plan that is tailored to their individual framework, you lay a firm foundation for both the conviction and the commitment to *act now.*

Section Four: language application
The Milton model

You are probably wondering just exactly what the Milton model might be. And it's really good to wonder in this way, as that causes your mind to search for links to other learnings and other associations. And searching in that way means that you remain open to new information for change. Of course, you have already gained many useful skills and resources. And of all these skills, there are some that you can use in every situation. You might like to think of the specific ones that you can and will use in the days ahead. They all exhibit the general possibility of utilisation in a variety of combinations for creative linguistic application. And you can do that easily. Haven't you?

And people can respond in many different ways, some more or less effectively than others. Of course, at this moment you are sitting, reading this paragraph. And in so doing, you are aware of certain things consciously, yet I don't know just when – perhaps now, maybe in a few moments, or even a little later – you'll realise exactly what it is that you have learned. But could you just stop for a moment? Because I was just thinking about a recent seminar with Richard Bandler when he mentioned how Gregory Bateson suggested that he should go and see Milton Erickson, who said to a medical colleague *'You're hear ... and what I'm saying is very important for you to understand it all completely...because consulting doctors provide therapeutic gains ... and speaking to you as an accelerated learning specialist, you know that buy now.'*

Whereas the meta-model gets very specific, more detailed information, the *Milton model* is at the opposite end of the spectrum. It deals in *artfully vague language*, the meaning of which is intuited by the listener according to their own internal experience at that time. It can be quite trance-inducing as you listen to it. Yet each person makes sense of it in a way that fits for them. And you can use it to impart important information very effectively. The first two paragraphs of this section contain multiple examples of the Milton model in action. In fact, each sentence is a specific example of each pattern. Let's elucidate.

Box 6.1:   The Milton model

	Distortions
Mind reading	Claiming to know the thoughts and feelings of others *'You are probably wondering ...'*

Lost Performative	Where the performer of the value judgement has been left out *'And it's really good to ...'*
Causation	Implied or stated that one thing causes another *'That causes your mind to ...'*
Meaning	When two things are equated to mean the same thing *'Searching in that way means ...'*
Presupposition	The linguistic equivalent of assumptions *'... already gained many useful skills and resources ...'*

Generalisations

| *Universals* | Words like always, every, never, all, none, etc.
'... of all these skills ...' |
| *Possibility/necessity* | Words like can, will, should, must, have to, might, could, etc.
'... that you can and will use ...' |

Deletions

Nominalisations	A verb (process word) changed into a noun (static word) *'... utilisation ... combinations ... creative linguistic application ...'*
Unspecified verb	Process words lacking a complete description of 'how' *'And you can do that easily ...'*
Tag question	Questions which displace resistance (e.g. polarity responses) *'Haven't you ... ?' (also didn't you, weren't you, aren't you?)*
Lack of reference	Deletes 'who' is doing the action *'... people can respond ...'*
Comparative deletion	Deletes what specifically is compared with what *'... more or less effectively ...'*

Other patterns

| *Pacing current experience* | Truisms about current, ongoing, sensory experience
'... at this moment you are sitting, reading this ...' |
| *Double binds* | Creating an 'illusion of choice' using the word 'or'
'... perhaps now, maybe in a few moments, or ...' |

Conversational postulate	Yes/no questions, yet the listener actually does what is implied *'But could you just stop for a moment?'*
Extended quotes	Designed to overload the conscious mind and remove resistance *'Richard Bandler ... Gregory Bateson ... Milton Erickson ... said ...'*
	Ambiguities
Phonological	Homonyms which can cause mild confusion *'You're hear (here) ...'* (also *right/write/rite, their/there/they're*)
Punctuational	Two sentences connected with one word, which acts as a link *'... very important for you to **understand** it all completely ...'*
Syntactic	A word's function is not immediately apparent from the context *'... consulting doctors ...'* (Who is consulting? Patient? Doctor?)
Scope	How much of one part of a sentence applies to another *'... speaking to you as an accelerated learning specialist ...'*

Of course you don't need to remember the terminology in order to use the Milton model effectively. You can simply write out some examples of the patterns as you weave them into your explanation and planning. They are very useful for allowing patients to make sense of what you are handing over in their own way. You can use the patterns in any order.

You're probably wondering just what can be done to help you overcome those panic attacks. And it's good to start thinking in this way because that means your mind is already seeking solutions. You may not know this, but you have many past experiences that can act as resources in this situation. And of all the experiences you've ever had, several will fit the bill. We should be able to unearth those ones which will have the best effect. And we can be quite creative in our utilisation of the various combinations. Can't we? Because that reminds me of a patient ...

Take the time now to create your own examples.

The SCORE model

This model, which was first introduced by Robert Dilts, is one that can be applied to virtually any situation. It can be used to order and sequence the type of information that patients typically seek in a consultation, and it can help you to cover all of the bases. All you need to think is *'What's the score so far?'*. The letters stand for the following.

- *Symptoms – what is initially presented.*
- *Causes – what has come beforehand, the reasons why.*
- *Outcomes – what you want instead.*
- *Resources – what you need to bring to bear on the situation.*
- *Effects – the short-term and longer-term consequences.*

This kind of structure gives patients the information that they really want – about diagnosis, causation, treatment and prognosis. Here are some examples.

> *Your anginal symptoms are caused by not enough oxygen getting to your heart muscle when you're exercising. What we want instead is for you to be comfortable going about your daily business. So what I'm going to suggest is that we add in a beta-blocker, a drug which will help your heart cope more effectively. All the evidence suggests that this kind of medicine can protect your heart over many months and years.*

> *You've got some pains in your knees. That's caused by osteoarthritis, some wear-and-tear changes over the years. What we want to do is to find the best way to manage this for you, so you can be more mobile. In the first instance we need to use some effective painkillers. Once I have the results of the X-rays, we can see about an orthopaedic referral. In the longer term we may need to consider a joint replacement.*

> *You've been feeling quite depressed for some time now ... certainly made worse by your housing situation and your husband's leaving. You want to start feeling better ... getting back to doing the things you enjoy. I think the time has come to help you do that more quickly ... by using an anti-depressant tablet. Most people start feeling better within two weeks ... many are completely better within two to three months. I usually keep this kind of medication going for about six months.*

These examples may appear like a monologue. In reality, the *SCORE model* is interspersed with the patient's comments, questions and your eliciting of yes-sets for agreement. I have presented it in this way to let you see how it frames most effectively the information you put across. I also use it as a framework for referral letters. I have used it to help to negotiate resources for service developments, even for the building of our new health centre. It's a very versatile model. You can perhaps think of other areas in which to use it.

Up until now you might have had that uncertain feeling, you know, the one caused by wondering if you can really use this material effectively. And, of course, my goal throughout this book is to present the information in so many ways that you come to find yourself automatically using it. You are probably realising by now just how many of the skills are beginning to integrate easily. Perhaps you will begin to catch yourself having successfully applied a pattern or two in the next few days. It is even more likely that, with a little practice, this material will wend and wind itself into all that you do over the coming months. What's your score now?

Utilising non-verbal communication

We have covered a lot of ground in this area already, especially in the gathering information and building relationships phases. As well as giving our explanations and plans verbally, we can use all that we have elicited to enhance our message non-verbally, ensuring to an even greater extent that it will be acted upon. Our posture, gestures and voice qualities convey vital additional signals. We need to be congruent, aligned in our delivery and committed to our intentions.

You remember that, in general, people store their representations of the past to the left or behind them, those of the future to the right or straight ahead, and their representations of now 'inside' their body or just in front of it. It's easy to calibrate to how each individual patient does this as they tell you what *had happened* (past), how they *feel now* (present) and what they *want instead* (future). You can gesture or look to these areas as you seed in appropriate information. When speaking about problems that they have *had*, gesture to the past. When talking about your agreed management plan, gesture to their future. You can even mark out days, weeks or months by slight 'chopping' hand gestures to their right (your left).

> *It'll probably take 48* (mark) to 72 hours* to start to get better. By the time 4* or 5* days have passed, you'll likely be completely better. Remember to take all of the 7*-day course.*

> *That was a terrible problem you had back then* (to past), and what's important right now* is that we begin to plan for a healthy future*.*

Remember the section on beliefs and expectations? In that section we noted that patients often made particular gestures about beliefs that were *'close to their heart'*. Or they used phrases like *'on the one hand'*, gesturing with the left hand,

and *'on the other hand'*, gesturing with the right, as if these beliefs were somehow projected out in space around them. You can replay these gestures to them as you fit your explanation to their current belief framework. You could even bring both your hands together as a non-verbal signal about *integrating* conflicting beliefs. Let your hands guide you through the next example.

> *So it's like on this hand* (left) *... part of you wants to give up smoking ... and the intention behind that is to have healthy lungs ... do more of what you want* (look for yes-set) *... And on this hand* (right) *... the smoking part ... wants you to have something to do with your hands ... be calm ... relaxed ... think straight ... time for you* (chunking up). *... So what if they could join together ... so that you have time for you to do more of what you want ... thinking straight about having healthy lungs ... calm ... relaxed ...* (bring hands together).

During the time when patients are telling you about their problem, the difficulties they have had and how it has affected them, you are in a particular body posture and using a certain voice tone. This anchors the problem state to your physiology and tonality. When you ask about what they want instead, their future expectations and how things will be different, it is really important for you to *change your physiology and voice tone*. Move a little in your chair, sit more upright, put a little more animation into your voice, and gesture to their right (future). Now you don't need to go daft over this, just enough to mark it out to their subconscious mind. Then when you are talking about agreed actions, management plans, investigations, etc., use *this* physiology and tonality instead.

Embedding language

We talked in Chapter 5 on building the relationship about embedding language by marking it out in some way. We do this all the time, usually unwittingly. How we do it can allow us to seem congruent or, at worst, incongruent. Say the following out loud:

'I'd like you to do that now'.

- First use a rising, questioning inflection on the word 'now'.

- Then make it a statement, flat across.

- Then use a commanding, downward inflection.

If someone asked you the above question, which of the three versions would probably cause you *to do that now?*

With a downward inflection on the words that we want to *emphasise*, we can mark out our intentions clearly. Consider the following examples.

> *Now I don't know how soon ... **you're going to get better** ... it may be within the next few days ... almost certainly ... **within the next week**.*

> *I'm really not sure if you're the kind of person who could ... **give up smoking now**. You probably wouldn't find it all that **easy** ... **giving up** ... **now**.... In fact, it's possibly unlikely that ... **you can do this** ... today or tomorrow ... and I don't even know if ... **next week's the time** ... all I know is that ... **the decision's yours** ...*

One complete message nestled and embedded within another!

You can practise this quite easily. Simply write out a few short messages like the ones shown in bold above, ones that you feel are important to get across. Then embed them in other, longer sentences, and practise saying them out loud. As well as tonal emphasis, you could also use a very short pause just before ... saying them, that is. As well as voice tone, you could also mark out by using a specific gesture each time. Watch how some politicians, like Tony Blair, do this. If all this seems not quite as easy as you would like, you can rest assured that simply having the *intention* of marking things out is all that is required. It will then happen automatically.

You can also use embedding within questions (with downward tonality), as in the following examples.

- *'I was wondering how easy you'll find it to ... **take your medication now**.'*
- *'Is there anything that might prevent you from ... **doing that now**?'*
- *'I'm curious ... are there times when you find yourself ... **relaxing easily, not a care in the world**?'*
- *'Which ways do you think will help you most to ... **lose weight effectively**?'*

Side-effects

In this day and age, with issues like informed consent, and the availability of so much information, we have an obligation to tell patients about the side-effects of medications and other treatment options. If you are anything like me, you'll know that this is a double-edged sword. We all have patients who simply read the drug leaflet, imagine having the side-effects, and then get them. They are hypnosis machines. Then, of course, some patients are suggestible to the extent that because you – an authority figure – are delivering the message about what to look out for, it's sure to develop. So how can we use what we have already learned to fulfil the obligation of informed consent, yet at the same time minimise side-effects?

What I usually do is to use a combination of embedding language plus an empty chair. I discuss the side-effects while gesturing to an imaginary patient in the other chair, gesturing to the real patient with what I'm marking out for them. Look at the following example.

> *Some people can get side-effects with medication* (gesture to empty chair),
> *but most people are fine* (gesture to them). *Occasionally they can get a bit of*
> *nausea, and stomach upset* (gesture to chair), *but the majority are OK*
> (gesture to them). *Rarely, maybe three in a thousand can get palpitations*
> (gesture to chair), *and need to stop immediately. The other 997* (gesture to
> them), *are fine. Any questions?*

Another way is to say what you have to, yet be *maximally incongruent* as you do so. Tell them about about side-effects as you shake your head 'no' in simultaneous incongruence. Use moving away or excluding gestures while you raise your voice tone at the end of the sentence, like a question. The more incongruent you are, the better. Of the two approaches, however, I generally prefer the empty-chair method. It's easier.

You can use either method in any area in which you have to cover important yet negative information that you want to prevent the patient associating into. You can fulfil the medico-legal aspects yet still maintain an appropriate dissociation.

Ending explanation and planning

The most important aspect of explanation and planning is that it needs to be a two-way, dynamic, interactive process between doctor and patient. It is not enough simply to give out your message, full stop. You must continue to *calibrate* to the verbal and non-verbal signals that let you know that it has been both received and understood. All that we have covered in this chapter presupposes that not only do we link our messages to our patient's beliefs and expectations, their framework and filters of communication, but also we provide the space to allow them to be fully involved in the process that leads to shared understanding.

We have seen that many patients' beliefs about their illness, and about what is happening to them and why, can be limiting – often markedly so. Whilst we need to build our explanations on their pre-existing frames, we must ensure that our seeds are planted in fertile soil. To that end, *verbal reframing* skills are paramount in gently yet surely expanding previously impoverished viewpoints to encompass a more health-giving outlook.

You will recall that the experts believe that utilising your patients' *meta-programs* in your explanations gives a finely tuned message that is more likely to be acted on. However, only you can decide whether or not to take that fully onboard and utilise it now. If you want to prevent mixed messages, poor outcomes and bad explanations, then both studying and using meta-programs effectively will markedly enhance your ability to help patients to go in the right direction, and will leave you feeling increasingly satisfied as you fulfil your own potential as a capable communicator.

Yet at what level of *chunk size* do your explanations need to be? Big picture or detail? How much *negotiation* do you need to do? Remember that behind every communication, whether in words or behaviour, there lies a positive intention. If you chunk up high enough you will find it. Then you can chunk down again only as quickly as you agree on other behaviours or methodologies that will meet the same underlying need. You are also likely to be wondering just how you can use the *Milton model* to artfully get your message across.

And as you do this, it's important to keep the *score*. Feeling good about communicating effectively is caused by attention to the ongoing process, not merely the story-line content. Focusing on the goal, target, aim and direction is the key skill on which the other skills are predicated. The short-term goal is an excellent consultation. The long-term aim is an increasingly satisfying relationship.

And last but not least, you need to consider the subtleties of the non-verbal nuances that make or break this and every other phase. So as you **contemplate** what you've just completed, before **you're curious** about moving on to the next stage, you might ... **begin to wonder** ... just exactly how ... **deep inside** ... these skills are ... **beginning to integrate** ... but only at the rate and speed that is ... **right for you**.... And I'm not sure if that is ... **happening now** ... or whether you'll only ... **be aware of it** ... once it's ... **successfully completed** ... is it not?

CHAPTER 7

Closing the session

Introduction

Often this part of the consultation is quite easy. Sometimes it is rather difficult. There's nothing worse from a doctor's point of view than when a patient brings up something completely new just when you think it's all over. Or it becomes painfully clear that your well thought out and delivered explanation has fallen on deaf ears. Then there are those peculiar circumstances, and I don't know if this has happened to you, when you know it's over, they know it's over, yet *they're still sitting there*! Perhaps engaging in social chit-chat, asking about your wife or children (or dog!). Maybe holding forth about a local or national political topic that is currently in the news. Or just not wanting to go back out into the cold and wet.

If you have followed and practised the various skill sets in the previous chapters, then you will have found that most of the problems that were associated with closing have all but disappeared. Usually problems at the end follow inadequate agenda setting and exploration in the earlier stages, and failing both to elicit beliefs and expectations about the patient's current illness and to explain what is happening in the words that fit their framework. Occasionally, however, some patients will keep their most important, pressing or embarrassing problem to the very end, until after they have fully tested the waters. So whilst you may want to close down and get on, you may need to be flexible enough to re-open if the occasion demands it. After all, the whole idea of a consultation is to deal with patients' issues.

There are also specific skills that are pertinent to this phase, which will bring it to a natural and satisfactory close for both parties. This is the time for clear backtracking and summarising of the plan so far, ensuring a safety-net by asking about *'what-if scenarios'* and follow-up arrangements. And, of course, the elegant breaking of rapport that allows you to disengage, take stock, regroup, look after yourself and move on to the next patient in line.

Aims of this chapter

The closing phase of a successful consultation is built firmly on the foundation of the skills that you have been learning so far. We shall revisit these, albeit very briefly in summary form, before moving on to the phase-specific skills. It's important to round off a session by effectively backtracking what has been agreed so far, talking about what to do if things don't go according to plan, before effectively breaking rapport in a way that allows you to pick it up again at a subsequent visit. And as well as continuing to look after yourself, it's important to allow some time for reflecting on what has happened, and to plan for the future.

We shall cover the following specific areas:

- highlighting the important topics in the previous phases
- *backtracking* revisited
- discussing *'what-if scenarios'* and *future rehearsals*
- *chaining* several consultations together
- the skills of *breaking rapport* (even in difficult circumstances!)
- continuing to *look after yourself*
- *reflecting* in four quadrants.

Skills review

Given that a satisfactory closing phase depends so much on what has gone before, what are the important skills that you need to pay attention to in the earlier phases? I shall simply list them below, but you can refer back to each section to remind yourself of the details.

Initiating the session
- Breaking state and then ensuring that you trigger your *consulting flow state.*
- Initial rapport: *matching and mirroring* body language and voice patterns.
- Eliciting the patient's *yes-set.*
- Using *backtracking* to establish a mutually agreed *agenda.*

Gathering information
- Noticing how information is presented through *meta-programs.*
- Exploring and formulating the patient's *beliefs and expectations* through the *meta-model* questions.
- Setting *well-formed outcomes* and becoming solution centred.

Building the relationship

- Utilising first, second and third *perceptual positions*.
- Noticing *congruence* and *incongruence*.
- Paying attention to *eye-accessing cues* and *projections*.
- Using *meta-comments* to structure the consultation.

Explanation and planning

- Utilising and expanding on the *belief* framework, with *reframing*.
- Using *meta-programs* and the *convincer channel* to get the message across.
- Keeping the *SCORE* in mind.

Backtracking revisited

Backtracking can be used in any phase of the consultation. Here we want to use it as a *final summary* of what has been agreed so far, and to delineate the next steps. It is very important at this point to look for a congruent yes-set. This lets both you and the patient know that everything has been covered appropriately and that the agreed action plan will be acted upon. Be very sensitive to anything less than a full yes at this stage. It is far better to spend a few moments re-opening an area of doubt than to press on regardless, jeopardising the next steps.

> *So in summary, it seems that these chest pains you've been having do sound like angina. It's important to use the spray under your tongue before you exert yourself. I will organise the exercise test and you'll get your appointment directly from the hospital. After that we can sit down with the information and decide the next step. Have we covered everything?*

> *So, just to backtrack. It seems that you had become increasingly depressed since your mother's death last year. And the symptoms you've had up until now are not a sign of madness, just a prolonged grief reaction. The tablets will start to help you get better within the next two weeks or so. And the counsellor will be in touch with an appointment shortly. I'll see you again in two weeks. Any gaps, or have we covered everything?*

At any stage of the consultation, if you are in doubt, backtrack and check for agreement. Assuming that you want patients to congruently follow an agreed management plan, it is far better to re-open and clarify any areas of potential confusion before moving on. You will always regret *not* having done so, and the reward for doing so is increased compliance and patient satisfaction.

What-if scenarios

What if things don't go according to plan? What if, before you next see the patient, something else has happened? Something that was unlooked for by them but which was a possibility that you could have covered. Successful endings always include the type of thinking that begins with the question *'What would happen if ... ?'*. We are projecting ourselves into the future to contemplate the possible consequences of our present decisions and actions. If it all goes according to plan, *this* will happen. If it doesn't, *that* will happen instead. Insurance companies call this downside planning.

Because patients cannot hear our unspoken thoughts (unless they are schizophrenic!), failure to address what might happen instead could leave us looking foolish. We have probably all read about, or maybe even experienced, the disgruntled teenager with a sore throat, given penicillin but still no better, who actually has glandular fever, making the subsequent consultation run less smoothly. Or perhaps a similar scenario springs to your mind. A few seconds discussing the potential possibilities develops deeper rapport and trust should the unexpected happen. Of course we can't, and indeed shouldn't, discuss all of the possible negative eventualities. The last thing we want to do is install the potential for iatrogenically induced side-effects. Yet we do need some way to cover the options.

- *'I expect this antibiotic will clear your chest within the next three to five days. If it doesn't follow that course, let me know.'*
- *'The vast majority of patients get better quickly with this medication. Occasionally, in the first few days it can cause nausea. Most people find that subsides quickly, so I would ask you to persevere with it if that happened.'*
- *'Sometimes after a steroid injection into the shoulder, the discomfort can actually increase in the first 48 hours or so. That's a good sign, as it's almost invariably followed by a complete resolution of the problem.'*
- *'I expect the blood tests to be normal, and you can phone my receptionist for the results in two days. If that's the case, we need do no more unless it flares up again. If the results are different to that, I'll leave a specific message about what to do.'*

Future rehearsals

Sometimes there is a particular behaviour or series of steps that you want your patient to take. And of course you want to markedly increase the chances of their complying. If you have framed these future actions within their own belief framework, this will already have helped enormously. But what else can you do? There are several options.

One is to give the patient a written instruction of just exactly what you want them to do – probably no more than three main points, otherwise it becomes too complicated. I often write these suggestions out on a prescription pad, with their name on the top. This seems to increase the chances of action, even (or especially) if I have not given a prescription for medication. The prescription pad is a very powerful compliance tool for some people, particularly those who are *external* in their meta-programs. Handing them a patient information leaflet can also fulfil the same function.

For those who are *internal*, I may actually ask them to write out their own instructions on the pad. Because they are more likely to act on their own decisions, getting them to commit in this way increases the likelihood of a favourable outcome. And of course I would say '*Only you can decide whether to follow through with this ...*'.

I have also rehearsed patients through future actions by getting them to imagine in their mind's eye, using all of their senses, exactly what they will be doing – seeing themselves (dissociated) carrying out the plan and succeeding. For those who are less visual and more verbal, you can ask them to talk you through the next steps. The kinaesthetics can give you a run through the actions that they will take. In all cases, by rehearsing in this way you are substantially increasing the chances of success.

Compliance, adherence or whatever name you give to carrying out future instructions is a vital part of medical care. There is no point giving masses of health information and management plans without some mechanism of ensuring that these are carried out effectively. A short time spent here (and honestly it only needs to be short) will repay you many times over.

Chaining consultations together

Sometimes it is possible to deal with the current situation within a single consultation. However, in these days of increasing complexity and more chronic disease management, our outcomes may need to be spread over several consultations. So whilst this particular consultation is coming to an end, both you and your patient may also need to be addressing just how far you have come and what still remains to be tackled.

At the end of this session you will then be looking towards what you both want to accomplish in the next consultation. It is often useful to break down larger outcomes into smaller chunks, using each as a stepping-stone to an important overall health gain. And you can do this whether the illness is depression, ischaemic heart disease, diabetes, multiple sclerosis, or anything else.

One simple way to do this is first to establish the main and most important outcome. Then decide what would be an outcome at a halfway point. Considering both of these, you can then establish three-quarter and one-quarter points, and before you know it you have a series of stepping-stones, each with their own specific sub-outcome. And you can appraise how far you have come, and what needs to be done before the next session, as you end this one.

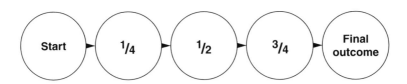

Figure 7.1:   Chaining outcomes together.

For example, with depression, the patient's final outcome may be a complete restoration of physical and mental well-being within three months. You will already have used the specific outcome questions to detail this in sensory terms. Yet part of this 'getting better' may also require the addressing of specific thinking skills, improving relationship issues both at home and at work, together with physical exercise and fitness. Each of these can be tackled incrementally over this time period as smaller chunk sub-outcomes moving towards the larger goal. So which outcome are you scheduling for the next session?

In diabetes there may be several tasks to co-ordinate, including overall control, medication compliance, dietary adherence, and assessing neuropathy, nephropathy, arteriopathy, ophthalmology, blood pressure, exercise regimes, concurrent medical problems, lifestyle, etc. Chunking these tasks down into specific outcomes and delegating appropriately allows for a more effectively targeted care programme.

In all of these cases, then, closing the session will also include seeing how far you have come, as well as thinking about and planning ahead for the next session. In this way, your consulting flows more easily from one session to the next in a less overwhelming and more manageable way that preserves your own health and sanity.

Breaking rapport

Why is it important to be able to break rapport effectively and still maintain a relationship? Why are some people good at establishing rapport, yet don't seem to be able to let go and move on? How do you give someone the hint that it really is time to go now, having already addressed all of their pertinent issues? What are the specific skills that you need to master?

For many people, establishing and maintaining rapport is second nature. It's so automatic, though, that they have difficulty breaking rapport without feeling that in some way they have violated the other person. And, of course, we've all had the experience of being caught in a conversation that we want to move on from, yet in some way the other person seems oblivious to our behaving like a cat on a hot tin roof. Can you remember what that feels like? So just exactly what are the signals that we can send out, in a gently escalating way if need be, that it's time to detach and move on?

You will recall that much of rapport at the level of behaviour is expressed in our physiology and voice qualities. To disengage and break rapport, we usually begin by starting to *mismatch* posture and gestures. We may sit up more erect, move faster with slightly jerkier movements, give less eye contact, and look more at the computer screen. Our breathing rate changes, often becoming quicker and shallower. This is accompanied by a more overt closing of the patient's notes, exiting the computer record and turning away. Our voices generally *speed up* and *get louder* as we say the words that bring the consultation to a close.

However, it's quite possible to say the words of farewell yet keep the same voice speed and tonality, matching and mirroring the patient's body language. Then the non-verbal message is *'Don't go … stay!'*. Guess which message they pay attention to. Yes, the non-verbal wins out every time. Or as you escort them to the door, another more social topic opens up, perhaps family, friends or some other mutual interest. And there you are, with the door half open – you half out, and the patient still inside!

Then, of course, there are those who just sit there and talk, oblivious to what's happening outside of them, completely engrossed in their own continuing tale, blind to your body language and deaf to your tones. They are in rapport with themselves, but not with you! Given that it's clear they have actually finished the medical part of the consultation, what should you do in these circumstances?

In a situation where the patient is still to some degree in bodily rapport with you, all you have to do is be more overt in your own body language. Speed up your rate of speech, increase the volume (but don't shout yet!) and notice whether they respond. Standing up and walking towards the door is a sure sign for most people that the consultation is over. It's interesting how, even as you are still conversing, just initiating the move to stand up triggers the patient to do the same.

For those who are only in rapport with their internal selves, subtlety is *not* the right strategy. You need to be really overt, even to the point of verging on apparent rudeness. Usually standing them up and holding them by the elbow will snap them out of their trance state. Very occasionally, using a pattern interrupt, such as knocking something off your desk, is required. Only once have I knocked my chair over! You will very seldom, if ever, come across someone who is so *self* oriented that they miss all of your cues. You may be concerned that this is a bit blunderbuss and will undermine your relationship. My experience, though, is the reverse. It's almost as if at a deep level you are treating them in the same way that they treat others, ignoring superficial cues. This is actually a more profound matching of behaviours that shows you understand their experience implicitly.

The following exercise will allow you to experience how body language and voice tone may help or hinder your efforts to disengage.

Exercise 15: Breaking rapport

1   Find one, or preferably two, colleagues with whom to do this exercise so that you have an observer position.
2   Person 1 chats with person 2 about a *pleasant event* (e.g. a holiday, sport, etc.). Ensure that you are *matching and mirroring* appropriately.
3   Person 1 decides that it's *time to go*. Say what you would say in order to go. However, *keep matching and mirroring* body language, keeping your voice tone and tempo the same. What happens? How easy is it to actually let go and move on?
4   Chat again for a moment or two. Now begin to say the words of farewell. This time *mismatch* body language and *speak louder and faster*. What happens?
5   Debrief with the observer prior to changing positions. What were the differences between failing to disengage, disengaging appropriately and *breaking rapport* too abruptly? How did those experiences feel in your body?

Learning how to break rapport gracefully, tailoring your method to the circumstances, is a very valuable skill to practise. You can develop it further by experimenting in other everyday situations – perhaps 'routine' conversations which are not that important in and of themselves. Notice how other people do it gracefully, or not! What about shop assistants, air hostesses, sales representatives and chat show hosts? You can learn a lot by observing their skills in practice.

Looking after yourself

One of the most important things that you can do is to continue to look after your own state of mind and body. You can really only give of your best by ensuring repeatedly that you take the time to fully disengage emotionally from the previous consultation before inviting in the next patient. We have come full circle from our beginnings in initiating the consultation.

At this point it is a good idea to consult the list of states in Appendix 1. Choose some states that are relaxing and peaceful. Fully access them and anchor them to a specific relaxation trigger. Ensure that you can quickly and easily re-enter each state at will. All it requires is 30 to 60 seconds for yourself between occasional patients if the going has been tough. Surely you're worth spending a minute on every now and again? Compared to the time you spend on everyone else, it's a small gift that you can gratefully receive.

Exercise 16:   A well-deserved break

1   Find a time and place where you can be by yourself, *undisturbed*, for 10 minutes or so.

2   Close your eyes and begin to *focus on your breathing*, the gentle in and out breaths. Let the out breath last twice as long as the in breath. Breathe into your abdomen, and as you breathe out imagine that all the care, all the worries, all the *stresses are being released* from your body. Imagine them *dripping off* the ends of your fingertips and toes, seeping into and being welcomed by the ground underneath. You can give them a colour and a sound as you *experience this happening*.

3   Now think of a *calming, relaxing memory*, maybe a holiday, lying at the beach or poolside. Perhaps *just drifting*, listening to your favourite relaxing music. Maybe the afterglow of achieving something really satisfying.

4   Now alter the pictures, the colours and the sounds so that the feeling becomes *s-o-o-o-o re-laaax-ingggg*. Now double those feelings with the next breath, then double them again.

5   As you *go deeply* into this feeling, *set your anchor*. Either a touch, a particular colour that reminds you of the feeling, or saying the word *re-l-a-a-a-a-axx* in that special way.

6   Before you arise, imagine that *you are using this anchor* at an appropriate time in the future, knowing that the more you use it, the stronger the effect will be.

Reflecting

The ending of a consultation, or a series of consultations, can be not only a time for reflecting on what you have achieved so far, but also marks a point in time for considering what to do next. A specific chapter on developing personally is coming shortly, but at this stage it is worthwhile considering four areas that can help us to consult more effectively.

The *four quadrants model* is drawn from the work of Ken Wilber, specifically *A Brief History of Everything* (Wilber, 1996) and *A Theory of Everything* (Wilber, 2000). We are well used to discussing the psychosociobiological aspects of disease and illness in medicine. Wilber's model adds a systems quadrant, and it can be a useful way to define further which aspect of a situation deserves our attention for intervention.

Briefly, Wilber is an integrationist who believes that there are several different ways to slice the pie of experience. None of the ways have the whole truth, yet when taken *together* the sum is greater than the parts. Sometimes we focus too much attention on one area to the exclusion of the rest. Consider Figure 7.2 opposite.

Basically, as an *individual*, we can do certain things (our actions in the world), and we can think certain things (make meanings and interpretations). And these things may be quite different from one individual to another. As a *group* (of doctors, patients etc.), we share certain cultural beliefs and we engage our practice of medicine within the constraints of our system, both local and national. And, of course, in different countries there are different systems for the delivery of healthcare, and even differing beliefs about illness causation and treatment (e.g. in China). So, you may be asking, *'How on earth does all of this apply to me?'*

Well, imagine that you are a stressed doctor, trying hard to cope with the ever increasing demands of patients and Government bureaucracy. You are struggling with the load, wondering what you can do. You have just finished a long series of consultations, with several extras, running way behind time. How do you feel? What can you do about it? Let's take this thought through the four quadrants.

Well, you can do something different, another behaviour, like jogging or some other form of exercise to relieve stress. This is in the 'body' quadrant, a physical answer. Or you could learn some new thinking skills, update your beliefs, and learn how to relax mentally. This is the 'mind' quadrant. You could decide that you would do better if you improved your interpersonal and communication skills so that you could deal more effectively with patients' demands, perhaps by learning negotiation skills. This is the 'culture' quadrant. Perhaps, however, your appointment system is letting you down. Maybe you

INDIVIDUAL	
Mind – Interior Beliefs and values Meanings and interpretations Psychoneuroimmunology Subjective	*Body – Exterior* Behaviours and actions Physical illness (orthodox medicine) Physical interventions Objective
Culture – Interior Group beliefs and values Shared communication Support groups Inter-subjective	*Systems – Exterior* Methods of access to and delivery of care Health economics Health centre layout Inter-objective
GROUP	

Figure 7.2:   The four quadrants model.

need a nurse triage system. Perhaps your reception staff need more training. This is the 'systems' quadrant.

There is no one 'right' solution, yet some may be immediately more effective than others. If you are consulting at 5-minute intervals, then no amount of jogging, thinking positively or better communication skills will make a great deal of difference. Yet changing your system to 10-minute appointments will have an immediate effect all round. However, we sometimes fail to look at some fairly easy system changes that can give long-term benefits to *all* of the quadrants. Let us address some of these now.

The ending of consultations is the time to make sure that your system for referrals is up to scratch. Do you dictate your letters there and then, or at the end of the consultation series? Heaven forbid if you take them home! Perhaps you have a fixed 'admin' time, or do you slot it in whenever you can? What about urgent referrals? What about taking telephone calls from patients? It's important to ensure that you set up your system to work best for you, allowing you to focus on the task in hand.

What about your appointment system? If you are always feeling harassed and running behind time, are you being realistic in your expectations for yourself and your patients? Do you have slots for routine, 48-hour and same-day urgent appointments? Or is it a free for all, with extras all round? Do you plan for partners' absences on holiday by blocking off more routine appointments and only making them available at the time of increased need? Or do you employ a locum? Could you manage your own system better, regardless of what your colleagues are doing?

Do you have nurse-run minor illness clinics to give you time to deal more effectively with more complex issues? What about triage systems? We have four minor-illness-trained nurses, two of whom also do telephone triage. This has markedly reduced the hassle of 'trivia', especially for the afternoon on-call doctor.

This is not a prescription for change to deal with all problems. However, it is often a very useful exercise to run a problem through the four quadrants before jumping to a solution. The often neglected systems quadrant is well worth more attention. You can also run clinical problems and various forms of treatment through it with interesting results. I'll leave you to think about which ones to use as your own exercise. You can also check out Wilber's *A Theory of Everything* (Wilber, 2000) for a description of the four quadrants in integral medicine.

Reflecting on your own skills developing

We shall deal in depth with developing personally shortly in Chapter 9. However, at each consultation's ending you can use the four quadrants to reflect on just which area of skills you can focus on next. The 'body' quadrant may include developing physical skills such as minor surgery or family planning (fitting coils, etc.). Much of medicine is in a sense 'physical' and includes diagnoses, investigations, treatment regimes and drugs. By this I mean that these are things which we 'do' to people. Perhaps you have identified learning needs in this area. This is the more 'traditional' material for educational courses, lectures and seminars.

The 'mind' quadrant is continuing to expand exponentially. Through psycho-neuroimmunology we now have scientific evidence of how our thoughts and emotions affect our physical and mental health for good or ill. Cognitive behavioural therapists have known this for a long time. Yet fields such as NLP are producing simple yet potentially profoundly effective tools which can be easily learned and applied in ordinary consultations. Perhaps your learning needs and skills development might usefully focus on this quadrant. There are plenty of examples in this book for you to adapt appropriately.

The 'culture' quadrant is essentially about effective interpersonal communication, much of which we have covered already. Again this is an exponentially expanding area of medicine that at last has some scientific evidence for efficacy and is now beginning to be taught in medical schools. So which of the communication areas do you feel will repay further study? Negotiation skills? Handling difficult situations (*see* Chapter 8 on special situations)? Looking back over your last series of consultations, which area shouts out loudest? Choose one to focus on next.

And, of course, there is the 'systems' quadrant, namely how effective healthcare is actually accessed and delivered. Managers often oversee the dynamics of service delivery, yet as a frontline professional there are many issues and developments to which you can make a palpable difference. What about information technology? The use of computer systems for appointments, disease management, Internet communication, etc.? And other skills such as financial planning and budget management? What are your learning needs in this area?

You can take a short trip through the quadrants any time you want to ensure that not only do you address all of the areas, but also you maintain your balanced development.

Ending the closing

Closing the session has been a relatively short chapter – because what you have already done up to now has removed the pitfalls that might have been. You have spent the time honing your earlier consultation skills to allow this phase to go even more smoothly. *Backtracking* and checking for agreement to the management plan via yes-sets are the fundamental phase-specific skills. Allied to *what-if scenarios* and *future rehearsals,* you have covered the upside and downside of what might happen next. Congruent acceptance here builds a very useful foundation for the next time you meet with this particular patient. And, of course, remember that the elegant *breaking of rapport* is a skill which is well worth mastering.

And finally, last but not least, is you. Take the opportunity to *look after yourself now.* Develop some really good states both to consult in and to relax in. Occasionally you can make some time for *reflecting* on your performance using the four quadrants. Doing so will form the kind of recursive loop that spirals you upwards in your continuing developing skills.

CHAPTER 8

Special situations

Introduction

This chapter is all about those situations which, up until now, you might have found challenging. And of course we all have our own particular pet hates which come to mind here. Yet as you read on you will find that you have already developed most, if not all, of the skills required for a successful outcome. The previous chapters have given you a firm foundation from which to approach any communication issue, no matter how daunting it may seem at first glance. In fact, these skills alone may in and of themselves prevent the undernoted issues from arising. What we shall do, then, is to highlight the various additional nuances you can add to your already integrating skills. So what situations specifically are we alluding to?

Have you ever been confronted by an angry patient? You know, nostrils flaring, red in the face, loud aggressive voice in your ear, finger pointing accusingly in your face? How did you feel? Frightened? Scared? Aggressive? How did you deal with them? What if it happened again? What would you do differently next time?

And, of course, we are currently in a climate where it seems that anyone who wants to is encouraged to make a written complaint about us to the practice manager. Have you had any complaints made against you lately? How do you feel when you or your management of a problem is criticised unfairly (or even fairly)? Do you get that awful feeling in your solar plexus? Do you feel guilty, even if you're not? Does it stop you getting on effectively with your other tasks until it's all over? Is your mind elsewhere? What if you could handle these situations in a better, more satisfying way? Interested?

How do *you* go about breaking bad news to patients, especially in the area of terminal illness? Is this something that you do well, sensitively and caringly? Or do invisible barriers seem to stop you in your tracks? Theirs or yours? Many doctors find this area to be one of the most challenging they have to deal with in medical practice. Can you guess which of the skills you have already integrated are paramount in this situation? How could you begin to utilise them even more effectively?

How about your ability to recognise depression – that enemy which can present in myriad disguises? Are you satisfied that you can diagnose most if not all of the cases that come through the consulting-room door? Or do you have that vague feeling that you're missing some? Dotted throughout this book are a number of references to depression. *You already know more than you think you know!* We shall pull together the salient threads shortly.

Here's a word that will provoke a familiar feeling. *Heartsink* patient! What happens when you think of that particular face? When you hear that particular voice? Do you have many patients who fall into this category? Or none at all? Have you ever thought about how heartsinks really come about? And why your heartsink may inexplicably be another doctor's favourite? What if you had the means to deal with this kind of situation far more effectively than in the past? Is this something that you want?

Increasingly these days, we seem to spend more and more time on the telephone. How are your telephone consulting skills? Are you comfortable giving advice to a faceless individual at the end of a line? Or does your tolerance of uncertainty decrease markedly, and you end up seeing them at the health centre anyway? Telephone triage is one of the methods that is increasingly being used to help to manage what often seems to be a chronic shortage of appointments. And, of course, out-of-hours co-operatives may give telephone advice only to at least 40% (or more) of callers. Are you interested in finding out how you can increase both your own and your patients' confidence and satisfaction with your improved telephone technique?

These are what I believe to be some of the more challenging issues that can face us in everyday practice. I may not have included your absolute favourite dislikes, but you can be reassured that if you simply apply what you have learned so far, then you will already have changed these other situations for the better.

Aims of this chapter

This chapter is set up slightly differently to the previous ones. Because these are individual topics for discussion, we shall be highlighting the specific additional skills that are required to manage each area successfully. You will most probably find these additional skills 'popping up' unexpectedly for your use not only in other parts of the consultation, but also in other areas of your life.

The following specific skill sets are covered:

- non-verbal skills for *handling anger and aggression* (no, not martial arts!)
- a strategy for *responding resourcefully to criticism*

- the salient non-verbal clues in *breaking bad news*
- how to recognise *underlying depression*
- dealing with *heartsink patients*
- strategies for *consulting effectively on the telephone.*

So without further ado, let's move on to the first section.

Dealing with anger and aggression

Thankfully, for most of us, outbursts of out-and-out anger and aggression are few and far between. Yet we can all probably remember specific instances, perhaps even quite vividly, when we had to deal with a simmering emotion that boiled over in a consultation. I recall one such instance when a patient came in bitterly complaining about how useless the practice, the out-of-hours doctors, the paramedics and the hospital doctors had been in the care of a friend who had died. He was breathing fast, his face was red and he was trembling with emotion, pointing his finger, speaking loudly, aggressively and vehemently – an intimidating sight. How do you deal with such a situation without being defensive, aggressive or simply wishing that you could run away?

The standard advice seems to be to speak sl-o-w-ly, clearly and carefully, in a quiet steady voice, asking them to c-a-a-a-lm down while remaining clear-headed yourself. Have you ever tried this? Does it work? My experience is that acting in this way more often conveys a patronising air, and may even paradoxically *increase* their anger, as they may feel that their concerns are not being taken seriously enough! From what you already know, why would this be the case? Well, in terms of rapport, there is a complete mismatch going on, especially at the level of physiology and voice qualities. Although your words may be those of understanding their plight, your posture and tone, which can convey up to 90% of the communication message, are completely 'out of sync'.

So what is it that you can do instead to ensure that you convey both verbal and non-verbal understanding, while simultaneously leading them into a more productive state? Let us look first at the physiology of anger. This is an intense, high-energy state. often accompanied by gesticulations, pointing fingers, quick movements, and a *louder*, often increased-tempo voice, with the *emphasis* on *certain* words which are *punched* out with venom!

It is important that you *match* this physiology with your own increased energy levels, voice volume and tempo. So speak a bit faster and a bit louder than normal, emphasising *certain* words (though no shouting!). You can gesticulate a little more with both hands from side to side, palms upwards, but don't point your finger directly at them! If you need to point your finger, point it at the ceiling instead. Make sure that you match to no more than *70 to 80%* of their level. If you match exactly at 100% intensity (or more), this may cause things to escalate! The 70 to 80% level lets the patient know subconsciously that you have heard *and* understood their complete message – verbal *and* non-verbal. By effectively pacing them in this way, you can far more easily lead them down into a calmer state, into problem-resolution mode.

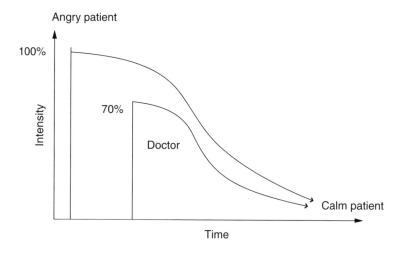

Figure 8.1:   Matching anger.

The words that you say are also important. However, they need to be geared towards the *process* of the communication rather than the content. Read through the following reply to an angry outburst (words to be emphasised are shown in bold).

> I can **see** that you're really ***angry*** about this. And I ***agree***, if I were ***you***, in ***your shoes***, I would feel ***exactly*** the same way. Now, ***like you***, I want to re**solve** this matter. I think it's ***really*** important that we take the time ***now*** ... to sit down together ... and find a way to ... resolve this ... to our mutual satisfaction.

Several things are happening simultaneously in the above. Start out *louder, faster* and more animated at the beginning, gradually lowering your voice and sl-o-owing down after the third sentence. This has the effect of matching the energy initially, allowing it to dissipate to a calmer state as you go on.

So what processes are occurring here? The first sentence gets the verbal message across that you acknowledge the patient's present state. The second sentence contains the magical word *agree* – usually music to one's ears if you're trying to get your point across. It's difficult to maintain an angry state if someone is agreeing with you. The bubble is burst. Where's the fight? But, you may be saying, I may *not* agree with them. However, all you are agreeing to is that if you *were* them, in their shoes, having had their history and their experience, you would feel the same way. How could you not if you are truly second-positioning them? You can still come back to your own first position viewpoint to put your side of things later. The objective right now is to defuse the situation. The rest of the statement sets out your intention to resolve the issue to the mutual satisfaction of both parties. You can now step in with your negotiation skills.

Yesterday morning, a Saturday, I spent 90 minutes on the phone to British Telecom trying to sort out an Internet problem. I was passed from pillar to post, cut off twice, and by the time I was reconnected to the seventh (!) person that morning I was feeling angry and frustrated. I said as much and more, to be met with the reply *'I can **imagine** just how **frustrated** you feel from the way you **sound**. And I **agree** it's really **important** to sort this out. Could you just ... bear with me ... a little longer ... and I'll do my best to help.'* I deflated like a spent balloon! This person had obviously been to an NLP course, unlike her colleagues.

In their book *Presenting Magically* (James and Shephard, 2001), Tad James and David Shepard deal with angry hecklers in the domain of public presentations. The *blamer* is the archetype of our angry aggressive patient, their finger pointingly accusing. They adopt their 'Don't shoot me, I'm only the trainer' response called *distracter*. This is a completely asymmetrical posture, with arms at different angles and heights, head tilted, spine twisted, and everything going off at a tangent, moving at random. The voice tone is up, down, slow, fast, deep and squeaky. They claim that this totally defuses the energy of the blamer and quickly brings the situation to a manageable level. Try it and see in more minor situations first. As far as I am aware, they don't advocate a *terminator* position!

The following exercise will help you to review similar incidents from your past, allowing you to update your memory banks in a way which will support your dealing with these situations more effectively in the future.

Exercise 17:   Re-editing past memories

You may want to do the following exercise with a partner, guiding each other through the steps. You may also want to anchor some powerfully resourceful states first, and then fire them off as you do the exercise.

1   *Identify a situation from the past* when someone was angry or aggressive, which you would like to update now. You are literally going to see it in a different way.

2   Allow yourself to close your eyes and *enter a relaxed state* with some easy breathing. Imagine that you have gone to *your own private cinema* in your mind. Picture a small screen down there at a distance, which shows only *black-and-white movies* from the past.

3   *Run the entire movie* of the event from a time *before* things started going wrong until after you were *completely safe* again. See yourself way down there, at a safe distance, in black and white. When you are safe again, after the event, *freeze the frame.*

4   Now, from there, *watch the movie going backwards, in reverse, at double speed.* All of the actions are in reverse, as are all of the sounds and words, like a Keystone Cop Movie. See them literally eat their words! Freeze the frame at a time *before* things started going wrong.

5   Now imagine that *you are a movie director* and you are going to splice in *a new piece of film.* See how you would have looked if you were *handling things resourcefully* instead. Look at your posture, your gestures and your breathing. Hear the difference in your voice tone, pitch, volume and speed. Listen to the process words. See yourself coping well. Play about with this new film until *it feels just right.*

6   Run the original film again from the beginning. However, just *before* the point when it had started to go wrong, *splice in the new film and run it all the way to the end,* with a successful outcome. Do this several times until the new film runs *smoothly,* and *you're satisfied with it.*

7   Now turn on all the colours, turn up the brightness, and *imagine jumping into the you in the new film.* Go through it from the beginning, all the way to the *successful ending,* until you literally 'pop' out again. Now look back at that new you with a *feeling of satisfaction* and allow your mind to *store this* updated memory in the most appropriate way.

The process that you have just gone through can be used for *any* less than positive memory from the past which prevents you from behaving as resourcefully as you want to right now. This particular technique works best for memories with negative emotions of moderate intensity or less. There are other techniques for 'heavy-duty trauma'.

Warning!

In any situation where you may be subjected to extreme anger or aggression, verging on violence, then press the panic button immediately. If you don't know where it is, find it! If you don't have one in your room, get one! Get help NOW. If you don't have a practice policy about how to handle these kinds of rare but potentially very serious situations, then institute one. It may be helpful to speak to your risk assessment officer and obtain their advice.

Occasionally, some people are not overtly angry on the outside, but are simmering away on the inside. They may not be comfortable with expressing what they feel, and they may even fear a backlash if they did so. Sometimes they may not even be consciously aware that they are angry because they have, in a sense, disowned it. They may be displaying 'passive–aggressive' behaviour, whereby their non-compliance with treatment or even a 'failure' to get better is in effect an expression of anger. When you are in rapport with this person, you will most probably get a sense of this feeling yourself. So what do you do?

Well, the simplest thing to do, if you want to address the problem, is to gently ask the following questions, with softeners of course!

* *'I may be wrong, but I get a sense that ... perhaps deep inside ... maybe even not yet fully aware ... that you're angry about something ... or someone ... (look for yes-set).'*
* *'I was wondering ... and this might sound a bit odd ... are you angry about something?'*

Hopefully by now you will be feeling a lot more comfortable about your ability to handle anger and aggression in whatever shape or form it presents. As you move on to the next section, keep these learnings in mind.

Criticism and complaints

It is a very rare doctor indeed who has not yet been subjected to criticism or complaint (justified or unjustified). And it seems that, as more and more people are being encouraged to complain as a fundamental right, we are all likely to face more such situations rather than less. It is vital to have a robust complaints procedure, one which does not simply pronounce judgement on the rights and wrongs of a situation in order to mete out 'punishment', but which also looks to implement the lessons learned at an individual and organisational level.

However, many doctors I have spoken to have been quite unprepared for the emotional turmoil that can surround a 'minor' complaint, let alone one for major professional misconduct. In general, we do our best to provide an excellent service while often working under considerable pressure, demand and constraint. A complaint, when we least expect it, can seem like a real kick in the teeth or a punch in the solar plexus.

I remember towards the end of a busy afternoon on call for the practice being asked to see a young child, carried in by his parents, who had fallen at a play park. Having ascertained that there seemed to be no serious problem, I sent them home with advice regarding analgesia and review if the child was not settling. A couple of days later one of my partners was called out to see him as he was still reluctant to weight bear. A subsequent X-ray showed a hairline crack in the lower tibia. The letter of complaint, with plenty of added vitriol, followed swiftly (not properly examined, not treated right, patronising manner, continued unnecessary pain, etc.). How would you feel in similar circumstances? Angry? Aggressive? Defensive? Worried? Guilty? Assertive? Numb? Fearful?

We each have our own particular types of reaction when we are criticised. And as you think about it now, you will have a sense of where in your body you feel that particular feeling. Perhaps in your gut, maybe in your chest, or your head, or elsewhere. Oddly enough, it's usually a feeling that has waves of familiarity flooding in from the past. Probably one that has lived with you for a long time. You might even find it connecting to particular childhood memories – perhaps a parent's voice, calling you in that particular tone that you know spells trouble, or a particular kind of look that means 'uh-oh, you'll be sorry'. It's often a reflexive, knee-jerk kind of reaction that comes out of the blue, even though you're an adult now. A reaction which leaves you being unproductive and feeling defensive, irritable and even down for the rest of the day, or longer.

So what would it be like if you could handle this kind of situation in a more resourceful way? What if you could deal with it without letting it intrude into the other parts of your working day, or worse still, your home life? What if you had a mechanism that allowed you to act with even more integrity? Interested?

Steve and Connirae Andreas, two American trainers, wanted to find out how people who dealt effectively with criticism, with respect for both themselves and others in the process, actually did so. They ran a modelling project in which they interviewed many people who responded resourcefully, and they elicited their strategy – their internal mental processing patterns for success in this type of situation.

They found that, in general, all of these people did similar things. They all had a way of stepping back and distancing themselves emotionally from what was going on, almost like a third-position observer. From here they could comfortably pay attention to the words and meaning of the criticism by running some internal movies of the description. They could then compare this with their remembered words and images from their own viewpoint. They noticed where things matched and where they mismatched. From the comparisons, they could choose their response accordingly, one that was appropriate to the situation and respectful of all concerned, including themselves. They noted if there was anything specific that they could learn from the criticism, and they thought about how they could apply that in future situations.

The exercise that follows is based on the findings of the Andreas trainers. You can use this to update old memories and allow yourself to become more comfortable when responding to future challenging situations of criticism or complaint. It's useful to do this with a partner so that you can really let yourself be thoroughly immersed in the process. As usual, it's good to have a powerful resourceful anchor set up beforehand to use as necessary.

Exercise 18:   Responding resourcefully to criticism

1   Choose a time in the past when you reacted badly to *criticism*, a time when you wished you had responded differently. In order to learn the technique effectively, choose an incident with a moderate emotional charge. Save your worst ones until later! Back up your memory to just *before* it happened.

2   Now imagine a *protective plexi-glass shield* in front of you. You can *see* what happens yet be protected from the feelings. This will help you to process the memory more comfortably. On the other side of the shield, see the *other you* who is about to be criticised. Notice that as soon as this other you recognises the criticism, they *dissociate* from it using their own plexi-glass shield. (Yes, that means two plexi-glass shields in total!)

3   See the *other you* as they make a *movie of the criticism*, attempting to understand the meaning behind the words. Notice that they can fill in any blanks by asking the critic specific questions to clarify the content and gain more information.

4   Now watch the *other you* as they review the *movie of their own recollection of events*. Notice as they compare where the two movies *match* and where they *mismatch*, asking appropriate questions for further clarification.

5   The *other you* can now choose an *appropriate response* based on the comparison. This can range from an apology, if warranted, through to stating that they continue to see it differently. They may agree on certain points and retain their own viewpoint on others. Listen to the words they use and how they say them. Continue to modify them until *you are satisfied* with the response.

6   The *other you* may decide to modify their behaviour in the future based on this re-run with the new information gathered. If so, see them at a future point *doing things differently*, and incorporating any *lessons learned*.

7   When you have finished, allow the plexi-glass shields to dissolve. Imagine bringing the other you *back inside yourself*, fully and completely, *integrating this new strategy* at a deep level.

You can use this strategy not only for professional issues but also in relation to family, friends and other areas of life where you might be criticised. The value of this approach is to allow you to listen to and evaluate more objectively any valid points that might require further action. Too often we take a criticism or complaint about our *behaviour* (what we do) as an attack on our *identity* (who we are). We react defensively, and we protect ourselves. This new approach allows sufficient emotional distance to enable us to comfortably agree or disagree, with the freedom to choose the most appropriate response.

Before you leave this section I suggest that you unearth another two or three examples from other life contexts and run them through the above exercise.

Breaking bad news

I was never taught this at medical school, nor did I find a suitable course to learn from. Probably, like me, you've had to suss a lot of it out for yourself. I remember some of my early attempts, most of which seemed to be taken up with trying to control my own emotions, let alone notice what was going on with the other person.

I recall as a young hospital doctor having struggled in vain to save the life of a man in his forties who had ruptured his mitral valve after a large myocardial infarction. He literally drowned in his own fluids, despite our best efforts in the small intensive-care unit of our somewhat remote district general hospital. Completely asymptomatic the day before, his death was a totally unlooked-for shock to his wife. I felt awful having to confront her with the terrible news. We cried in each other's arms as we both tried to come to terms with this tragedy. I had little idea of what to do, and was working on instinct. Thankfully, I have been able to move on since those days, yet still retaining the ability to give an appropriate empathic response.

So what are your memories of breaking bad news? And how do you feel about your ability to deal effectively with these situations now? Is this something for which you have developed your own style? Or do you still feel a level of discomfort that prevents you from fully engaging in the process? Do you have the words to say or the gestures to make when the inevitable is staring both you and the patient in the face?

Some people believe that breaking bad news requires quite different, special, issue-specific skills to the ordinary consultation. However, it is my belief that the vast majority of the skills required have already been covered in the five consultation phases. *You already have the skills*. What we shall do is to highlight some of the more important ones in each phase. One generalisation of note, though, is that the reading of non-verbal cues becomes even more important.

Initiating the session

Although there is no one 'right' state to be in for breaking bad news, it is important that you prepare yourself by having to hand not only your *consulting flow state*, but also any other additions that might be useful, perhaps states such as *calm, caring, compassionate, hopeful* and *optimistic*. Maybe there are other ones that spring to mind. Of course you can elicit these, anchor them to your trigger and have them available as and when needed. Because you want to pay particular attention to the non-verbal elements, the uptime *peripheral vision state* is a must. Make sure that you have used a *break state* anchor first, if appropriate, to disengage from any other issues that are playing on your mind.

Sometimes, even before you start, you may feel apprehensive because of past experiences. If that is so, you can use the exercise on re-editing past memories to help you. Simply go through it with that particular experience, updating it with your newly anchored states.

It is important to use your initial rapport skills to set up a comfortable environment both for the patient and for any relative or friend who may be present. It is useful to set the scene by doing a *backtrack* of all the relevant history, investigations, etc., to date. During this you can notice the patient's yes-set, which is vital to the following phases. Some mutual *agenda setting*, what you both might expect from today's consultation, enables this to be a two-way process.

Gathering information

You may already have some idea from previous consultations about the patient's preferred meta-programs. Some are perhaps more useful to consider for breaking bad news. Do they move *away from* problems or *towards* solutions? Do they prefer the *big picture*, what's going to happen in general, or the *specific details*, with all the nitty-gritty? Are they *proactive*, keen to find out now and get on with it, or *reactive*, requiring the information to be carefully considered and circumspectly given.

You will also want to consider just what you know about their beliefs and expectations up until now. This is not yet the time for any further detailed enquiry, although you will want your subsequent comments to fall within *their* framework. Giving and receiving bad news is a very significant emotional event. This may cause old beliefs to fall rapidly away, new ones to form quickly or, most likely, a kind of mind-numbing vacuum, even confusion, as models of the world turn upside down and inside out. Like emerging shell-shocked from a car crash. Be prepared.

At this stage you may ask the kind of direct question that follows. I usually like to use softeners, structuring the question to pay special attention to non-verbal yes or no.

> *I was just wondering ... if this were the kind of condition that turned out to be serious ... whether you were the type of person that would like to know exactly what's going on ... or not?*

If you leave a slightly longer gap at the last pause, you will get your answer non-verbally first, before any words follow. On the face of it, it seems a fairly direct, up-front question, yet those who answer in the negative often seem amnesic for the sentence and its meaning, as if their denial mechanism kicks in to protect them. Of course *you* know that it's serious, and that knowledge *will* leak non-verbally from you to them at some level. Usually, however, it doesn't come up for conscious processing by the patient until they're ready – perhaps days, weeks or months later.

Sometimes I ask a variation of the following question.

> *Well ... as you know ... we've done all the tests ... we have all the results back now ... the picture is quite clear ... I've spoken to the consultant ... and we feel as certain as we can be about the diagnosis ... (pause) ... What questions do you have for me right now?*

In this scenario the patient has complete control over the direction of the ensuing conversation. Those who want to know the details will ask, and those who don't will invariably go off at a tangent. Of course, these types of questions may need to be repeated over several consultations, since patients' information requirements change as they work through a bereavement process.

Building the relationship

You will recall that the skills that are relevant to this phase are useful at any stage of the consultation. It is here that developing and sustaining rapport at the level of identity and beyond is vital. Just what are your patient's religious views and beliefs? Is faith something that sustains them or not? Will they be able to continue their role at work? And in the home? You can ensure deepening rapport by providing your information within this framework.

The *meta-mirror* can be a very useful tool at any stage of the process. You can use it to help patients to think through and resolve various relationship issues that often arise when the ultimate prognosis is dire – the finishing of 'unfinished business'. You can use it to help yourself in your own relationship with this particular patient.

And what about the non-verbal cues of shutdown? How do you know when they've switched off and stopped listening? Is there information overload? Perhaps they have a semi-glazed look, staring into the middle distance, breathing more slowly, with cataleptic limbs, facial pallor, or a trance-like state. And whilst they may have stopped listening at one level, at a deeper level communication is still taking place. Words need to be chosen *very carefully* here, as too often negative connotations can act as deeply embedded post-hypnotic suggestions. Like the patient who was told he would 'live with pain', and who couldn't understand why he got very anxious when he was told that we could 'take his pain away'. Yet trance logic dictates that if 'life = pain', then of course 'absence of pain = death!'. So be careful with the words that you use during shutdown, as they can be more powerful than you think.

Explanation and planning

This is where the 'meat' of handing over bad news resides. This is the time to use the patient's meta-programs to get the message across sensitively and caringly in such a way that they can not only understand the content, but also begin to think about the implications for the future. The convincer channel and mode are very important here. Do they need to see what you're saying, perhaps by your drawing a picture or diagram? When patients ask about the prognosis, I usually draw out a skewed bell curve to indicate potential survival. I draw their attention to the right side of the curve, which I have elongated and which fails to return to the baseline. I tell them about exceptional cancer survivors and how we in the medical profession know little about why certain people survive much longer than others. As I say this, I am *non-verbally marking out* by gestures and voice tone the messages that I want them to take away.

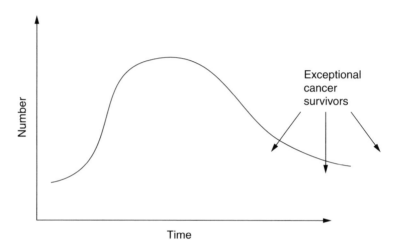

Figure 8.2:   Survival curves.

Some people may have a few weeks to a few months (gesture to empty chair) *... others can ...* **survive John** (use patient's name!) *... **for many years** ...* **perhaps five to ten years ... or longer** (gesture to patient).

That would be a far nicer post-hypnotic suggestion to receive during shutdown, would it not? You can adapt the words you use to fit conditions such as rheumatoid arthritis, multiple sclerosis, strokes or indeed any condition which the patient themself perceives to be bad news.

So will it be the actual words you say and how you say them that allows acceptance? Maybe it's something you do that makes them feel supported. Some patients may appreciate you holding their hand or even giving them a hug. There is so much non-verbal communicating about caring, empathy, trust, and willingness to support, to be there no matter what, in a well-timed hug. The caveat here is that the hug is because it's appropriate for the patient, not simply for you! Some people, who are more auditory digital, will abhor a hug but find that a thoughtfully prepared list of resource material makes complete sense.

You will have noted your own preferences with regard to the above by your reactions. Be flexible, and experiment with all of the approaches. Your patients will thank you for it.

Of course, what you say may mean different things to different people. So it's important to check out what meaning they take from your utterances. And this may not be the same as the one that you intended. You will need to give time to exploring how this new information fits with their beliefs, ideas, concerns and expectations. You may also need to reframe some of the limiting beliefs that arise during this phase. Some people may interpret what you have said as a death sentence. Whilst I would not want to offer any platitudes here, some *verbal reframing* patterns may help.

- *'Perhaps the question is not how much time one has left, but more about what you really want to accomplish with it'* (values hierarchy).
- *'Some people think that in reality, life itself is a death sentence, eventually. Yet none of us know the exact timing'* (model of world).
- *'For many people, death is failing to live whatever life you've got to the full'* (redefine).
- *'So tell me, what's the difference between a death sentence and a life sentence?'* (reality strategy).

Beware! The vacuum that opens up when one is receiving bad news can be filled with any belief, new or old, that stumbles by. You can use these patterns to help to direct thoughts towards life-affirming purposes.

Although much of bad news may seem to present problems to move away from, it's important to begin to explore what patients can move towards instead. What are their *expectations* of the future? Is what they want possible? Are they capable of achieving it? Do they feel that they deserve it and that they are worth it? This is where *well-formed outcomes* come into play. I remarked previously how, anecdotally, some patients can set themselves important goals to live for, such as the birth of a grandchild, the holiday of a lifetime, etc.

Now is the time to begin to set not only these large important goals but also the smaller ones, the next steps in treatment, what to tell one's spouse, family and friends, what benefits they can claim, and a host of other potentially helpful issues. Of course, this can be spread out over the course of a few consultations, thereby preventing overloading and overwhelming of the patient. Remember to check their *SCORE* from time to time.

Closing the session

This is the time for some safety-netting, which is often best dealt with by *back-tracking* of the major points, followed by some *what-if scenarios*, and *rehearsals* covering the future possibilities and eventualities.

> *I've given you quite a lot of information today ... and you'll need some time to digest it. Sometimes that brings up some new questions ... and you can make a note of these so that we can deal with them at our next session.*

> *Sometimes, after hearing this kind of news, people can find themselves feeling confused, or getting a bit spaced out, feeling off balance or maybe even quite emotional out of the blue. That's quite natural, you know, and it simply means that, at a deeper level inside, things are beginning to sort themselves out, in a way that best fits for you.*

At this stage, it's time to make the arrangement for the follow-up consultations, perhaps with some contingency plans for how to deal with anything unexpected that might arise in between. This might involve ensuring that there are adequate support systems such as relatives, friends, carers, etc. When you finally close the session, ensure that you check for a congruent yes-set that you've covered the main points and they know the next steps.

Although the patient may have left, this consultation is not fully over until you have accomplished one further task, and that is *looking after yourself!* Breaking bad news can be emotionally draining no matter how well you've prepared yourself beforehand. Ask yourself *'What do I need right now?'*. You may get an answer such as time out, relaxation, a cup of coffee, a short walk, or something else altogether. Perhaps you have other patients waiting and little time left for yourself. Make use of this short period by triggering your break state anchor first, and follow this with 30 to 60 seconds of your anchor for calm relaxation. You deserve it, and you're worth looking after, too.

Recognising underlying depression

In society today, depression seems to be on the increase. One or two out of every five patients we see may be suffering directly or indirectly from it. The ones who tell us they are depressed are easy to diagnose. Yet because depression can present in myriad ways, it's easy to miss it completely. Are you certain that you are uncovering all of the hidden depression in your practice? Or do you have that uneasy feeling that you could do better? Although I could easily write another whole book about this condition, just for now we shall focus on the salient points from an NLP perspective.

Depression is a *nominalisation*, which is a word that turns an ongoing process into a static or stuck event, like taking one still frame from a video and using it to represent the entire film. Diagnostic labels (hypertension, rheumatoid arthritis, cancer, etc.) can be helpful in medical practice, yet it is sometimes more useful to turn the label back into a process again, to allow movement to take place. Using various meta-model questions, we can open up other avenues for exploration. *Who* is depressing *whom* and *how exactly* are they doing it? *What* is it that they are doing? What would they rather do *instead?* And *how* do they go about doing this? You can use these questions at every logical level.

Meta-programs and the structure of depression

There are certain meta-program patterns that seem to go along with depression, and in combination they can give a less than useful response to the vicissitudes of life. They tend to be past oriented, move away froms, big-picture generalists, emotive feelers, reactive to circumstances, swayed by externals, and procedural to boot.

Depression is primarily a *past*-oriented condition whereby an excessive focus on previous problems frames the present and future. Today and tomorrow, if they are seen at all, are experienced through a veil of past negativity. Even if they do see a future, it looks bleak, black and foreboding. There is often a search for 'why' something has happened.

- 'Because my mother died when I was young, I'll never feel safe or secure.'
- 'Because of my redundancy, I'm on the scrapheap of life.'

There is an excessive preoccupation with moving *away from* problems. Issues are gone over and over again as if the solution can be found by simply identifying what to avoid. If you are only looking at what to avoid, you won't see any solutions. And of course solutions are what you need to move *towards*. However, with an away-from orientation, patients are skilled at finding out why something won't help, what the problem is with any solution.

- 'I just want to stop feeling sad and lonely.'
- 'I don't know why my relationships are such a failure. What am I doing wrong?'

Depressives usually chunk up on information – they tend to be *general* rather than *specific*. They often use words like *all, every, always, never, no one* and *everyone*. By failing to find out what specifically went wrong and what specifically they could do instead, they leave their problems looming large and looking unmanageable. They chunk up problems from the level of behaviour to that of identity. Doing something wrong (behaviour) means that *they* are a failure (identity).

- *'I never seem to get anything right. I'm just a no-good failure.'*
- *'It always seems to happen to me.'*

Many people with depression associate into painful memories of the past and dissociate from good memories. They are *feelers* when it comes to pain, and *thinkers* when it comes to pleasure. They easily re-live traumatic experiences and find it difficult to think of any of the times when they were happy. Or if they can, it seems so far away now, and almost unreachable.

- *'I live with the pain of her death every day.'*
- *'Happiness just seems so elusive.'*

Depressives may see themselves as victims of unavoidable life circumstances. In this way they are *reactive* rather than *proactive*. Because things happen *to* them, it's as if they have no choice about what to do for themselves in the future. They may feel unable to take action. For example, in a relationship issue, if only the other person would change, things would be all right.

- *'I can't challenge him about that, he'll only get upset with me again.'*
- *'I suppose I'll just have to wait until it all blows over.'*

The meta-program pattern *internal and external* is closely connected to *proactive and reactive* in further defining a victim stance. The 'locus of control' for decision making either rests within oneself, or outwith oneself and with some external authority. This in turn is connected to whether or not you feel that you have personal mastery in a particular context, whether or not you feel that you are responsible and able to make changes. If you are depressed and *external*, you may be letting outside events or people control your thinking about what is possible. If you add *reactive* to this, then you may never get round to getting better. Someone or something else has to make you better.

- *'My friend tried counselling, but she said it made her worse. I'm not sure what to do.'*
- *'I've heard you can get terrible side-effects from antidepressants. Do you really think I need to take them?'*

People who are more *procedural*, who like order and sequence, have an increased tendency to get depressed. They are full of *shoulds, have to's, oughts* and *musts*. In other words, rules dominate. They may carry on doing things in a certain way because they have to, regardless of their health. They may not like the thought of letting other people down, and so they carry on despite increasing symptoms. They don't like changes to routine, and since life seems to be an ongoing process of change they feel ill equipped to deal with it. They need *options* thinking to help them, although they may need a procedure to generate the different possible options!

- *'I know I'm working too hard, but they're depending on me. I have to carry on.'*
- *'We've always done it this way, but since the reorganisation I'm just not coping any more.'*

These are some of the main meta-programs involved in depression. It is the combination of them together in action which can generate much of the symptoms and behaviours.

The physiology of depression

Depression appears to have a fairly characteristic physiology. Posture tends to be more slumped over, with the shoulders in, and the eyes often looking down at the floor. Energy levels are often reduced, everything seems an effort, and the patient may be *'tired all the time, doctor'*. Eye contact is less frequent, and the eyes themselves often move from down left to down right. Depressives are 'inside' themselves, in a recursive negative loop of talking to themselves about how bad things are, and then feeling worse. Their breathing may be slower, with the occasional sigh before answering a question. Their voice may be flatter, more monotone and less expressive.

Try this physiology on for size right *now*. Just *do it* for a couple of moments and notice how it feels in your body. Now stand up, shake it all off, look up to the ceiling and put a huge grin on your face before reading on!

When you are in rapport with someone who has this physiology, you may quickly get caught up in their state. This can be a very useful early warning sign that you need to consider the diagnosis of depression. In fact, I now have a rule that states that *'anyone who makes me feel depressed has depression until proven otherwise'*. Although this may not be completely true, I find it a useful generalisation to keep the diagnosis in mind.

Uncovering questions

Sometimes patients may come in and tell you that they're not certain what's wrong, or that they're simply tired all the time (TATT syndrome). Maybe they're not coping well with a stressful situation at work, at home or in a relationship, and you're wondering if they're stressed or really depressed. Occasionally, depression presents as somatisation, where a list of physical symptoms is presented with many ensuing investigations but no diagnosis. This type of patient may be unwilling to entertain depression as a cause of their ailments. At other times, such as a few months after a bereavement, or in the year after childbirth, you know that there is an increased risk of depression, but may be uncertain how to ask about this sensitively.

In these circumstances there are a number of approaches that you can use to get to the heart of the issue. As usual, when questioning in this way, it is useful to use softeners. You can also incorporate *meta-comments* to help to frame your statements. It's often a good idea to start with a description of observable behaviour and lead on with a question.

- *'I was wondering, what with all that's been going on for you lately, whether you might be feeling down, or even depressed?'*
- *'When you were speaking about your mother's death you sighed, looked down, your hands were trembling and I wondered if you were holding back some tears ... can you bear to tell me just exactly how you've been feeling?'* (fairly indirect).
- *'I had a patient once, a bit like you, lots of aches and pains, lots of investigations ... but no obvious diagnosis. It turned out he was really very depressed ... although he couldn't see it himself. After a few weeks on an antidepressant he was much better ... and hasn't looked back ... I wondered about you ... ?'* (metaphorical).
- *'Some people, when they have had the kind of symptoms you've been having, think they may have depression. Is that what you were thinking?'*
- *'In the first few months after childbirth it's important that we don't miss any symptoms of depression. Would it be OK if I asked you a few questions about how you've been feeling?'*
- *'Quite frankly, John, you look very depressed. We need to discuss this now'* (very direct!).

Suicidal thoughts

At some stage, patients who are thought to be a suicidal risk need to be asked *the* question. Usually it's quite a relief all round to get it out on the table, and the act of discussing it seems to markedly reduce the risk of its occurrence (not always, though).

I often frame it as if a *part* of the patient may want them to die, because that seems to be a pathway to relief from an intolerable situation, a step into peace. (Of course, the hidden presupposition in that sentence is that a part also wants them to live.) You can chunk up the answers to a higher intention, like a negotiation, while calibrating to their yes-set. Then I agree that it's really good to have a part that wants us to have peace, and that up until now it's only had one stark choice. I reiterate that the aim of our treatment is to help them to get the peace they want *and* to live. You can do that as a two-part negotiation on each hand, and then bring them together in integration (*see* Chapter 6 on explanation and planning).

Once again there is a choice between being obliquely indirect or quite to the point. Calibrate closely to the patient's non-verbal cues.

- *'Sometimes, when people feel as low as you've felt, they might wonder about ending it all ... is that something you had thought about?'* (fairly indirect).
- *'I'm not sure whether you're the sort of person who might think about taking your own life ... or not'* (quite direct).
- *'Some people, almost against their will, have irrational thoughts that keep coming up, thoughts that they push away, about death and dying ... have you had thoughts like these?'* (indirect).
- *'You could always jump off the viaduct ... head first ... make a terrible mess though ... not a pretty sight for your parents to identify what's left'* (*very* direct! I said this to a young woman whom I knew very well and with whom I had great rapport ... she burst out laughing!).

Treating depression

The use of NLP methodologies to aid the treatment of depression is beyond the scope of this book. Having said that, you can utilise much that you have learned already to make a big difference. The essential point is to get the patient to adopt a solution orientation, by building a *compelling future* that they want to move into. The *well-formed outcome questions* and the *miracle question* can help here. Changing the physiology (posture, etc.) of depression is vital. Exercise (especially aerobic exercise) is very useful. I sometimes get my patients to dance to upbeat pop music! Set small, realistic, achievable goals so that they can experience success. Use *reframing* skills whenever you can. Use some of the exercises that you have learned already in this chapter with your patients. And how about helping them to set their own positive anchors? You might want to check through the rest of the book and adapt other processes as appropriate. They can all be utilised.

Heartsink patients

What exactly is a heartsink patient, and how do you deal with them? I can think of several people who, for a variety of reasons, have fallen into that category. You know, chronic recurrent attenders, unresolved (perhaps unresolvable) clinical issues, difficulties in actually making a diagnosis, and *'Well, you're the doctor, doctor. You tell me!'*. You probably have one or two, maybe more, that you can bring to mind right now. Are they *your* particular heartsinks, or do you share the same ones with your partners? Do they feel the same way? And, have you ever wondered, is there such a thing as a heartsink doctor?

Some patients may be your own *personal* heartsinks. By that I mean that other doctors may see them quite differently, and they are only heartsinks to you. Yet your colleagues may agree unanimously that a particular name will bring forth unresourceful feelings in all. So that raises some fundamental questions right from the start. What is it that makes one person heartsink and the next one not? Does the heartsink label belong to the patient themself, or to the feelings engendered in the consulting doctor? Or is it a product of the *relationship* between the two individuals? Whose heart sinks? How do these feelings come about? And how can we change them into something more resourceful?

Heartsink patients are certainly not malingerers. Studies show that at least one in every three will have significant medical pathology, often multiple medical pathology! This in itself gives some clues, because it is often challenging to manage simultaneously the demands of differing diseases and illnesses, with differing treatment requirements, in the time allotted. Perhaps what we feel is the incongruence that comes with conflicting demands. We shall return to that later.

So, as you think of one of your heartsinks now, picturing what they look like, and hearing how they sound, what is it that you are feeling? And where do you experience that feeling? In your chest? In your stomach? The very label suggests a feeling that sinks down, that moves, that has a direction, from heart to solar plexus. And how would you know, on encountering that patient again, that things had changed for the better?

As I see it, the heartsink response is something that happens *inside us*. It is *our* feeling *about* that particular patient, and how we relate – they to us, and us to them. They may be the external trigger, yet we own the feeling. And therefore, in order to do something about it, to make positive changes, we need to acknowledge that ownership first, otherwise we shall remain victims of its effects. Once it is accepted, we can explore several areas fruitfully. These are our own *past history*, the notion of *incongruence*, and our *communication patterns* (especially *meta-programs*).

Past history

There was one particular thickset middle-aged man with black-rimmed spectacles who was my personal heartsink, although not that of my colleagues. His voice used to grate on me like a physical pain. I would notice he was number seven on that morning's list, and the countdown would begin. Six to go, five to go, four to go, etc., etc.! And for me, the heartsink feeling was definitely in my solar plexus.

It was only when I really got in touch with that feeling again, listened to the particular voice tones once more, and asked myself, '*Where has all this come from? Where does it originate? Where in the past does it belong?*' that it all started to make sense. I got some flickering images, and the smell of school (you may know that smell and feeling). And then, suddenly, there he was. My old primary school teacher, who shall remain nameless. My unfortunate patient not only looked like him, but he had the same spectacles, and the same vocal qualities! That particular feeling had been an anchor to the dim and distant past, replaying negative emotions in the here and now.

And these personally idiosyncratic heartsinks are usually of that nature, either a visible or an auditory resemblance to someone from the past. A particular posture, gesture or mannerism. An *anchor* which can trigger off an unresourceful state. Not belonging to them as such, but belonging to you and your own personal history. So what can you do about it? Well, often simply knowing and acknowledging the source is a good start. That, together with noticing just how this particular person is different, and what specifically marks them out as dissimilar, may well be enough to break the link.

Of course, there are some other things you can do. If you consult the list of states in Appendix 1, you can choose three or four to anchor together, states such as feeling strong, curious, connected, accepting, dynamic, resilient, compassionate and energised. Find examples of each one from your past, or imagine how you would be if you had them already. Using what you know from previous sections, you can step inside each state, brighten up the pictures, turn up the sound and intensify the feelings. As you reach a peak, anchor it. Repeat this for the other states, joining them together on the same anchor. When you have a robust 'super state', you can then picture your patient, hearing their voice tones, as you fire off the anchor. Not only will this change your memory of the experience, but you will also find that the next encounter goes quite differently.

I'm not certain whether I could suggest your doing what I did with one of my patients who had a person who made her feel small, insignificant and overwhelmed. She imagined an image of that person on her inner mental screen. Then she added a red clown's nose, very frizzy orange hair, a painted clown's mouth, a teardrop from the left eye, and a multicoloured revolving bow-tie. Then she imagined that person saying what she had said in Donald Duck's voice, then Mickey Mouse, and then Sylvester the Cat! We did this several years ago, and not only do the changes persist, but her relationship with the other person improved markedly. Just a thought ...

Incongruence

You remember the feelings associated with incongruence, when you were in two minds, the *'but'* in the *'yes ... but'*? Well, it seems to me that one thing many heartsink patients express is a degree of simultaneous and sometimes sequential incongruity. Simultaneous incongruity is when the verbal and non-verbal messages are expressed differently at the *same* time. Sequential incongruity is saying one thing verbally and non-verbally at one time, and something different at a *later* time.

When you get into rapport, especially deep rapport, with someone who is displaying a large amount of incongruity, guess what? You get to experience those feelings, too. And sometimes you can wonder who the feelings really belong to, them or you. Those heartsink feelings at one level feel really uncomfortable. Yet at another level altogether, they are presenting you with very important information about this particular patient, here ... right now. They are a *signal* to you, a signal that something isn't quite right yet. A signal for you to explore in just what way their incongruence not only manifests itself, but also how you can use it to lead them towards congruence and resolution instead.

Whilst we can think of symptoms in many different ways, one way to do so is as a message of incongruence. A message that one part of the mind–body interface is 'out of sync', out of sorts with the rest of us. And multiple symptoms, multiple dis-ease and pathologies allow for multiple incongruencies, something that many heartsinks possess. Of course, health is more than the mere absence of symptoms. It is about a state of congruent inner alignment, inner harmony, a state that in itself can be profoundly healing.

So we shall now turn our attention to those areas of communication in which incongruency in heartsinks and our relationship with them can manifest.

Communication patterns

Sometimes that heartsink feeling can manifest itself because you and your patient have different communication patterns. Remember representational systems (VAKOG)? Occasionally, if you both operate mainly out of one system, and that system does *not* coincide (e.g. V versus K), then neither of you will see eye to eye, or feel that you have a firm grasp of the situation. The easy remedy to this is to ensure that you are flexible enough to use all of the representational systems equally, and be able to translate between them.

More often, however, the heartsink feeling can arise due to meta-program pattern differences. You probably now have some clue as to your own preferences, having read the previous chapters. Often the people who challenge us most are those who are very different to ourselves. The more they are at the opposite pole of each of your own meta-programs, the more likely there is to be a mismatch. When you are attempting to get your message across using your own preferred patterns rather than theirs, it can seem as if you are communicating with an alien, and vice versa! That heartsink feeling that arises is again a type of incongruency in information processing, rather like the square peg and the round hole syndrome.

This type of heartsink problem is usually idiosyncratic. Because your other colleagues will have differing communication patterns, they may not see your patient in the same light. Once again, the solution is to develop your flexibility in using the whole spectrum of each pattern. Ensure that you give your information in a way that best fits them. Use the heartsink feeling both as a signal that differences exist, and as a prompt for you to put your information in another way.

However, some patients, unfortunately for them, seem to give everyone with whom they come into contact that particular heartsink feeling. What is it about them that engenders this almost universal response? There are certain combinations of meta-programs which, when taken to the extreme, can set all our teeth on edge!

The combination of the extremes of *general* and *away from* with a *kinaesthetic* lead can be quite troublesome. These patients can be so 'big picture' that what they say is rather like abstract art, interpretable by the cognoscenti only. They may describe very vague indeterminable feelings and symptoms that they want to get rid of. However, they present their information quite randomly, often jumping from one piece to another as if they are connected in some way. They defy attempts to chunk down, and to get more specific, by remaining tantalisingly in the stratosphere. This is made all the worse if they actually have multiple pathologies that you are trying to get to grips with.

Another deadly combination is *specific, procedures, mismatch* and *away from.* They will insist on telling their story, step by step, in the most minute way. If interrupted, they will start at the beginning again, or at one of the story's many offshoots, some of which are undoubtedly red herrings, no matter how far you're running overtime. They tell you about what they definitely *don't* want, yet are unclear about what they *do* want. They have a '*Yes ... but*' for most advice that you give, being able to pick out potential problems like using a dentist's drill! Does this ring any bells? I had one patient like this and eventually he did choose to leave my list. This tells you a lot about my personal patterns.

Obviously there are no magical solutions to these types of scenarios. Yet for the most part you can handle the situations with far more grace and aplomb, even with a sense of achievement and deep connection, by simply wondering which meta-program pattern the patient is taking to the extreme. And discussing these types of management issues with your partners in these terms can allow you all to deal more concertedly and effectively with heartsink issues.

Heartsinks: embodying the beliefs of excellent communicators

If you cast your mind way back to this book's beginning, you can bring to mind the various presuppositions underpinning effective communication, NLP style. In effect, these are the beliefs, the operational rules, which when carried bodily into any interaction will enhance every consultation. These beliefs are not necessarily 'true'. However, if you act *as if* they are true, stepping into them, trying them on for size, allowing them to filter what you say and do, they will enhance your results immensely, even in the most challenging of heartsink situations. Let's revisit some of them now.

- *Everyone has their own unique model of the world.*
  Ask yourself 'Am I communicating this in a way that fits for them?'.
- *Behind every behaviour is a positive intention.*
  Ask yourself 'What is the positive intention behind this behaviour for the patient?'.
- *The meaning of your communication is the response it gets.*
  Ask yourself 'Are they interpreting my message in the way I intended?'.
- *Present behaviour is the best choice available.*
  Ask yourself 'If this is their current best choice, how can I help to expand their choices?'.
- *There is only feedback.*
  Ask yourself 'How can I utilise this response as feedback?'
- *Resistance is a sign of a lack of rapport.*
  You could say 'There are no resistant patients, only inflexibly communicating doctors'. Ask yourself 'How can I re-establish rapport with this person, and at what logical level?'

These are six of the important NLP presuppositions for communicating effectively. We are going to use them in the exercise below to get a sense of how having them already in place can really turn a difficult situation around, to everyone's advantage.

Why don't you choose a difficult encounter from the past to use this process on, one that you would like to explore profitably? One of my suggestions would be to choose your 'favourite heartsink' patient. So far we have found that our own personal heartsinks are usually those people who have a totally different way of thinking and being in the world to us. Their internal maps may be at complete odds with our own. You may gain a lot more than you think by doing this exercise.

Lay out the following places on the floor as shown in Figure 8.3. You could use a few sheets of paper to mark out each spot.

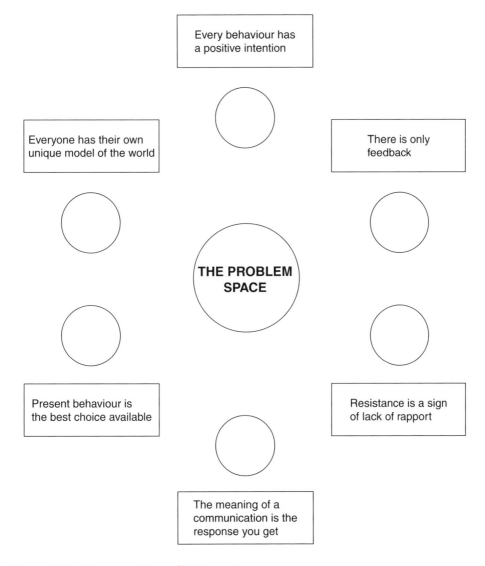

Figure 8.3: Presuppositions of NLP exercise.

Exercise 19:   Presuppositions update

1   Choose the particular *heartsink situation* you wish to review. As you stand in the *problem space*, imagine being right back in it. *Relive* the key moments, then step outside and 'shake it off'.
2   Choose one of the presupposition spaces to enter first. Imagine what it would be like if you could *try this presupposition on for size*. See yourself in the situation (dissociated) with this resource. How does it alter your experience? What new feedback do you have? What are you *doing differently*? How are they responding?
3   Now, *step inside* the problem space, *fully associate* with the experience and 'be there' in the situation again, *with this new way of thinking*. How does it feel on the inside? What are you learning now?
4   *Repeat the process* with each of the remaining presupposition spaces. Revisit them in any order as you wish.
5   As you finish, think about the *next time* you see this person. What is it that you will do *differently*?

The above exercise is modified from the original developed by Tim Hallbom and Suzi Smith. It is a very useful exercise which can be utilised in a variety of ways and in a variety of circumstances, not only heartsink situations. You could simply choose one of the presuppositions each day and ask yourself '*What if I were to see the world through this lens for a day? How does that enhance and enlarge my perceptions? How am I experiencing things differently?*'.

Or you could take a recurring situation that you wish would turn out differently – at work, at home, sport or leisure – and go through the process. You may find that it quickly streamlines and becomes an automatic part of your perceptions.

We have now completed our section on heartsink patients. As you think about it, who really owns the feeling response? Remember to use that feeling as a signal for you to explore the situation afresh, wondering about communication patterns, incongruencies and your own states of mind and body, and do something different. Avail yourself of all the other communication strategies in this book, especially the section on negotiating. And when you do, let me know your results.

Telephone consulting strategies

Nowadays, for a variety of reasons mainly related to working more effectively with time constraints, we consult far more frequently on the telephone. Sometimes this is at coffee time, when we are 'free' to respond to the various demands that are being made. Some doctors enjoy the verbal jousting that takes place, while others abhor it! More and more frequently we are beginning to organise it in a type of triage system to allow better use of available appointments. Telephone conversations can range from the minutiae of everyday practice to the strident demands of dire emergencies. Yet consulting over the phone is quite different from a face-to-face meeting. There is greater potential for misunderstanding, and an increase in the level of uncertainty to cope with. Do you relish the challenge, or are you campaigning for telephone-free coffee rooms?

So just what are the particular skills that we need to focus on? How can we train ourselves to manage telephone conversations more effectively? What if you could actually enjoy looking forward to using the phone more frequently and getting the results you wanted? Is this a dream or a definite possibility?

Phone physiology

The biggest difference when comparing phone with ordinary face-to-face consultations is the lack of visual input to enable you to calibrate patients' responses. Of course you could always get engrossed with doodling on bits of paper, playing with the computer, going through your mail or signing prescriptions, but that's not the kind of visual input I mean. The 50% or more of information that we normally obtain from posture, gesture, eye movements, etc., is completely lost. Voice qualities, tone, tempo, timbre, pitch and volume now account for more than 80% of the incoming information, whilst the words themselves convey less than 20% of the meaning.

But before we go on, let's back up a little. There is something that comes before all of this, before you even pick up the phone. And that is *your own state*. Are you often exasperated, harassed, frustrated or even angry when called to the phone? Are you trying to do several things at once? What do you think that might convey to the person on the receiving end? Regardless of the words you use, the emotional tone will win through and give the true message, even if it is out of conscious awareness. The same is true if you are distracting yourself by doing something else at the same time, such as signing prescriptions.

Your *consulting flow state* may be the best one to trigger as you reach out for the phone. What if you could *anchor the state to the phone itself* so that you automatically go into a good state, whatever happens? Perhaps you want to experiment with some of the other states in Appendix 1 to find the best fit. You can imagine rehearsing this a few times in your mind's eye so that it happens naturally. Perhaps the sound of the telephone ringing, or reaching out with your hand, will be a natural trigger. If you have a dislike of phones, maybe even a phobia (!), then you can adapt one of the processes described earlier in this chapter to help you to feel comfortable. Remember the BT commercial 'It's good to talk'.

But are you a right- or left-eared phone person? By that I mean which is the natural ear you listen with? Just watch other people. Which ear do they use? Does that seem like a crazy question? Well, we each have an ear that we're more comfortable with on the phone. Try using your other ear to hear the difference. I've noticed, and this is a generalisation, that many people use their left ear to get more in tune with the emotional nuances of the conversation. The right ear, on the other hand, is far more business-like and 'distanced'. I utilise this by using my right ear for potentially challenging calls and my left ear for all the rest. You can swap over when needs must. Don't take my word for it, though. Experiment for yourself.

So having got yourself into the right state, and decided which ear to use, what do you do next? Well, the most important thing is to immediately *match* your voice qualities to those of the patient. Speak at the same rate, rhythm, volume, tone and relative pitch as them. Remember that one way to quickly get yourself into the groove is to repeat simultaneously in your mind's ear what they are saying as they say it. Then, when it is your turn to speak, you will gain an almost immediate rapport that you can subsequently deepen.

Of course you remember that one very effective way to establish rapport is to match the patient's breathing rate. This is quite easy on the phone, as breath sounds are more readily heard. And no, I'm not meaning those kinds of heavy breathing sounds! If you fail to hear their breathing, remember that they can only speak on the out breath. Pacing their breathing in this way will deepen the connection.

Words and other strategies

When people are talking to you on the phone, they are usually in one of two camps – faster speakers or slower speakers. Those people who have been trained in telephone cold-calling techniques know this well. If the respondent speaks quickly, they will use more visual and auditory words in their presentation. However, if the respondent speaks more slowly, they use kinaesthetic and auditory digital words. This seems to give a better match to the predicates that these people use naturally. One way to get off to a bad start, and then fade, is to mismatch speed and predicates. Mutual understanding may well be the first casualty.

One strategy that successful telephone callers use can make up for the lack of visual face-to-face input. What they do is to *imagine*, in their mind's eye, just what the other person might look like based on their voice qualities. This internal imagery not only prevents them from being distracted externally, but it also actually increases the quality of attention that they pay to the call receiver. If you know the patient already, picture them in their natural surroundings. This seems to make a successful call more likely. Smiling as you answer the phone (yes, I know that's a definite stretch!) conveys a more open welcome. Try it and see. *Literally!*

When speaking to patients it is important to let them have their say, so that they feel satisfied they have been heard, and told their full story. Earlier on in the conversation it is useful to utilise your non-verbal and verbal equivalents to *'go on ... tell me more'*. Ensuring that you have your patient's complete tale fosters their willingness to listen to you in return, and pays longer-term dividends. Of course all the other consultation skills that you have learned so far can come into play, especially the softeners.

If you are on telephone triage and you want to persuade a reluctant patient to forego the house call and come to the health centre instead, you can remember to *use embedded language* with a downward tonality. You can see more patients in the time available, and I believe this is an ethical use of persuasion skills.

> *I agree that it's important to ... **sort this out quickly** ... and I don't know if you could ... **come down to the centre now** ... but if you could ... **do that now**, that is ... I could ... **deal with it effectively** ... let's say ... **at 10.40** ... does that ... **sound OK?***

If *you want to*, you can perhaps allow yourself to *write out* several more *examples*, and this will give you even more *practice* in the skill of *embedding language*, having things come out the way *you'd like to*. Of course, don't *just do this*, simply because *I've said so*. Find your own reasons to *do this now*. (Yes, I know this last paragraph was more than a bit over the top.)

Difficult calls

There are some calls that you might need to make which you may find challenging. Perhaps they are to the kind of people who up until now have left you feeling emotionally mauled. Or maybe you have to make a complaint but you're just not the type of person who likes doing that. Perhaps you simply want to get your point across firmly yet fairly, yet you wonder if you can handle it effectively. You may even have to break bad news and wonder if the recipient will cope, let alone you.

People who manage these challenges resourcefully have a strategy for their success. They don't just simply pick up the phone and get stuck in! They spend a few moments preparing themselves, setting themselves up in a way that increases their likelihood of achieving the outcome that they want. So what is it that they actually do?

First they set a well-formed *outcome* for the call. They decide specifically what points they want to get across and how they will frame them. They may even jot this down on paper. They have already considered the *consequences*, what will happen if they get their outcome, and the downside plans in case they don't. They picture in their mind's eye what a successful conclusion would look like, sound like and feel like from all three *perceptual positions*. Then, based on that, they decide what *state* they would need to be in from the start of the call that would support that conclusion. Having accessed that state (and chosen which ear to use!), they make the call. Try this strategy on for size with your next challenging call, and notice the different outcome.

There is a tip from professional sales callers who are effective not only in getting heard but also in having their advice acted upon. Before launching into their spiel, they ask how the other person is feeling at that moment, and then leave a space for them to answer. Whether the answer is good, bad or indifferent they acknowledge it (pacing), and then they move on in the direction of their choice. This simple technique doubles their success rate (*see Influence: Science and Practice,* by Robert Cialdini).

Ending the call

Have you ever had the experience of knowing that you had other things to do, itching to get on with them, yet you couldn't get off the phone because the other person was oblivious to your discomfiture? This often happens with in-laws, and sometimes with patients, too! Have you ever said your goodbyes several times, yet there you are, still talking to them? What is going on in these situations? And what can you do instead?

Well, as you may have already guessed, ending calls when you want to depends on *how* you use your voice. Once again, because there is no visual input for calibration, the person on the end of the line cannot see your increasingly frenetic body language as you fail to disengage. You really must not only say the words of farewell and mean them, but you will also need to *exaggerate* them somewhat. That means talking *louder* and *faster* than normal as you say good-bye. Visualise the other person putting the phone down, too, as you do this.

I know one person who, when he can't get the message across that yes, he really has to go now, disconnects the phone with a finger while he's in mid-sentence. The other person then thinks that they have been cut off. Sneaky, I know, and not a method that I would necessarily recommend, but it does show an admirable flexibility of behaviour.

Well, I hope that this tour through various telephone techniques and approaches proves useful to you. As usual, the proof of the NLP pudding is in the eating, the experience itself. Take it step by step and you will find that your telephone skills improve rapidly.

Summary

We have covered quite a bit of ground in this chapter, focusing on some of the commoner yet diverse issues in general practice communication today. Hopefully you'll be unlikely to find yourself giving bad news over the telephone to a suicidally depressed and very angry heartsink patient who is critically complaining about your telephone manner! But if you do, you'll cope.

Joking aside, these are all very pertinent issues that in my view are often not discussed or, worse still, that are poorly taught. I cannot over-emphasise that all of the core skills you have already learned so far form the foundation for success, even in these challenging areas. With the addition of the issue-specific skills you may find yourself unstoppable in achieving your communication outcomes. Remember that anything less than allowing this to become a fully automatic part of your developing excellence just won't get you the results that you deserve. Think about that as you move on to the next chapter.

CHAPTER 9

Developing personally

Introduction

I wonder if you can remember back to just before you made the decision to pursue medicine as a career. What was going on in your life at that time? What was it that influenced your choice? Did you 'always' know that this was what you were going to do? Or were there some other factors that came to bear on your decision? Such as family? Friends? The media? Something else?

There were a number of things that influenced me. In my teens I was heavily into athletics, especially middle-distance running. This developed a twin interest of wondering just how my body worked, and why it sometimes got injured. My coach at the time was quite fanatical about exercise physiology, and his intensive training methods often led to consulting sports medicine literature! Several of my classmates at school were considering medicine as a career, and our teachers at that time pushed this idea for the academically bright. I sometimes wonder, though, whether it was really the television programmes of the day, *Doctor in the House*, *Doctor at Large*, the Carry On films, and so on, that really made my mind up. These young doctors seemed to have a whale of a time, getting up to all sorts of antics!

What was it that led *you* to choose this path? What fuelled your desire? Has whatever flame that was lit at the time continued to burn fiercely? Or is it a flickering candle in the wind, in danger of being snuffed out altogether? As time goes on, have you sometimes wondered whether it was all worth it? As I write this, we are at a time when four out of every five general practitioners are dissatisfied with the pressures of their work, feeling overburdened with bureaucracy, and wondering if they can cope with the ever-increasing demand, both in and out of hours. Many are looking for early retirement, or a sideways step on to another career path, demotivation and demoralisation being the order of the day. Going through the motions. Do you feel like this? Is that really what you want for yourself?

And of course we are also on the verge of being besieged with personal learning plans, continuous professional development and even organisational learning plans. All well, good and laudable. Continuing education is very important. Yet even more so, I believe, is the link between all of these and their connection to those deeper aspects of ourselves – our *dreams*, our *visions* and our *sense of purpose* in what we are doing. The kind of inner fulfilment that lets us know, when we look back at the end of our lives, that we counted, we made a difference, our passing deeply touched many people, and we lived up to the best of our expectations.

So for me, personal development is not just about deciding what new things to learn, which new courses to go on, and what new skills to 'bolt' on. Important as these may be, I believe that before all that, as a foundation, we desperately need to reconnect with our flickering inner candles and turn them into roaring flames. We need to reconnect to our passions, our dreams, the things that got us started off in medicine. The vision we once had, the beliefs that sustain us, and the values that nourish us. Reconnecting to the times when we have been at our best, gathering these perhaps disparate resources together again, harvesting what we already have, and aligning ourselves with a new found congruence. Building the kind of *compelling future* that we really want to move into.

Wow, you may be saying. This sounds a bit heavy! Well maybe, maybe not. My experience is that when we get back in touch with our core values, what really makes us tick, then it becomes so much easier to decide just exactly what new things we want to do, learn and acquire. And we do them because *they fit* with who we are at the deepest level.

Aims of this chapter

So this chapter is about uncovering. Uncovering what is already there, perhaps hidden away in the mists of time, or buried deep in the attics of our memory. We shall explore the various logical levels of experience as they impact on these deeper aspects of ourselves. We shall bring to light, dust off and nourish those elements which up until now may have lain dormant, yet which when realigned together will allow us a far deeper level of sustenance.

We shall cover the following elements:

* bringing forth your *best self*, firing on all cylinders!
* utilising the *resonance pattern*, with your mentors
* discovering the *values* that really drive your behaviours
* uncovering your *beliefs* about you as a doctor, and updating them if need be

- rediscovering *vision and purpose* in your life
- the *levels alignment process*, nesting it all together
- building your *compelling future*.

There are a number of exercises that you can do in this chapter, although not necessarily all at once. Because you can revisit each section as often as you like, it may make more sense to focus on one area at a time, being as thorough as you can, in the knowledge that the effects are cumulative.

Being your best self

There are times, and we've all had them, when we wished we had said something different, done something different, held back in some way, or come forth in another way. Times when we know we were performing below our capabilities, below our standards, and below the best that we knew we could be. And there may have been all sorts of external constraints, pressures of work and time, other commitments and other people that prevented us from accessing our best selves. There may also have been various internal constraints at different levels of our own being that obstructed the outpouring of the best we can be in any given situation. And to be totally frank and honest, no matter what the external constraint, the only person who can make a difference, the only person whom we can pay attention to, the only person who can bring forth our best selves is ... *our self!*

And as you think about it now, you know there have also been times when you have been really in the flow of things, saying and doing the right thing, at the right place, at the right time. Times when, despite so-called 'outside forces', you came up with the goods, maybe even against the odds. Times when you may have delightfully surprised yourself. And these times did not necessarily occur only in your medical practice. They will also have occurred in every other context of your life, with family, friends, in sport and leisure, or with your hobbies and interests. And what is more, they have occurred *throughout* the times of your life, from childhood through to the present day.

So in the next few paragraphs we are going to do an inventory of the best times in your life so far. If anything less than positive comes up as you do this, leave it on the side just for now. We want to focus on the things you're passionate about, the things that move you, that make you laugh and love, the kind of experiences that have made you who you are today, when you're being at your best. You might want to get some paper to write down what comes up. Often when remembering times seemingly long since forgotten, you will spontaneously relive the memories, accessing those really good feelings as if they are happening

right *now*. Of course you can feel free to anchor these as they arise to a particular finger, knuckle, word, sound or movement. Remember, in the paragraphs
that follow, that we want to explore *all* contexts of your life, not just medicine.

So let's start with the things that you're most passionate about. What are
your interests, what gets you really motivated? What are the things that, once
you get started talking about them, you just can't stop, you're so enthusiastic?
Is it sport, your hobby, or something else altogether? Think back to the last time
you were feeling this passion. Imagine stepping into the memory of the event.
Relive it now and experience the feelings. Then make a note of it as you move on.

If someone were to ask you *'What have been your greatest achievements in life
so far … ?'*, what would you answer? What are the things that you look back on
that you have accomplished, the things you're proud of? What have you built
in your life? A family? A practice? A garden? A kid's football team? A sanctuary?
A business? Let your mind roam over the years. Maybe you were determined to
do something and you achieved it against the odds. Maybe you were instrumental
in setting up the practice computer system. It doesn't matter how big or small
it appears in other peoples' eyes, it's *you* that counts. Jot down your answers.

Everyone has had times in their lives when they've been having fun, for fun's
sake. Often spontaneous, these moments usually occur with family and friends,
at home and on holiday. I remember being at a water-park with my kids and
racing down those yellow slides that go up and down before they hit the water.
We raced over and over again. It was mindless, childlike fun! Just thinking
about it brings the feeling back. What similar fun-time memories do you have?
When did you last have some childlike fun? Make a note of these memories.

We all have certain skills and talents, things that we do really well. What are
your particular ones? What do other people compliment you on? What do they
say you're good at? Perhaps it's an external skill, like being good at minor
surgery. Perhaps it's more internal, like having determination or perseverance.
Maybe you're really good with kids or animals. Perhaps you have skill as a
public speaker, or maybe a negotiator. People may applaud your teaching skills,
or your ability to be well organised, or on time. You may be skilled at handling
difficult situations effectively and sensitively. You may be a great cook, chef,
gardener, football player, artist, dancer or writer. These all have within them
certain skill sets. Which ones shine out in you?

Who are the people you look up to, who inspire you? What is it about them
that resonates with you? They could be people you know personally, or you may
see them in the media. You may have read their books, or read about them in a
book. They may be living, dead or even purely fictional. NLP trainer Peta Heskell
was my inspiration for this section of the chapter. I've never met her, nor have I
trained with her, yet I've read some of her writings on the subject. You see the
thing is, those people who inspire us are simply shining out a particular quality

that attracts us because it is already within us, lying dormant, ready to be awakened. So write down the names of those individuals who inspire you and the qualities that they demonstrate.

What could initially seem like quite a sombre thought is the eulogy that someone would say once you had departed this mortal life. What is it that people will remember about you at your passing? What are the positive qualities over your lifetime that will have caused you to be an inspiration to others? What things would you like them to remember about you? As you think about them now, you can make a firm commitment to continuing to develop these qualities as you *live* your life.

What is it that you really like about yourself? Be honest! You might not mention these things to anyone else lest they thought of it as bragging. But what are they specifically? In your private moments, when there is only you, what do you think are your best bits? If you could use three positive adjectives to describe yourself, what would they be? What is the specific evidence that lets you know this? What do you see, hear and feel as you think about these things? When you are at your absolute best, what is true about you? And how do you know this?

So how easy did you find it to come up with all the myriad things that represent you as your best self? Maybe you're still writing them down and thinking them over. Or have you been terribly British and thought how one mustn't blow one's own trumpet? How sad if that were true. Of course the real truth of it is that, if you allow yourself to soak up these memories, you will have already begun the process of re-igniting them in your life, reconnecting them to the you of the present moment. And what a present that is to give yourself.

Exercise 20:   Being your best self

1   Find yourself a quiet time and place where you can be *by yourself*. Take your notes and your *memories with you*.
2   Decide which *anchor* you are going to use. Will it be a finger, a knuckle, a gesture, or a word said in a particular way?
3   Select *the highlights* from each paragraph. Ensure that you *select memories* that come from every decade and every context of your life so far.
4   *Relive each memory*, making it big, bright and close, with surround sound, intensifying the feelings. *Anchor* each memory at its peak, in the same way *each time*.
5   As you luxuriate in *being your best self*, imagine taking these feelings *into the future*. Visit *each context* of your life as it is now. Be with the key people in each place, noticing not only your feelings but also their response to you. *Enjoy the experience!*

The more you use this anchor in everyday circumstances, the more you will automatically seed it into each area of your life. As you do this now, you will find that the very environment you are in, and the people you are with, will begin to trigger off this state out of your conscious awareness. They will have become a reinforcing anchor. Nothing is a panacea, though, and it is useful to repeat the exercise over time to both strengthen and deepen your resources.

The resonance pattern

Do you remember those people who inspire you, who mentor you, and who attract you to their own characteristics? Do you remember that they are simply reawakening and resonating with your own dormant qualities? These are ones that you may have deeply buried and don't feel really belong to you ... *yet*. It is as if they are dissociated aspects of yourself, projected on to other people, and waiting to be reclaimed. As if you have the intellectual map but have not yet embodied the experience. British trainer Ian McDermott introduced me to the *resonance pattern*, which I believe was originally modelled by Robert Dilts. It is a way of reclaiming those dissociated and projected aspects of ourselves, allowing the already installed seeds to grow, flower and blossom.

Have someone guide you through the following exercise.

Exercise 21:   The resonance pattern

1   *Identify three mentors* who have particular characteristics that inspire you. They can be living, dead, or even fictional. They could even be things such as mountains, sea, trees, etc.
2   Lay out the four positions as described opposite.
3   Standing in the self-position, look over to *mentor number 1*. Imagine that you can see them over there *displaying the particular quality* that inspires you. Even if you can't see them clearly, pretend that you can! Notice their posture, gestures, voice qualities, etc.
4   Now, leaving your self-position safely behind, *step into and 'become' your mentor*. See through their eyes, hear through their ears, and feel their feelings. Adjust your posture so that you are just like them.
5   Focus your attention on *the particular quality* that this mentor has. As you *access this*, look across at the self-position, and imagine 'that you over there' ready to receive this gift. Then imagine *beaming it across to*

'*that you*', in a beam of light, a stream of sound, a radiation of feeling, or any other way you wish.

6   With the transmission complete, step out of your mentor and back into the self-position. Now *imagine receiving the gift fully inside you* so that it bathes every cell in your body. As you receive it mentally, thank your mentor.

7   Do the same process with *each mentor in turn*. When you have completed all three, imagine the *resources integrating* inside you. As you do this, think of the particular situations in the future where these resources would be useful. Imagine being there, and the difference that it now makes to your interaction.

Again, this is another useful process that bears repeating in the future. We can easily do a 'quickie' variation of this in seconds. When you are in a particular situation, perhaps stuck in some way, wondering about what to do, ask yourself '*What would (mentor's name) do in this situation?*' The answer can be both surprising *and* informative.

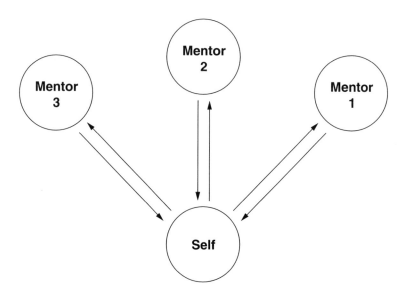

Figure 9.1:   Resonance pattern.

The values that drive our behaviours

Behaviours do not exist in a vacuum. If they did, they would be easy to change. But often they are not. How many times have you told someone to change their behaviour (e.g. stop smoking, lose weight, take exercise) and they did it immediately? I'll bet you can count the times on one hand! How many times have you told yourself that you were going to change your own behaviour, yet after a very short time you found yourself doing the same thing again? That's because our behaviours are closely, nay intimately, linked to our deeper values from which they arise. Changing behaviour becomes a lot easier when we chunk up the positive intention that underlies it to the value which drives it.

What we do in our everyday consultations, the behaviours that we wish we could do more of, and those we definitely want to do less of, are all driven by the values that govern them. And when we get that incongruence signal (you remember that one!), this is often a message that two or more of our values are in conflict. So what are typical values? Well, words such as honesty, integrity, truth, service, making a difference, achievement, learning, love, respect, honour and job satisfaction are all values words. They are the answer to the question *'Why?'*. And if you take any behaviour and keep chunking up by asking *'Why is that important to you?'* for each given answer, you will soon arrive at a values-based word.

For many of us, our values are not something we think about on an everyday basis, although our behaviours reflect them to all and sundry. Do you walk your talk? Do your espoused values, the ones you 'consciously' know and say you live up to, actually match up to your actions? It is often very useful to get some clarity about what your own individual core values really are.

Becoming more conscious of those values that are 'hidden away' in the depths, at your core, can be a very liberating experience. Finding out what is really important to you actually frees up your decision-making processes. It allows you to act more congruently. You can quickly identify where any conflict lies and more easily resolve it. You may end up feeling far less at odds with yourself, with more energy to do what you really want.

In the following exercises we are going to identify what is important to you in your work. We shall find out which values you move towards, and those that you move away from. These are very valuable exercises, so do them now in order to reap maximum benefit.

Exercise 22:   'Moving towards' values

1   Think of *three experiences* at work that for you were most rewarding. They need to be *significant ones*, ones that you might think of as the 'very stuff' of general practice, the *raison d'être* of why you do what you do. They may have occurred during consultations or home visits or at special clinics. Get three different types of experience in different contexts.

2   Now *relive each experience in turn*. Write down the key words and phrases that best describe them. Ask yourself '*What was important about that? What did that do for me? Why was that significant?*'. Keep going until you have a cluster of between four and eight words. These are your *core values*. If you need to, look at the examples of values words above.

3   Now compare and contrast each of these four to eight words. Which of them appear more important than others? If you could *rank them in a hierarchy*, what would that look like? Which would be at the top? What about second and third?

These are the 'hot' words that give direction and meaning to our lives in that particular context. By delving deeply in this way you open yourself up to having a more fulfilling life at work. Knowing your values can streamline your actions because you are simply 'being' and 'doing' *you* in a more effective way. Previously difficult decisions are much easier to handle. You may find yourself more in the flow in your consultations. Of course, you can repeat this exercise for all the other contexts of your life. What would that be like if you began to feel more aligned throughout your life? We shall have more dealings with alignment processes later.

We also have 'moving away from' values, the types of words, meanings and experiences that we want to avoid, such as embarrassment, shame, guilt, humiliation, blame, hurt and despair. In the next exercise we shall explore the types of situations that you would want to steer clear of. Knowing these 'down-side' values can also be useful in helping us to get what we want, and sometimes they can point us to specific areas that we need to work on.

Exercise 23: 'Moving away from' values

1 Choose *three consultation experiences that went badly*, ones that you wouldn't want to repeat. Choose different contexts; include a home visit as well as your consulting room.
2 Write a list of the *key words* and phrases that come up for you. Keep going until you have four to eight words that best fit the situations.
3 You don't need to rank them in order, but do *choose one that feels worse* than the rest.

These 'moving away from' values were possibly quite unpleasant to experience. If you are still feeling them in your body, get up, move around and change your state. It is good to know what you want to avoid as well as knowing what you want to move towards. This can give you added impetus when making decisions about what to do in difficult circumstances.

Occasionally, when you are doing this exercise, some of the values words can invoke quite negative states. Sometimes, even though the experience you chose was in the fairly recent past, you may have felt pulled back into much earlier times, perhaps to a time when you were much younger, perhaps into a memory of the first time you experienced that particular feeling. This simply lets you know that there is an as yet unhealed memory from your past that needs to be updated. You can use the processes from the last chapter, such as the strategy for *responding resourcefully to criticism*, or *re-editing past memories*, to help you. Remember that you are an adult now, and you were much younger back then, doing the best you could in the circumstances. From this perspective you can allow yourself to learn whatever was of importance in that event, and let go of any residual negative emotion.

Getting values met

Before ending this section, there are some useful questions to ask yourself about your values. Words like honesty, integrity, achievement, etc., may mean different things to different people. So how do you know that your values are being met? What rules do you have to let you know this? What behaviours are acceptable and fit your criteria?

If your rules are too strict, you might find yourself frustrated that your values are being met quite infrequently. This doesn't mean that you should change your values, but simply that you might want to check that your standards are not set frustratingly high. If every consultation needs to be perfect before you allow yourself to feel that you've achieved something worthwhile today, you might become quite exasperated. You can keep the value intact yet change the evidence required to meet it. For example, you could set your level at 80% rather than 100%, or you could start to look for the one small thing that you did in each consultation which achieved something worthwhile for the patient. You set the rules originally, and you may have forgotten why they were set that way. You can change them ... if you want to.

Lastly, you may want to ask yourself whether you are satisfied with the core values on your list. You may want to experiment with adding some new ones to which you aspire. You can do this by thinking what types of behaviour would satisfy that value and then imagining using these behaviours in the future. You can do a kind of mini-rehearsal in your mind's eye, perhaps imagining using these behaviours in three or four different situations over the next month. Remember that this is an experiment, and you can check in from time to time and see how it's fitting together.

Beyond belief

You will probably recall from Chapter 4 on gathering information that *beliefs* are our guiding principles and generalisations about the world at large, what we can and can't do, who we are and who it is possible for us to become. They are the operational rules through which our values are expressed in our day-to-day behaviours. Our beliefs are important to us. They are the reasons *why* we do what we do.

You probably have many beliefs about general practice. Beliefs about your patients and their behaviour patterns, beliefs about the environment in which you work and how the NHS functions, beliefs about the politics of healthcare provision, beliefs about what it means specifically for you to be a general practitioner or hospital doctor, beliefs about how well you provide your services, beliefs about your skills levels. As you think about some of these beliefs now, you will notice that some of them enhance what you do, opening up new possibilities. You may also notice how some of them limit you, like a straitjacket.

Yet up until now you may not have thought that your beliefs were change-able, that they could be updated, or you could even choose some new ones – but only if you really wanted to. Many people think that beliefs are pretty much fixed and unchanging. Yet a few moments' thought will let you know that this is not the case. Do you still believe in the Tooth Fairy? Or in Santa Claus? Do you still believe that the clothes, hairstyles and music fashions of your early teenage years are as pertinent now as they were then? What about your religious beliefs? As we grow, change and evolve throughout the various stages and transitions of our lives, many of our beliefs do the same. Of course, our core fundamental beliefs about ourselves may remain relatively fixed and stable over a long period of time. Yet our beliefs about the world and the people in it may change substantially, and sometimes unexpectedly, at short notice.

Robert Dilts thinks of beliefs as having *natural life cycles*. They come into being at times of openness to change, and they serve a useful purpose for that particular time-frame. Then, as you begin to doubt their effectiveness in changing times, they die off, to be replaced by updated beliefs. Of course, you can always harvest the best intentions of the old ones along the way. Then what you used to believe can be given a place in your own personal history museum of old beliefs, together with the Tooth Fairy *et al*!

As you think about all of your life transitions now, from childhood to adolescence, choosing a career, adulthood, marriage, raising a family, children flying the nest, and retirement, you will be aware of this cycle operating at many levels. *Beliefs change!* Respecting this cyclical wave of change, and utilising the process, can help you to let go of limiting beliefs and open up to life-enhancing ones.

Beliefs are self-fulfilling prophecies. Whether you believe something is true or not, you will generally get to prove yourself right each time. Because of cognitive dissonance, that feeling we get when the outside world seems at odds with our inner world, we will reject any incoming information that fails to conform to our belief structure. Or at best, we will fit the new material in such a way that it is organised by our current belief. Just think about it. How many times have you provided masses of data about the harmful effects of smoking and the patient says *'You know, you are absolutely right, I am going to change this behaviour immediately'*? Not likely!

It is very useful to take stock of your present beliefs about a particular context. This can provide you with information that affirms your sense of purpose. It can also identify areas where updating and even changing your beliefs would be useful. You might like to remind yourself of your values words first.

Exercise 24:   Your current beliefs inventory

Take a few moments to think about the following questions. Allow yourself the time for answers to come up. The ones on the surface will appear quickly, but the deeper-level ones may surprise you. Write down whatever arises, no matter how relevant or irrelevant it first appears.

1   Why are you a general practitioner? Why are you a hospital doctor? Why do you do this job?
2   What do you believe about yourself as a doctor? How should you behave? How should you not behave? Why?
3   What do you believe about the patients you serve? Are they deserving, or not? Why?
4   What are your strengths and characteristics? Why are those particular strengths important to you?
5   What do other people believe about you? Why do they believe this?
6   How easy is it for patients to change what they do? Why is that the case? How easy is it for you?

There are no right or wrong answers here. For each answer, allow yourself to get curious, and gently ask 'Why?' again until you have enough information to move on.

These are your current beliefs about yourself as a medical practitioner. You will probably have many answers that sit comfortably with you. There may also be some that do not, and some that you may wish to think about again, to update or even change. Yet before that, it is useful to ask some more questions, this time about your potential as a doctor – what you could accomplish if you really believed you could. Perhaps, as you look around you, there are other colleagues who have different beliefs from you. What would it be like to try them on for size?

Exercise 25:   Your potential beliefs

Once again, think about the following questions, mull them over, and note down your answers.

1   What beliefs would you really like to have about yourself as a general practitioner? And as a hospital doctor? Which ones could you try on? Who could you model?
2   If you really were fulfilling your potential as a doctor, what would be happening? What would you be doing instead? Why?

3 What kind of feedback from patients and colleagues makes you feel good? What could this lead you to believe about your potential?
4 What beliefs about your patients might serve you (and them) better?
5 What stops you from implementing these beliefs right now?

These questions will have given you some ideas not only of what currently limits you, but also of how you would like to be instead. If you were to be the *best you* that you could possibly be in your present post, which belief would you like to update? And what would you like to replace it with?

Look through your list of current beliefs and choose one that limits you. Look at your potential beliefs and select one that you would like to strengthen and have in its place. Now go through the following belief change process exercise (opposite).

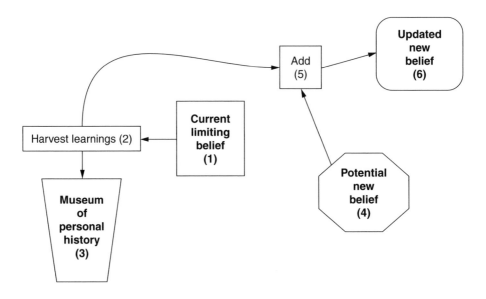

Figure 9.2: Belief change process.

Exercise 26: Updating your beliefs

For this exercise, lay out two chairs side by side, and sit down on one of them. Or if you prefer to stand, mark out two positions on the floor and stand in one of them. You might like to have a colleague lead you through the exercise.

1   Think about your *current limiting belief*. How does it limit you? Why do you want to change it? What does it prevent you from achieving? Write down your answers if you want to.

2   Now ask yourself how that limiting belief may have served you well in the past. What function did it perform? What is the *positive intention* behind it? What could you *harvest* from it? Note down your answers.

3   In your mind's eye, imagine placing the remains of this limiting belief in your *museum of personal history*. As you do this with a sense of reverence for what was, take what you have harvested with you as you get up and move to the other chair.

4   Now think about the *potential belief* you would like to embody. Why is this important to you? What are the benefits of embracing it now? How do your *harvested learnings fit* with this new belief?

5   Watch yourself in your mind's eye as you try this updated new belief on for size. See how it alters to give you a *'best fit'*. Watch yourself go through a day, a week, a month, noticing and incorporating any feedback.

6   When you are *certain* that it fits like a glove, imagine stepping inside the image, seeing through those eyes, hearing the responses, and experiencing what it feels like. When you are ready, stand up and take this *embodied* belief out into the world with you.

We are always changing beliefs, at some level, throughout our lives. Usually this happens outwith our conscious awareness. Occasionally it can happen after a significant emotional event, both positive *and* negative. However, the vacuum created at those times may be filled by any belief that 'happens along'. Does it therefore still seem somewhat odd to you that it is possible to choose which beliefs you want to have? One of the many fruits of NLP is that by modelling the process of natural belief change, we can encourage ourselves not only to utilise it to make the changes that we want, but also to 'step into' the beliefs of excellent communicators.

Rediscovering vision and purpose

Back at the beginning of this chapter's introduction I told you a little of the things that were going on in my life around the time when I was deciding to pursue a medical career. What got *you* into medicine? Why did you choose this career pathway? What burning ambitions did you have? What was calling out in you to be fulfilled? You may not have any answers to these questions yet, but mull them over in your mind.

You might want to think about it this way. Purpose is all about expressing our deepest sense of self – who we really are in the world. As such, it grows out of and connects our past to our present, on into our future. Our goals, which we may or may not achieve, are future-oriented expressions of our expectations. However, they spring from and are nourished by our sense of purpose, which has a here-and-now timeless quality to it. We may or may not know what that purpose is. Yet most people, when connected to it, recognise it as a whole body and mind experience, a sense of feeling complete congruence with their life's direction – a resounding and unequivocal *'Yes!'*

We connect our sense of purpose through our everyday roles in life, express-ing our closely held beliefs and values in our daily activities. We are congruent through all levels of our being. We may have a great sense of fulfilment in what we do. Yet many of us do not have this sense of inner congruence. We feel con-flict caused by differing goals and demands. We do *this* today, and its opposite *that* tomorrow. We may have a vague sense of heading somewhere, yet wonder if it's a dead-end street. We may even begin to believe that what do lacks any coherent purpose, other than as a means of survival. We are purposeless.

So how do you feel as you read this? Congruent or incongruent? Practical or impractical? Airy-fairy stuff and nonsense or complete sense?

Personally I believe that fulfilling our purpose, being the best we can be, and expressing that through our chosen roles, gives an immense feeling of satisfaction – a satisfaction with which we can look back on our lives and say *'I counted, I made a difference, I lived up to the best of my expectations'*.

So far in this chapter we have considered how we are at our best, explored our values at work, and delved into our core beliefs. Now is the time to ask the kind of questions that can begin to connect all of that to our deeper *sense of purpose*, and the kind of edifying *vision* of our future potential that can draw us like a magnet. There is a sense in which this goes beyond ourselves, *beyond identity*, to incorporate other people in our sphere, our wider community. For some there may well be a religious or spiritual component – a feeling of con-necting to the underlying pattern that unifies all.

Exercise 27:   Exploring purpose

1   What are the things that you are *really passionate about?* At work? At home? Your hobbies? Choose something in one of these contexts that *really interests you*, about which you are enthusiastic, switched on and alive to. Something that *really involves you totally*. You could choose your important 'moving towards' values words and their experiences already identified.

2   As you *immerse yourself* in these thoughts and feelings, ask yourself 'What is really important about this? What does this really do for me? What does this get for me?'. You will recognise that these *questions 'chunk up'* to higher levels of personal significance.

3   For each answer that you get, ask the same questions of that. *Keep chunking up* until you can go no further. You may even get to a point where there are no words that adequately describe your experience. At this stage you are very close to *discovering the purpose* that underlies your passion.

4   Think about what was important to you in your childhood and teens. What were you immersed in? What were you fascinated by? Are you still connected to that today or has it been somehow 'lost' in the mists of time? As you *reconnect now*, ask yourself the chunking up questions again.

5   As you allow yourself simply to be with those feelings, images and sounds, let yourself wonder about the pattern that connects, the *underlying purpose*. Who else is connected in this way? How does this interact with the larger community to which you belong?

Of course, an exercise like this is not something you can simply do in a few minutes and then have 'the answer'! You have started a process that will continue, perhaps over several days, maybe for longer, mostly out of conscious awareness, although perhaps with a significant 'Aha' now and again. It is as if the answers are revealed, they come bubbling up to the surface. Resist the attempt to make logical or rational sense of them. Let them speak for themselves. Listen to your *calling*.

You may find that as the dust settles, a clearer picture begins to emerge, a kind of *vision* that, with your *sense of purpose* at its root, shows you a path towards fruition. For some people this is expressed through fairly concrete images of the types of actions that will take place – what they will actually be doing. For others, the images may be more metaphorical or even symbolic.

Whatever form the images take, go with the flow in the knowledge that you can revisit this exercise from time to time.

For those of you who are interested in exploring this area in more depth, I suggest reading *Living Awareness,* by Peter Wrycza.

Aligning the levels

We have gathered a lot of information in this chapter, and you may be asking yourself *'What on earth is this all for? Where is he heading to with all this "stuff"?'.* We have certainly gone from the more superficial issues of what states you are in when you are *being your best self,* peeling back the layers of the onion skin of *values and beliefs,* to reach the central kernel of *purpose.* And you have found out a great deal about yourself in the process.

When you look at people who are really in the flow of life, enjoying the journey, achieving major and minor outcomes with apparent ease, making a real difference, yet graceful with it, undulating with the ups and downs yet keeping their balance, you may wonder *'How is this possible? How are they able to do what they do? What is their secret? And is it available to me?'.*

I don't know if you have come across people like this in your everyday life. Or whether there is someone you look up to and respect, who lives life in this way. Perhaps someone you've read about, seen in the media or heard on the radio. When you examine these people closely, and model them, as some in NLP have done, one thing stands out clearly. They all seem to have aligned themselves in such a way that their daily actions and interactions are a direct expression of their *purpose and vision* which, through their *beliefs and values,* infuse and inform every *behaviour.* They have a degree of congruence that radiates from every pore, and often simply being in their presence can have a calming, almost healing effect.

The *levels alignment process,* based on the work of Robert Dilts, can start to bring those almost disparate parts of ourselves into a greater degree of congruence and inner harmony. It joins together all that we have been working on so far in this chapter, in a way that allows its fuller expression in our various day-to-day contexts. Initially I suggest that you take your everyday consulting as the first context with which to work. You can explore other areas of your life in the same way in due course.

Find yourself some space and lay out six areas on the floor as shown in Figure 9.3. Allow the distance of one step to separate each of the circles from the next. You can do this exercise yourself or with a colleague to guide you.

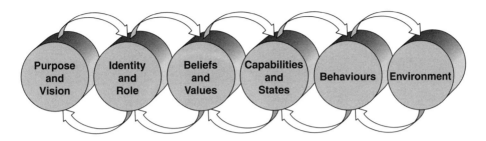

Figure 9.3: Logical levels alignment.

Exercise 28: Levels alignment process

1 *Stand in the Environment circle* and imagine being in your consulting room. See the layout of the room in your mind's eye, hear any sounds (e.g. the hum of your computer) and feel what it's like to be there. Think of the people who come in and out. Is this a morning or afternoon session?

2 Take a *step back into the Behaviour circle*. What is it that you are actually doing there? What are your movements? Your posture? Your gestures? Do you feel balanced? What does your voice sound like? Which part of your body does it seem to arise from? Your nose, mouth, throat, chest, abdomen? If you were completely balanced, what would that feel like?

3 *Step back into Capability and States*. What skills are you using? Rapport skills? Diagnostic skills? Computer skills? Other skills? How are you communicating? Fire off *your consulting flow anchor*. As it builds, add in *being your best self*.

4 *Step back into Beliefs and Values*. What is important to you about general practice or hospital medicine? What do you believe about yourself as a doctor? What would you like to believe about yourself? *What is worthwhile about what you do?* What do you believe about patients? What would you like to believe about them? Think of your 'moving towards' values. Name the word and get in touch with the feeling.

5 *Step back into Identity and Role*. Who are you as a doctor? What is your role, your function? What do you want to accomplish? What is *your vision, your metaphor, your symbol?* What are you *called* to do? How does being a doctor *connect with all of these things?*

6   *Step back Beyond Identity.* Think of how you are connected to your patients, partners, community and beyond that. What is your *sense of purpose?* Who else might share that with you? You may have religious or spiritual beliefs. *Get in touch with all of this* as a deeply felt mind–body experience.

7   Now, taking all of what is *beyond identity, step forward into Identity and Role.* Let this *sense of connectedness infuse* your role, enriching it and blending with it. Let it mix with *Vision and Calling, informing* your metaphor, your symbol.

8   Now take all of this new blending, this enhanced sense of self, and *step forward into Beliefs and Values.* Again let it mix and re-infuse, *changing and rearranging.* What is important now? What do you believe now? What do you value now?

9   Take all of this further enhancing and *step forward into Capabilities and States.* How does this greater depth enhance your skills? Your diagnostics? Your communication? Fire off *your consulting flow anchor, and being your best self.* Luxuriate as everything continues to *mix all together.*

10 *Take all of that* and *step forward into Behaviour.* What are you doing now? What are your actions? How are you moving now? How does your voice sound? What if you imagined being *completely balanced? Enriching yourself.*

11 *Now, bringing all aspects of this with you, step forward into Environment.* Be in your place of consulting. See the images, hear the sounds and experience the feelings. Notice how all of this gives you greater depth, greater clarity and a greater sense of being in the *right place,* at the *right time,* for the *right reasons.* Simply allow yourself a few moments to *integrate all of this in the way that best fits for you now.*

This exercise links what is really important to us deep down inside to our everyday life. This can have quite profound effects, especially if we have been feeling out of sorts, or 'out of sync' with the world. You remember those times when you felt as if you were going through the motions, fed up with what you were doing, wondering if you were in the right job? Trying to get on with things as you 'survived' the latest onslaught from the corridors of power? Well, at those times, you can let that feeling of being at odds with yourself and the world be the signal that it's time to do the *level alignment process.* Time to take your destiny out of the lap of the gods, and into your own hands. And *now's* the time.

Building your compelling future

Now that we have all of the above 'under our belt', we need to turn our attention to the future. Does your future happen in the way that you want it to? Or does it happen *to* you instead? And what's more, is it really *your* future that happens? Or someone else's plan for it? The processes that we have covered so far will have unleashed a degree of inner congruence such that you may find your goals becoming more easily achievable. When what you want comes from and resonates with a place of inner alignment, your outcomes become a more natural expression of who you really are. They flow! And if what you want doesn't fit, you will more readily recognise the feeling of incongruence that lets you know either to do something different or to change your outcome in some way. A great feedback mechanism.

Way back, if you can remember that far back, in Chapter 4 on gathering information, we laid out the criteria for a *well-formed outcome*. You know, *stated in positives, started and maintained by you, sensory-based evidence, consequences and by-products*, and *ecology concerns*. And in general that is a good way to start off the process of getting what you want.

However, one thing I have learned over the years is that goal *setting* is not the same as goal *getting*! The well-formed outcome process is a good way of setting up your goals, ensuring that they fit with you, your sense of self, and the important people in your life. However, actually reaching your goals, achieving your outcome, may require an additional process. Some time ago I came across the notion of setting up and sequencing your own internal states in such a way that they automatically help you to achieve your desired outcome. I put this on the back-burner, forgetting about it for a while, until I more recently looked at the idea again, simplified the process somewhat and experimented with it in my own way.

This book is the fruit of that process. I had been thinking of writing a book like this since 1995. I had lots of thoughts, a few scribblings, but no real output. I never seemed to get round to it. It was like a dream without a deadline, almost as if it had been parked in the back corner of the furthest recesses of my mind. Now I don't know if you can resonate with that experience. Perhaps you have dreams that are not as yet fulfilled. How many times have you set yourself a goal that fizzled out like a damp squib? Things that you really wanted to do, yet they didn't materialise. All I know is that, within a few short days of running my outcome through this process, I was full of energy, itching to get started! And that enthusiasm has sustained me through the five short months it's taken so far. Plus working full-time as a GP, and all the other things I do. Also getting it published at the first attempt! Coincidence? Possibly, although I think not!

At first glance you may think that this whole business seems rather odd. We are going to be externalising thought processes that are usually well out of conscious awareness. And of course it all usually happens automatically, at the speed of thought which, if you think about it, is pretty fast. It might seem quite daft to lay it all out in the way you're going to do this. You might initially even feel that only a ninny would act like this. Yet the people who get their outcomes met successfully time and time again have a formula, an internal strategy. They weren't born like that. They learned it along the way, although not necessarily as easily as you're about to.

You are now going to get the opportunity to own it for yourself, if you really want to. Only you can decide whether to participate fully, or not. Yet if you really think about it, anything less than fully acquiring this strategy just won't get you the outcomes that you deserve.

The really good thing about this process is that you have, in your own mind, all of the main parts pre-assembled. It is simply a case of *sequencing* what you already know, a bit like joining the dots. Once learned, it will streamline quickly so that just thinking it through will start off the action. Again I suggest that you lay out on the floor the spaces shown in Figure 9.4. Do the exercise with a partner or colleague.

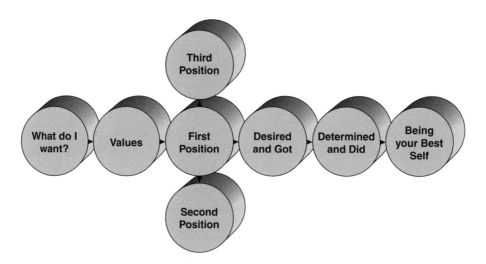

Figure 9.4: Compelling futures.

Exercise 29:   Building your compelling future

Part One: setting up

Between each step of the following process, *ensure that you break state cleanly* before going on to do the next step.

1   Set out a space for what you want, your *outcome*, but leave it blank for now.
2   Step inside the *Values space* and remember each of your 'moving towards' values. Reconnect to each experience so that you have a full sense of them all before stepping out.
3   In *First Position*, step inside and simply be yourself. In *Second Position*, imagine being someone else who will be affected by your achieving your outcome. In *Third Position*, imagine being the fly-on-the-wall observer of an achieved outcome.
4   Step into *Desired and Got*. Think of times when you really, really wanted something, you got it, and looking back on it, it is still *a good decision* today. This could be something you wanted to have (a car, a holiday, etc.), a skill you wanted to develop and did, or something you wanted to be, and evolved into. With these examples in mind, go *back before* you achieved the outcome, when you're feeling the want, the desire. Focus on that feeling as you make the picture big, bright and colourful, turn up the sound, and *at the peak of the feeling step out of the circle*, leaving the feelings inside.
5   Now step into *Determined and Did*. Think of times when you were absolutely determined to do something, you did it, and it is still *a good decision* today, looking back on it. It could be studying to pass an exam, an experience from sport, or a short-term or long-term objective in which you succeeded. Go *back before* the achievement and get in touch with the feeling of determination. Focus on the feeling as you make the picture big, bright, colourful and close, turn up the sounds and *at the peak of the feeling step out of the circle*, leaving the feelings inside.
6   In *Being your Best Self*, step in and fire off your previously set anchor. Really build the feelings up and, at the peak, step out of the circle.

Congratulations! You have finished the first part.

Setting things up correctly is always the most important part of any venture. It is well worthwhile spending just as much time now as will allow the process to streamline as you do it. You have now set up a template through which you can put any well-formed outcome – large or small, major or minor. I suggest that you practise by taking some fairly simple outcomes through it first. Leave your most important life's dreams until a little later!

Exercise 30: Building your compelling future

Part Two: goal getting

1 *Choose an outcome* that you want for yourself. One that relates to your work context. One that you have already put through the well-formed outcome process, and that you know fits. *Step inside the 'What Do I Want?' circle as you think about it.*

2 *Holding that thought, step into the Values space.* Notice how this outcome fits with those deeper aspects of yourself. Search for your *feeling of congruence*, the signal that lets you know it's all right. If you keep getting your incongruence signal instead, step out. This means that the goal, as formulated, does not fit with your deeper sense of self. This is valuable information that lets you know you need to alter the goal in some way so that it does fit. *Only move on to the next stage when you have a congruent feeling that your goal fits.*

3 *Step into First Position,* imagining that you have achieved your goal. You are 'trying on' success to see and hear how it feels. Then *step into Second Position,* and through the eyes of another, see that you as he or she succeeds. *Step into Third Position* and watch the success as a neutral observer. Glean any new information from all of these positions to update your goal as necessary, *ensuring that you have your congruence signal* before moving on.

4 When you are ready, *step into Desired and Got.* Picture your outcome as something that you really, really want. Make it big, bright and colourful, coming closer. Turn up the sound. *Intensify your feelings of wanting as you look at it.*

5 When you are ready, *step into Determined and Did.* Picture your outcome as something that you are really, really determined to do. Make it big, bright and colourful, coming closer. Turn up the sound. *Intensify your feelings of determination as you look at it.*

6 When you are ready, *step into Being your Best Self.* As you experience those feelings, imagine that you are now at the time of *successfully achieving your outcome.* Bask in the feelings of success. Hear the sounds of success. Look around you noticing what else is happening. Notice the date. *When you are ready, step out of the circle. Leave the image of your success inside the circle, now a dissociated picture, with the date and time of completion indelibly stamped on the bottom!*

Having completed this exercise, you may still be wondering whether this is a crazy kind of thing to do, or not. Really the only thing you can do is to *give it a go*, and test it thoroughly by using all kinds of outcomes – large, small, important and not so important. Modify it to suit yourself. You can actually shorten the process if you want to. If you are certain, having asked the well-formed outcome questions, that this is what you want, you can simply do the last three steps instead. Take your outcome into the *Desired and Got, Determined and Did* and *Being your Best Self* circles, with your completion date attached.

As you think about it now, you will see how this process helps to both pull you and push you towards your goal. The combination of these two feelings, push and pull, connected in this way seems to allow you to glide effortlessly to your outcome. It is important to end up with a dissociated picture of your having achieved your goal. Why is this? Well, it lets your mind know that you have not yet achieved it, and every time you think about that image you will experience a strong, almost magnetic attraction to it. Leaving it as an associated picture, as if you're there fully inside it, fools your brain into thinking that you have achieved it already. This actually reduces the attraction, making it less compelling.

Congruence about what you want in a particular context is vital. If part of you wants one thing, and part of you wants another, that is a sure-fire recipe for inner conflict. Or worse! You will feel torn about what to do, in two or more minds. You may even successfully achieve the outcome yet feel strangely unfulfilled, perhaps as if you are 'going through the motions', at odds with yourself. You can treat this like a negotiation between the two parts, chunking up to find the higher intention that lies behind each part. Then, having established agreement at this level, you can chunk back down to a practical, shared outcome that fits with both parties. This will then be a *congruent*, agreed goal about which you can feel really good at all levels of your self.

Enjoy experimenting. Happy outcomes!

Continuing developing personally

We have now achieved the outcome of reaching this chapter's ending. It has been quite different to the other chapters in the book. This has been a chapter specifically about *you*. Too often we spend our time thinking about and helping other people, often to our own neglect. This chapter has been about redressing the balance. The focus has been on delving beneath your surface exterior to unearth the gold nuggets that may have remained hidden and dormant for too long – the kind of inner wealth that can provide the foundation for what you do with the rest of your career.

And you can, of course, continue your personal development in many ways. There are several books in the Bibliography that can help you on your way. Tape-assisted learning may suit some. Courses and seminars can give you the kind of time out that is needed not only to do these exercises, but also to contemplate your future directions. They can provide the type of environment that can both sustain you and allow accumulative change. In ending, however, I reiterate my own belief, which is that *personal development* is not only about acquiring new skills, important as these are. It is also about *unlocking the potential that is already there*, and channelling it within your own definition of a worthwhile direction in which to move forward. So finally, consider this.

When you are *being your best self*, you really flow, life happens spontaneously, you cope, even enjoy it, and ride the waves easily to the shore. This is a nourishing, health-giving state of mind and body. When you uncover your *values*, what is important about what you do, you get the chance to begin to line up with some very powerful forces for sustained endeavour. Your *beliefs*, which act as your *values'* operational rules, help to channel these energies in a worthwhile direction. And you the person, a unique *identity*, presently in a *role*, perhaps even a *calling*, as a general practitioner or as a hospital doctor, can set the course with a compelling *vision*. Something that attracts you and that propels you forwards. Something that connects you at your deepest and highest levels to an overarching *sense of purpose*. Something that moves you *beyond identity*, into a larger world, a bigger frame, a broader breadth, a deeper depth. Something that makes life worth living. Your *compelling future*.

CHAPTER 10

Before we finish ...

Introduction

Finishing, ending or completing a project brings with it a certain set of feelings. These could be feelings of satisfaction, the kind of repleteness that accompanies a delicious meal and the ambience of pleasant surroundings. Or perhaps basking in the afterglow of knowing that you have succeeded in an important endeavour. Savouring the moment like breathing in the heady aroma of a fine wine. Maybe there is a sense of relief, or even release. A time to gather your thoughts together contemplatively, wondering where all of this will begin to take you now, what new pathways are emerging, and which direction you will take.

And yet before that, we also need to consider that there is of course a fallacy about endings, an untruth about finishing, a lie to completion. Because what we are really experiencing is a feeling *about* a body of knowledge that we think we have understood. And understanding is merely that feeling we get when we have everything tucked away in the right boxes, the right compartments, the right intellectual categories. And the problem with understanding and completion is that, unless we are careful, very careful, it can get in the way of future learning.

Eventually you are going to close this book, yet the subject matter is not a closed book. If you cast your mind back over the past 50 years or so of medical developments, the one constant is that change is always taking place. You only have to look at the field of transplant medicine, joint replacement technology and the developments in molecular biology to see that what was once fact has been replaced with new and updated fact. Sometimes there has been a complete paradigm shift, to use a much-abused phrase. We do not know where the boundaries, the limits, the ceilings lie. In NLP there is always more to learn, much more. And because we don't yet know what is possible, now and in the future, we need to keep an open mind, a Zen mind, a beginner's mind.

So when you get that feeling of completion, of finishing, of understanding, recognise it for what it really is – simply a breathing space, a resting point, a well-earned break. A signal that your internal map has had a reasonable amount of updating and expanding, for the moment. Time for some recreation, refreshment, revitalisation, prior to engaging in the ever ongoing upward spiral of learning once again.

And now is the time to begin to think about your future possibilities. Time to speculate about just how this book, full of information and skills, will best serve you. Time to consider the consequences and ramifications of your successfully using this material, not only today, but also tomorrow, next week, next month, next year, perhaps in five years or maybe ten years from now, or more.

But just before that ...

Mapping across and updating maps

Way back in Chapter 1, I outlined the Calgary–Cambridge model with its five stages and 70 individual skill sets, built on academic, scientifically based communication research. Over the course of *Consulting with NLP* we have systematically mapped across the pertinent NLP approaches, skills and techniques to each phase. In this section we shall not only show the individual elements of this mapping, but we shall also expand this into an NLP-based consulting model.

Box 10.1: NLP meets Calgary–Cambridge key skills

1	*Initiating the consultation*	• Flowing consulting state and break state anchors
		• Developing rapport, matching, mirroring
		• Opening statements, backtracking, agenda setting
		• Calibrating non-verbals, yes-sets
		• Psychogeography of room set-up
2	*Gathering information*	• Meta-programs, unconscious filters
		• Meta-model questioning
		• Beliefs and expectations; verbal/non-verbal expression
		• Use of softeners
		• Well-formed outcomes and miracle question

3	*Building the relationship*	• Rapport at the higher logical levels
		• Perceptual positions and meta-mirror
		• Peripheral vision state, relaxed consulting
		• Congruence and incongruence
		• Eye-accessing cues
		• Structuring with meta-comments
4	*Explanation and planning*	• Verbal reframing of beliefs
		• Meta-programs and convincers for information transfer
		• Chunking skills, induction, deduction, metaphor
		• Negotiating skills
		• Languaging with Milton model and SCORE model
		• Non-verbal placing of relevant information
5	*Closing the session*	• Backtracking and summarising
		• 'What-if' scenarios and future rehearsals
		• Chaining consultations together
		• Breaking rapport elegantly
		• Looking after yourself
		• Reflecting in four quadrants

We can of course look at this from a slightly different perspective, which will also add in the various skill sets from chapters such as that on *special situations*. This forms the kind of foundation whereby not only can you use the model for consulting more effectively, but you can also begin to experiment actively with using NLP therapeutically, for patients and yourself, if you've not already done so.

Figure 10.1 illustrates the flowing nature of *Consulting with NLP*, together with the essential skills for each phase.

1   *Your state*: Remember to *break state* after each consultation and get into your *flowing consulting state* with *peripheral vision* throughout. It's really important to *look after yourself*, because the better you feel the better you will perform.

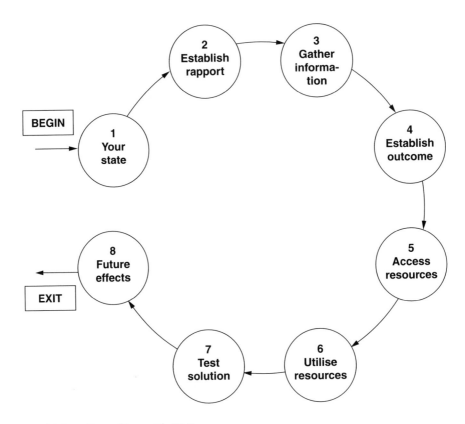

Figure 10.1: Consulting with NLP.

2   *Rapport*: This is the *sine qua non* of effective consulting. You can *match and mirror* at the level of physiology and voice, plus the higher *logical levels* of capability, beliefs and values, and identity. Use your *second-position* skills to further develop genuine empathy. Continue to maintain rapport throughout the consultation.

3   *Gathering information*: From their first utterances you will notice the patient's *meta-program* patterns. Allowing an *opening statement* together with *backtracking* and *yes-sets* establishes today's *agenda*. You can, with *softeners*, use *meta-model* questions to enquire sensitively about *beliefs and expectations*. Of course, continuing to *calibrate* to the patient's verbal and non-verbal responses is vital.

4   *Outcomes*: What is it that they (and you) really want? Use the *well-formed outcome* criteria and the *miracle question* to delineate further and dove-tail these together. Are you planning to *chain consultations* for multiple outcomes?

5   *Access resources*: Which resources does the patient need and at what *logical level*? What are the leverage points for change? Do they need investigation or onward referral? Do you need to do some *verbal reframing* of beliefs? Or do you just need to explain things using their *meta-programs*? Would they benefit from accessing and applying a *resource state anchor*? Perhaps the *meta-mirror*?

6   *Utilise resources*: Which ones are you actually going to bring to bear on the current situation? And how do you *chunk* the information appropriately? Could you think of applying the various *NLP patterns and resources* that you have learned in other chapters (on special situations and developing personally)? Ensure that you are using their *convincer channel* to best effect, together with the *Milton model, SCORE model* and *negotiating* as required.

7   *Test solution*: So have you successfully reached your joint outcomes? *Calibration* skills and *yes-sets* are important here. If there is not a significant change in the patient's condition, you may need to *do something different*.

8   *Future effects*: How will what you have done today generalise and be effective in the future? Have you built a *compelling future*? Have you covered all the '*what-if*' scenarios and *future rehearsal* of actions? What are the next steps?

This eight-step model has given excellent results in many fields of application over the years. Utilising it in everyday consultations will allow you to make the most of every patient contact. And not only that. You will also gain immeasurable benefits for all concerned. But of course, as always, only you can decide whether to use it now.

What would happen if ...

Just before we finish, before we cross the line, there are still a few things left to address. What if you were to ask yourself some useful questions? How might that be of benefit right now? There are many questions that you could ask, and many ways of asking them. But if you really think about it now, what would happen if you were to apply this material in your everyday consulting? Just exactly how will you be doing things differently from now on? And in what way will your current and future patients reap the benefits of your integrating skills? These are the kinds of questions that we shall be considering in this section. A sort of '*What if you could ... ?*'.

At this moment in time, I'd like you to cast your mind back to the beginnings of this book, and to the various chapters and sections that you have come through so far. Some of the things you have learned already will spring to the forefront of your mind, while others will be nestling in the background, operating at a much lower level of conscious awareness. Yet what are the things that have really struck a chord with you? What approaches look right to you? What in particular gives you that good feeling – you know, the one that feels intuitively correct? Which of the areas have made complete sense so far?

Think of this now as you do the next exercise.

Exercise 31:   What would happen if ... ?

1   Look back through the book and *choose five areas* that stand out for you. The five particular areas that would *make the most difference* for you if you incorporated them into your future behaviours. Write them down.

2   For each area, *get really specific* about what it is that you are doing differently. As you *picture yourself*, notice how you move, walk, talk and gesture differently. *Listen* to the sound of your voice and to your words as you say them. Adjust your images and sounds until they give you the best kind of *feelings inside.*

3   Take each area in turn. *Notice now how others are responding differently* to you in each scenario. Look at the expressions on their faces, and their body language. Listen to their replies, their words and their voice tones. Notice their different behaviours.

4   Now settle back in the theatre of your mind's eye. *Allow these five scenarios to coalesce* in a kind of collage. It doesn't matter whether you *see them clearly* or not. Just pretend that you do. Imagine that the skills from each area are *merging, integrating.* As this happens, *step inside*, try them on for size, feel the feelings and luxuriate in them.

5   Let's go for a *journey through time.* Take all of these feelings and imagine that you are in *next week*, in the place where you work, a particular context. Look around, and notice how things are different. Now take the feelings into *next month, then 3 months from now, then 6 months.* Imagine going out to *1 year, 2 years, 5 years, and more.* Notice what has changed, and enjoy yourself.

6   And from that point, beyond 5 years, turn and *look all the way back towards now.* Sense how *your skills have developed over this time*, connecting together, perhaps in ways that you're not yet fully aware of. Allow yourself to come back to the here and now, only as quickly as *you're integrating everything* in your best interests.

This exercise is very useful for seeding changes into the future direction you want to take. It's almost as if, by thinking about it in this way, you are creating a natural, self-fulfilling pathway of developing excellence. You might want to wonder what would happen if you were to revisit this exercise again, choosing five different areas with which to work. What if you could sow these seeds into other life contexts as well? What changes for the better would then ensue?

And they all lived happily …

Once she had reached, in fact overachieved, exceeded her goal of 125 kg, a strange thing happened. She described it as if she had an internal knowingness, a kind of inner certainty that things were going to be different now. And it wasn't as if she did a great deal that was really different. In fact, she was hard-pushed to describe what was new. It was just that, automatically, gradually and without much effort, her weight started to drift down. And not only has she lost well in excess of 10% of her body weight for the first time ever, it is as if weight is no longer the issue it once was. She feels more settled, more confident, and more able to 'be myself'.

And it was only by following Erickson, by learning from his experiences, that I chose to use this superficially at least, somewhat contrary to logic approach. Yet deeper down, below the surface, you will find that it fits the situation beautifully, like a glove. The deep structure of this intervention was to 'prescribe the symptom'. All her life this patient had tried to lose weight, yet instead imperceptibly gained it. By reversing the process, by prescribing what was happening anyway (a weight gain), yet this time with conscious application, the tables were turned. And if you can, by conscious choice, make something worse (e.g. gain weight), the inherent assumption is that you now have the degree of control necessary to make it better (e.g. lose weight). You have choice. And my patient didn't have too long to wait for the result.

Of course, Erickson was a master, if not the master, of noticing fine detail. His students asked him how he had known, in such a short period of time, that his beautiful blonde in the two-piece suit, with stockings that went all the way up, was really a man dressed up in woman's clothes. And he replied that whilst on the surface he had appeared to make that diagnosis very quickly, at a deeper level, it had sprung from a skill that he was continuing to develop all his life. And his students asked just what that meant.

So Erickson told them a little about developing, from child, to adolescent, to adult and beyond. And he told them that it was so very important to pay attention to all of the significant things that you can see and hear all around you. Because he had noticed, in developing, that girls, even before they had actually developed breasts, would reach out in a particular way with their hands. It was as if, even at that early prepubertal stage, their hand and arm would make a circular detour around a breast that had still to develop fully. Yet in their mind, the patterns were already set. And as for the blonde, he had reached straight across to remove the lint, *with no diversion at all!* He agreed that yes, it was a small, almost tiny detail. Yet actually it was the pivotal point in therapy, establishing a deep rapport. Hence his adage to all students, young and old: *'Take all the time you need to develop your ability to notice fine distinctions.'*

Some three weeks after he had accused me of reverse psychology, looking terribly confused as he left the consulting room, my rock-climbing smoker and I had a chance encounter. At the time, one of my daughters was taking her first swimming lessons at the local pool. I had arrived early to pick her up, and it just so happened that he worked there as a pool attendant. It was raining outside, and I was glad to be going inside where it was more comfortable. I noticed him at the far end and remembered how he had polarity responded both into and out of trance. I had an inward chuckle or two. Then he noticed me out of the corner of his eye and slowly began to move in my direction.

He gradually sidled up to me, although I continued to have a semi-glazed look – you know, that feeling you can sometimes get when light sparkles on water and reflects into your eyes. He stood alongside me, and as I looked out ahead I could see him out of the corner of my eye. I said nothing and he shifted a little, from one foot to the other. He had a big grin on his face, and I could sense that he was eager to tell me something. Still I waited, saying nothing, not even giving a nod of acknowledgement. Eventually the silence got too much for him. You know what it's like when tension builds up inside and there's something that you just have to do. You have to get it out, get on with it!

However, for some reason, time seemed to slow down, as if everything was moving in *sl-o-o-o-w* motion. I was reminded, somewhat strangely, of one of Clint Eastwood's films, one of the Westerns. I just can't recall the name of it. A gunfight of some sort. But I remember there was a pocket watch, and some music that played the same tune *over and over and over again. Monotonously.* Getting *slower ... and slower ... and slower ...* as the mechanical spring wound down. And the *slower* it went, the more you knew that soon ... very soon ... it was going to *stop. Completely.* And then, the action would start.

He could bear it no longer. He turned to me and blurted out *'I've been stopped smoking now for three whole weeks, no cravings, and I've never, ever felt better in my life. What do you think of that then, Mr so-called Doctor?'*

So I turned to face him, and looked him directly in the eye. An intense sort of look. He flinched a little, yet held my gaze. I opened my mouth to speak, and I said:

*You know, I'm not ... (head nods) ... **absolutely certain** ... but I really don't think that ... **these changes you've made ... and all the good feelings you've got ... are really ... and I mean really ... going to last ... for the rest ... of your life.***

And every time I saw him after that I would make a special point of going up to him and asking if he had started smoking again. And when he replied *'No!'*, with a cheeky grin, I would say it was *only a question of time*, and march off. And he didn't know, he really didn't know, and I never, ever told him, that I had used his polarity response to help him to get the changes he wanted.

Concluding

Have you noticed that once you get past halfway, and especially after three-quarters, things just seem to accelerate exponentially right up to the end? Like a great movie that you have been waiting to see. Once you're there, engrossed, identified with the characters and deeply involved in the plot, then time just flies by. And afterwards, when all's said and done, you think back on a tremendous experience, time well spent, a sense of satisfaction. We have covered a great deal of ground and material in *Consulting with NLP*, and if you have gained anything near as much as I have through writing it, then I hope that leaves you well pleased, yet still wondering about more.

So as you think about it now, what is it exactly that you have gained for yourself?

As the brave hospital doctor, having made it all the way through, what is it that you will be highlighting in the days to come? What are the particular skills that will make your task easier? How will you be handling potentially challenging situations differently now?

And as the health professional, nurse, counsellor, psychologist or PAM personnel, just what is it that is going to allow you to be ahead of your field? What information have you already adapted to fit your circumstances? What more is yet to come? What's next?

What about you, the medical student? Have you begun to realise just exactly how task and relationship fit synergistically together? What if you were to continue developing your expertise over the many years of your newly starting career? Just how good a doctor do you really want to be?

Perhaps as a retainer or part-time doctor you have already found yourself juggling with increasing ease. Perhaps you have found your niche in the team. Maybe you have also developed a better sense of your own confidence. Now what if you were to allow that feeling to spread into other areas of your life? Who else might benefit? And how?

As an 'ordinary GP' (whatever that is!), you may have found that both old and young dogs can easily learn new tricks. You already know the man (or woman) who can. It's you. Just exactly how are you going to take what you already do well and enhance that in the coming days and weeks? And in what way will that stimulate you to do more?

Now for you, the trainee registrar, grappling with the uncertainties of every-day practice. What are the particular areas we have covered that are going to help you most with summative and formative assessments, video-recordings and the like? What if you were to picture yourself having already successfully mastered these areas? Just how good a GP do you want to be?

As the GP trainer and educator, which parts have you marked out as the ones you will begin to teach straight away? How have you already started to incorporate and integrate these new perspectives with what you already know about consultations? As the teacher, nay mentor, of future generations of young general practitioners, look ahead in time and notice the profound effects that you have had on the cascade of knowledge and skills emanating forth.

I am an ordinary GP with an extra-ordinary passion. I want to know what makes people 'tick'. I want to know how to formulate my communication so that I can *get the message across*, no matter who is sitting in the consulting-room chair. I want to know how to be flexible enough to adapt my behaviours as circumstances dictate, yet allow them to come from the core of who I am. I, like you, in later years, want to look back and know that I made a difference, I counted, I lived up to the best of my expectations.

And so, finally, in this book at least, I am going to ask you to do one last thing. I am going to ask you to get that faraway look in your eye ... as you *go inside* ... and begin to conjure up a dream ... a Martin Luther-King kind of dream ... *your dream* ... a dream of what might be ... what could be ... what *will be* ... when you allow yourself to ... *fulfil* your goals ... and more ... to *achieve* your ambitions ... to be the *best you* that you can be .... To notice just how *you can* ... make a difference ... allow your life to *count* ... *really count* ... and at the end of the day ... know that you ... have gone ... way ... way ... *beyond expectations*.

And if anyone should ask just what it was that you got from reading this book, you might reply:

'I HAVE A DREAM'

Further training in NLP

I hope you have enjoyed reading *Consulting with NLP*, doing the exercises and utilising your learning in everyday consultations. Once you start using the tools that NLP has to offer, you may be wondering just how to develop an even greater proficiency in both this and other areas of application. I have included in the Bibliography a list of useful books which can help you to broaden your horizons even more. There are also some audiotape sets from well-known trainers, ranging from short seminars to full-blown NLP training.

However, a menu is not the meal, and a holiday brochure is not the experience of the destination it portrays. Because NLP is very much a hands-on, experiential discipline, the best way of learning it is simply to *do it*. By attending a skills-based course, using accelerated learning strategies, you will be able to assimilate a great deal very quickly. And not only that, you will be able to *do* NLP rather than simply talk *about* it intellectually. Over the past few years there has been an explosive proliferation of trainers and courses. So just how do you choose wisely?

The Association of NLP (ANLP) (www.anlp.org) is a UK-based organisation which provides information about training companies in your area. Although it is not a regulatory body, it also oversees the syllabus for the two main certification trainings, Practitioner and Master Practitioner. Traditionally these are 20-day training courses, usually spread over several months, which cover all of the agreed material for basic and advanced NLP. More recently, tape-assisted 7- or 10-day accelerated courses have also been approved. These are usually done as intensives, completed in one sitting.

I have trained with three UK-based organisations whose type and formats of training suit a wide variety of needs and learning styles. All of them are based in London.

International Teaching Seminars (ITS) is directed by Ian McDermott and is one of the most long-established UK institutes. I completed both Master Practitioner and Health Certification trainings with ITS, which involved not only Ian McDermott but also NLP pioneer Robert Dilts, Tad James, Tim Hallbom and Suzi Smith – an international array of respected trainers. These were 20-day courses spread over several months in a modular format. Ian, a consummate trainer with extensive experience of health applications of NLP, has also trained with a group of general practitioners in Scotland. The ITS website is www.itsnlp.com.

David Shephard, director of the Performance Partnership (PP), specialises in accelerated tape-assisted Practitioner (7-day) and Master Practitioner (14-day) courses. You prepare beforehand by listening to course material on tape and consulting a selected reading list. Having completed both short course and Hypnosis Trainer courses with PP, I can attest to David's expertise in Timeline Therapy for many medical conditions, and to the integrity of his training style. The PP website is www.performancepartnership.com.

More recently I completed the Society of NLP Trainer Training with McKenna-Breen. This is the only UK organisation to host Richard Bandler, who is accompanied by Paul McKenna and Michael Breen at a variety of different levels of training. Their accelerated formats are quite different experiences to standard NLP training, with 7-day courses and no prior preparation requirements. They focus more on unconscious skills acquisition, rather than on conscious intellectual knowledge. If you believe that learning should be fun and entertaining as well as educational, then Richard Bandler is a master of the art. You can check their website at www.mckenna-breen.com.

Because there are a number of different approaches to NLP, and differing schools of thought about methods of application, it goes without saying that there is no one correct way to learn and utilise the material. Each approach has both strengths and weaknesses. I have found, by experiencing a number of methodologies, that each has its part to play in an integrated understanding of the whole. Certainly, for me, it is important to close the learning loop by having a conscious working knowledge of unconscious competencies.

On a personal level, I provide both short introductory workshops and longer certification-type training. These can be tailor-made to address your specific learning needs independently, regardless of group size. In liaison with other top-flight trainers, there will be a series of advanced seminars on the application of NLP to health in a variety of contexts, including communication, management and therapeutic issues. For more details you can contact me at lewis.walker@ardach.grampian.scot.nhs.uk.

Or if you prefer:

Ardach Health Centre
Highfield Road
Buckie
Banffshire
Scotland AB56 1JE
Tel: 01542 831555
Fax: 01542 835799

Glossary

Accessing cues The subtle behaviours of eye movements, postures and gestures indicating which representational system (VAKOG) a person is thinking with.

Anchoring Associative classical conditioning whereby an external trigger is linked to an internal response or state. This can be re-accessed overtly or covertly.

Association Seeing, hearing and feeling the world as if one is completely inside the experience, whether it be right here and now, or a remembered or imagined event.

Auditory The sensory modality of hearing, speaking, sounds and words.

Behaviours External observable actions. 'What' we do.

Beliefs The operational rules connecting values to behaviours. Beliefs form three main categories about (a) causation, (b) meaning and (c) boundaries in (1) the world around us, (2) our behaviour, (3) our capabilities and (4) our identity.

Break state An abrupt interruption of the current state, especially if it is negative or unresourceful.

Calibration The ability to read non-verbal responses and behavioural cues accurately, linking them to specific internal states.

Chunk The amount of information that is considered at any one time. Chunking up leads to more abstraction, chunking down leads to more details, and chunking laterally leads to analogy, simile or metaphor.

Congruence A state in which all parts of yourself are aligned and working together in harmony.

Content The who and what of a situation.

Context The where and when of a situation; the environment in which it takes place.

Criterion The standard by which something is evaluated; a value.

Critical submodality The driver submodality which, when changed automatically, changes the rest.

Dissociation Experiencing an event as if you are outside yourself, observing.

Ecology The study of consequences; ensuring that outcomes and changes fit with the rest of the system.

Embedded commands Using a downward tonality to *mark out* what you want someone to do.

Environment Where and when something takes place; the context.

Eye-accessing cues The specific eye positions for remembered and constructed pictures and sounds, feelings and self-talk.

Feedback The external response to your behaviour which gives you information about what to do next.

Future pace A rehearsal of future actions connecting present resources to specific behaviours.

Gustatory Relating to the sense of taste.

Incongruence The experience of being at odds with oneself, in inner conflict, wanting one thing yet doing another. Simultaneous incongruence occurs when both parts of the conflict are expressed together. Sequential incongruence occurs when one part is expressed at a later time.

Kinaesthetic Relating to body sensations, feelings and emotions.

Logical levels The various levels of experience divided into a hierarchy of environment, behaviours, beliefs and values, identity and beyond. Useful for organising thinking about problems, resources and interventions.

Matching and mirroring The behavioural elements of establishing rapport at the level of physiology and voice.

Meta-model A set of questions to specifically explore deletions, generalisations and distortions.

Metaphor The process of thinking about one thing in terms of another. A story that can be used to generate change.

Meta-program A fundamental out-of-awareness information filter that acts across many contexts and determines our general responses to experiences.

Modelling The 'how to' of finding out about and replicating another person's skills. Finding the difference that makes the difference.

Model of the world A description of a person's internal map of experience.

Neuro-linguistic programming The study of the structure of subjective experience. The process of creating models of excellence.

Olfactory Relating to the sense of smell.

Outcome A goal which meets the criteria for a well-formed outcome.

Pacing and leading Building rapport by matching part(s) of another's experience prior to moving in a direction of mutual gain.

Parts A metaphorical way of talking about our needs, desires and behaviours in differing situations. 'It's like part of me wants X and part of me wants Y.'

Perceptual positions Moving mentally between being in your own shoes (*first position*), the shoes of another (*second position*) and a fly on the wall (*third position*). Very useful for negotiating successfully.

Predicates The words that indicate which representational system is being used: visual, auditory, kinaesthetic, olfactory, gustatory or unspecified (digital).

Process The 'how' of a situation, as opposed to the content (the 'what').

Quotes Richard Bandler was quoted as saying 'You can give people information by saying what someone else said, thus removing your overt influence'.

Rapport The mutual dance of responsiveness as you align with another person.

Reframing Changing the meaning of an event by changing the frame that surrounds it. There are many ways to do this, including the 14 verbal reframing patterns.

Resource state Usually a positive past experience which can be brought to bear on the here and now to effect change.

Sensory acuity The ability to detect the more subtle nuances in what is seen, heard and felt.

Sensory-based description Describing what is happening or has happened in terms of what can be seen, heard and touched.

State The sum total of all mental and physical activities and feelings that are going on at one time.

Strategies A set of explicit thinking and behavioural steps to achieve a specified result.

Submodalities The basic building blocks of experience. The qualities of each of the five sensory modalities (VAKOG).

Synesthesia See–feel and hear–feel circuits whereby accessing the first automatically accesses the second simultaneously. Phobias are a prime example of this.

Timelines The unconscious arrangement of past experiences and future expectations, usually seen as a line from left to right or from front to back.

Translation Rephrasing words from one representational system to another. For example, 'see what you mean' (V) and 'loud and clear' (A).

Values The answer to the question 'What is important to you?'. Important standards that we aspire to, such as honesty, integrity, making a difference, achievement, etc.

Visual Relating to the sense of sight.

Well-formed outcome criteria Goals that are stated in positives, initiated and maintained by the self, have sensory-based evidence for evaluating success, preserve current by-products, and have an ecological fit.

Bibliography and other resources

In this section I list the books and audiotapes that, over the years, I have found useful in expanding my knowledge and skills base in NLP and consulting. Because NLP steps back and looks at the underlying process, the deeper aspects of effective communication and change, much can be gleaned and learned from the study of apparently diverse fields. I shall give details of resources on *general NLP reading; training, education and management; books on Erickson; the consultation; other useful books; audiotape resources;* and *Internet resources.*

General NLP reading list

- Andreas S and Andreas C (1990) *Heart of the Mind.* Real People Press. Each chapter details a client problem together with NLP tools for change. Useful patterns.
- Andreas S and Faulkner C (1996) *NLP: the new technology of achievement.* Nicholas Brealey Publishing. An American-based introduction to NLP with lots of submodality exercises. Comprehensive.
- Bandler R and Grinder J (1975 and 1976) *The Structure of Magic 1 and 2.* Science and Behaviour Books. An in-depth study of the meta-model.
- Bandler R and Grinder J (1979) *Frogs into Princes.* Real People Press. The first edited transcribed seminar. Lots of techniques. Fun-filled and irreverent!
- Bandler R and MacDonald W (1988) *An Insider's Guide to Submodalities.* Meta Publications. An intriguing look at various submodality patterns for change.
- Bandler R and LaValle J (1996) *Persuasion Engineering.* Meta Publications. A radically different approach to influencing skills!
- Dilts R (1990) *Changing Belief Systems with NLP.* Meta Publications. Several approaches to belief change, mainly using kinaesthetic timelines.
- Dilts R (1999) *Sleight of Mouth: the magic of conversational belief change.* Meta Publications. A cognitive and categorical approach to verbal reframing patterns, which is a mine of information.

- Dilts R, Hallbom T and Smith S (1990) *Beliefs: pathways to health and well-being.* Metamorphous Press. An in-depth look at various belief change mechanisms in health.
- Gordon D (1978) *Therapeutic Metaphors.* Meta Publications. Generating and applying isomorphic metaphors for change.
- James T and Woodsmall W (1988) *Time-Line Therapy and the Basis of Personality.* Meta Publications. Excellent sections on the development of meta-programs via Jung and Myers-Briggs, and on beliefs and values. Interesting model for change work.
- McDermott I and O'Connor J (1996) *NLP and Health.* Thorsons. An excellent application of the basics of NLP to health and disease. Well worth reading.
- McDermott I and O'Connor J (1996) *Principles of NLP.* Thorsons. A good short introductory overview. Easy to read.
- McDermott I and Jago W (2001) *The NLP Coach.* Piatkus. Combines NLP with the field of coaching, providing many useful approaches that are adaptable to everyday general practice.
- McDermott I and Jago W (2001) *Brief NLP Therapy.* Sage Publications. Key concepts and applications of NLP in clinical situations. A good overview, plus two detailed dissected case histories.
- O'Connor J (2001) *NLP Workbook.* Thorsons. A practitioner-level training in workbook form, from one of the best NLP authors in the field. An excellent resource that is well worth the investment.
- O'Connor J and Seymour J (1990/1994) *Introducing NLP.* Thorsons. A comprehensive introduction and clear overview.
- Wrycza P (1997) *Living Awareness.* Gateway Books. A heart-warming NLP approach to personal and spiritual development.

Training, education and management

- Charvet SR (1995) *Words That Change Minds.* Kendall/Hunt. The definitive book on meta-programs. Published for business yet applicable in every context.
- Dilts R (1998) *Modelling with NLP.* Meta Publications. A description of the NLP modelling process and its application.
- Dilts R and Epstein T (1995) *Dynamic Learning.* Meta Publications. The application of NLP to various learning strategies, such as memory.
- James T and Shephard D (2001) *Presenting Magically.* Crown House Publishing. The best book to date by far on the use of NLP in training and presentation skills. Excellent value.

- Knight S (1995) *NLP at Work.* Nicholas Brealey Publishing. An introduction to NLP from a business perspective. Well written and easily readable.
- Knight S (1999) *NLP Solutions.* Nicholas Brealey Publishing. The application of NLP modelling tools to business, yet with many useful insights for medical practice.
- McDermott I and O'Connor J (1996) *Practical NLP for Managers.* Gower. Ostensibly for managers, although the communication strategies will be familiar.
- O'Connor J (1998) *Leading with NLP.* Thorsons. The 'how to's' of effective leadership. Essential reading for developing leaders.
- O'Connor J and Seymour J (1991) *Training with NLP.* Thorsons. An excellent guide to using NLP in teaching. Very useful for GP trainers and educators.

Books on Milton Erickson

- Battino R and South T (1999) *Ericksonian Approaches: a comprehensive manual.* Crown House Publishing. An in-depth guide to learning the fundamentals of Erickson's approach.
- Grinder J and Bandler R (1975 and 1977) *Patterns of Hypnotic Techniques of Milton Erickson, MD. Volumes 1 and 2.* Meta Publications. How Erickson used language exquisitely to obtain therapeutic results.
- Haley J (1993) *Uncommon Therapy.* Norton. The various psychiatric techniques of Erickson applied across all ages and all problem areas.
- Overdurf J and Silverthorn J (1994) *Training Trances.* Metamorphous Press. An integration of Ericksonian and classical strategies for change. A truly outstanding example of multi-level communication with individuals and groups.
- Rosen S (1982) *My Voice Will Go With You.* Norton. The teaching tales of Erickson. Many, many short stories about Erickson, his patients and his unique approach.
- Zeig J (1980) *A Teaching Seminar with Milton Erickson.* Brunner/Mazel. The man and his approach to therapy.

The consultation

- Byrne PS and Long BEL (1976) *Doctors Talking to Patients.* RCGP Publications. One of the first explorations of the 'ins and outs' of general practice consultations.

- Greenhalgh T and Hurwitz B (1998) *Narrative-Based Medicine.* BMJ Books. The patient's story in everyday consultations. Using narrative in diagnosis, treatment and making meaning out of illness.
- Miller W and Rollnick S (1991) *Motivational Interviewing.* Guilford Press. A book about consulting with patients who have addictive behaviours. Strategies for change which can be adapted to everyday consultations.
- Neighbour R (1987) *The Inner Consultation.* Churchill Livingstone. A blend of NLP, Ericksonian and Eastern philosophical approaches to the consultation. Beautifully written, a classic!
- Pendleton D, Schofield T and Tate P (1984) *The Consultation: an approach to learning and teaching.* Oxford University Press. An all-encompassing, detailed if somewhat bland approach. Broke my first consultation teeth on this one!
- Rollnick S, Mason P and Butler C (1999) *Health Behaviour Change.* Churchill Livingstone. A well-written book about how to motivate patients to make changes in hospital and community settings.
- Silverman J, Kurtz S and Draper J (1998) *Skills for Communicating with Patients.* Radcliffe Medical Press. This and its companion volume, *Teaching and Learning Communication Skills in Medicine,* gives a complete evidence-based methodology of communication skills in the consultation. An absolute mine of useful information which laid the foundation for *Consulting with NLP.* I am indebted to the authors!
- Tate P (1997) *The Doctor's Communication Handbook.* Radcliffe Medical Press. A small book that is packed full of helpful strategies and communication tips. Worthwhile reading.

Other useful books

- Assagioli R (1965/1990) *Psychosynthesis.* Mandala. A manual of principles and techniques for psychological change and growth. In many ways a forerunner of NLP.
- Bridges W (1991) *Managing Transitions.* Nicholas Brealey Publishing. About helping people to cope with organisational change. Many good adaptable individual strategies.
- Cialdini R (1993) *Influence: science and practice.* Harper Collins. A professor of social psychology, Cialdini expounds on the six fundamental rules of influence. Backed up by an impressive array of research evidence, this is a best-seller!
- Csikszentmihalyi M (1997) *Living Well.* Weidenfeld and Nicolson. The psychology of flow states in everyday life.

- De Shazer S (1994) *Words Were Originally Magic*. Norton. Solution-focused approach incorporating the miracle question. Plenty of client transcripts.
- Devito J (1997) *Human Communication: the basic course* (7e). Longman. A textbook for students on college communication courses. Well researched and well written.
- Ellis R and McClintock A (1994) *If You Take My Meaning* (2e). Edward Arnold. A wide-ranging discussion of communication issues in individuals and groups, with excellent chapter references.
- Farrelly F and Brandsma J (1974) *Provocative Therapy*. Meta Publications. Farrelly's approach to therapy and change is fun-filled, humorous and para-doxical, yet it gets results. A good read.
- Gleick J (1987) *Chaos: making a new science*. Viking. A very readable intro-duction to complexity and chaos theory.
- Kopp S (1972) *If You Meet The Buddha on the Road, Kill Him!* Science and Behaviour Books. An enjoyable read that cuts through the myths and legends of psychological treatment.
- Lawley J and Tomkins P (2000) *Metaphors in Mind*. The Developing Com-pany Press. Using symbolic modelling to effect client transformation via 'clean language'. Contains interesting applications for medical practice.
- O'Connor J and McDermott I (1997) *The Art of Systems Thinking*. Thorsons. A practical introduction with everyday examples, including health applications.
- Rinpoche S (1992) *The Tibetan Book of Living and Dying*. Rider Books, Random House. A Buddhist text which is a mine of information for palliative care.
- Rossi E (1993) *The Psychobiology of Mind–Body Healing* (2e). Norton. Detailed explanations and evaluations of the bodily chemical changes caused by thinking processes.
- Rossi E (1996) *The Symptom Path to Enlightenment*. Gateway Publishing. The application of complexity and chaos theory to biological systems, with specific reference to psychological change mechanisms. Outstanding!
- Senge P (1990) *The Fifth Discipline*. Doubleday. The art of the learning organisation and an approach to systems thinking in business. Also incorporates personal mastery, mental models, shared vision and team learning.
- Senge P (1994) *The Fifth Discipline Fieldbook*. Nicholas Brealey Publishing. Multiple examples of the above in action.
- Sinay S (1997) *Gestalt for Beginners*. Writers and Readers. The life and times of Fritz Perls, and the precepts of Gestalt therapy. All in cartoon form!
- Stevens JO (1989) *Awareness*. Eden Grove. A book about Gestalt therapy, with many exercises.

- Watzlawick P (1978/1993) *The Language of Change.* Norton. A clear exposition of the elements of therapeutic communication.
- Watzlawick P (1983) *The Situation is Hopeless But Not Serious.* Norton. How people make life miserable, and what they can do about it.
- Watzlawick P (1988) *Ultra-Solutions: how to fail most successfully.* Norton. 'The operation was successful but the patient died' sums this book up perfectly.
- Watzlawick P, Weakland J and Fisch R (1974) *Change: principles of problem formation and resolution.* Norton. One of the original Palo Alto group studying effective communication in therapy.
- Whitmore J (1992) *Coaching For Performance.* Nicholas Brealey Publishing. One of the leading business coaches for personal enhancement using the GROW process.
- Wilber K (1996) *A Brief History of Everything.* Shambhala. A four-quadrant, multi-level approach to integrating diverse life views into one coherent model.
- Wilber K (2000) *A Theory of Everything.* Shambhala. Integral visions of business, politics, medicine and education. Thought-provokingly practical.
- Wilber K (2000) *Integral Psychology.* Shambhala. A fascinating integration of Western and Eastern psychology from its beginnings up to the present day.
- Wolinsky S (1991) *Trances People Live.* The Bramble Company. How to step out of dysfunctional patterns of behaviour. Multiple strategies for change based on developments from Erickson.

Audiotapes

- James T. *The Master Practitioner Collection.* A set of 28 advanced training tapes, the next step up from Practitioner. Well edited and professionally produced by the originator of Timeline Therapy, a well-known US trainer.
- McDermott I. *The NLP Professional Development Programme.* A six-tape set by one of Europe's leading trainers, covering leadership, managing people and powerful presenting. It includes several processes, including the *levels alignment process*, and the *resonance pattern*, from this live seminar.
- McDermott I. *Tools for Transformation.* A four-tape set, extracted from a Practitioner-level training course, covering several useful skill sets.
- McDermott I. *Freedom from the Past.* A two-tape set with demonstrations of the NLP phobia cure in trauma resolution.
- McDermott I and O'Connor J. *An Introduction to NLP.* A two-tape introduction with several easy yet powerful exercises.

- McDermott I and O'Connor J. *NLP Health and Well-Being.* A single tape with several health applications.
- O'Connor J. *Leading with NLP.* A two-tape set with multiple strategies and exercises to complement the author's book.
- Overdurf J and Silverthorn J. *NLP Practitioner Tape Series.* A set of 32 tapes of a live Practitioner level training by two of the best American trainers in the field. Well edited, the material flows and is an outstanding resource in place of doing the training yourself. Contains lots of material about using NLP for therapeutic change.
- Overdurf J and Silverthorn J. *NLP Master Practitioner Companion.* For use in preparing for their accelerated training, this has sections on verbal reframing, meta-programs and values.
- Overdurf J and Silverthorn J. *Beyond Words.* A six-tape set from a live seminar, with plenty of demonstrations of the use of language patterns for change.

Internet resources

- www.itsnlp.com The website of Ian McDermott. Articles and training schedules for a variety of short and longer seminars.
- www.performancepartnership.com The website of David Shephard. Schedules and discussion forum.
- www.nlptrainings.com The website of John Overdurf and Julie Silverthorn. Schedules and articles.
- www.mckenna-breen.com Host to Richard Bandler in the UK. Information schedules and articles.
- www.anlp.org The Association of NLP (UK). Has a quarterly magazine, *Rapport.*
- www.nlpu.com The website of Robert Dilts. Many excellent articles and extracts from the *Encyclopaedia of Systemic NLP.*
- www.anglo-american.co.uk The Anglo-American Book Company specialises in mail-order NLP books. An extensive catalogue.
- www.iash.org The International Association for the Study of Health. Linked to Dilts, Hallbom and Smith's Health Certification Trainings.
- www.nlp.org A large collection of articles and links to other sites. Includes reviews of trainings and books.

These are just some of the possible websites that you can visit. You will find some of them more worthwhile than others in terms of information provision. All of them have links that will take you elsewhere, at the speed of thought!

Great states

I have listed below a large but not exhaustive number of different positive states. You can choose the ones that attract you and you vividly remember, with all of your senses, past memories with that particular feeling. Or you could just as easily imagine what it would be like if you had that state right now, and build it up, intensifying it so that it is strong and stable. Then, of course, you can attach it to any anchor of your choosing. Experiment, like a great chef, with mixing several of them together, and imagine what it would be like to experience that mixture in some future event. The choice is yours!

Alive	Autonomous	Wide awake	Adaptable	Appreciated
Great beauty	Bright	Calm	Cheery	Compassionate
Committed	Challenging	Courageous	Creative	Curious
Determined	Decisive	Dignified	Dynamic	Delighted
Elegant	Excellence	Excited	Energetic	Enthusiastic
Focused	Free	Fulfilled	Friendly	Fascinated
Full of fun	Forgiveness	Flexible	Graceful	Grateful
Grandiose	Glamorous	Caring	Happy	Healthy
Honest	Harmony	Helping	Humour	Hopeful
Innovative	Inspired	Integrity	Interested	Keen
Playful	Joyful	Jovial	Justice	Learning easily
Loving	Luscious	Loyal	Laughing	Making a difference
Mastery	Optimistic	Organised	Ordered	Peaceful
Persevering	Passionate	Powerful	Revolutionary	Relaxed
Resourceful	Resilient	Safe	Secure	Stimulated
Service	Simplicity	Problem solving	Sharing	Successful
Truthful	Unique	Useful	Unstoppable	Vitality
Wisdom	Warmth	Zest	Centred	Grounded
Synergistic	Winner	Wonderful	Brilliant	Contented
Carefree	Confident	Cool	Collected	Fabulous

Educationalists now know that the state you are in at the time of learning is very important, not only for short- and long-term memory recall, but also for the behavioural incorporation of skills. What if you could choose some states right now to build into a *learning state?* A state in which you could more easily absorb information, skills and behaviours – effortlessly. Which ones would fit the bill? How have you learned most easily in the past? How about the following recipe of states?

- *Fascination*: A time when you were watching, listening to or doing something that completely held your interest, your full attention.
- *Curiosity*: A time when you were really intensely wondering what was going to happen next.
- *Surprised yourself*: A time when you thought you couldn't do something, yet you succeeded anyway!
- *Playfulness*: A time when you were having fun simply for fun's sake.
- *Automatic skill*: Something you already do without thinking, such as driving your car or cooking a meal.

Take all of these examples, re-live each one vividly, and anchor them to the same trigger. Imagine mixing and coalescing them together to form a *super state for learning.* Then wonder what would happen if you were in this state each and every time you were learning something new.

You can, if you wish, apply this principle not only to learning and memory strategies, but also to how to make better decisions, how to increase motivation, how to use beliefs more effectively for change, and how to be even more creative. What about persuasion states? And negotiation states? You might like to think about which recipe of states fits each category.

Most of all, though, use this list to access and bring yourself home to some great states to live out of on a daily basis.

Submodality charts

You can use these submodality charts to explore the structure of any subjective experience. They are the brain's basic building blocks. You will find that changing them will change the coding of the experience itself *and* its meaning. Certain submodalities are drivers. Shifting them will cause others to shift, too, like a ripple effect. Sometimes one apparently small shift can cause major therapeutic change.

It is often useful to compare and contrast the submodality structure of different experiences. NLP calls this *contrastive analysis*. You can elicit the submodalities of the problem in its context and compare this with different contexts where the problem is absent. *Mapping across*, whereby the submodalities of the first experience are changed into those of the second, can have a profound effect. You can compare pairs such as boredom and curiosity, failure and success, grief and gratitude, problem and opportunity, doubt and belief, or confusion and certainty. Experience what happens when you change one into the other.

Submodality chart		
Visual	*Experience 1*	*Experience 2*
Black and white or colour		
Associated or dissociated		
Bright or dim		
Near or far		
Location in space		
Still-frame photograph or movie		
Bordered or panoramic (all around)		
Clear in focus, or fuzzy out of focus		
Life size, bigger or smaller		
Three- or two-dimensional		
Single or multiple images		

Auditory	Experience 1	Experience 2
Loud or soft		
Near or far		
Surround sound or point source		
Location in space		
High or low pitch		
Clear or muffled		
Normal speed, faster or slower		
Rhythmic or arrhythmic		
Moving or stationary		
Kinaesthetic	Experience 1	Experience 2
Location of feeling		
High or low intensity		
Hot or cold		
Continuous or discontinuous		
Still or moving		
Fast or slow		
Heavy or light		
Small or large area		
Direction of spin		

Have fun exploring the various submodality shifts. You can make any experience appear, sound and feel better than it was originally. Use these submodality shifts to make your outcomes more attractive, more motivating and more compelling.

The meta-model

Below is the complete meta-model, in detail, as it appears on standard NLP trainings. You will recall that *distortions* operate on *generalisations*, which in turn operate on *deletions* in a linguistic hierarchy. You will get far more impact and potential for change by challenging distortions first. However, you are *not* from the Spanish Inquisition! Remember to use the appropriate softeners to gently extract the appropriate information.

The meta-model			
Distortions	*Example*	*Intervention*	*Effect*
Mind reading	'You're angry with me'	'How do you know I'm angry?'	Recovers the source of the information
Lost performative value judgements	'It's difficult to get better from this'	'Who says?' 'According to whom?'	Recovers the source of the belief
Cause and effect (X causes Y)	'Not having a job makes me depressed'	'How does not having a job make you depressed?'	Recovers the choice. Provides a basis for alternative choices
Complex equivalence (meaning)	'Asthma means I have weak lungs'	'How does having asthma mean that your lungs are weak?'	Further specifies how X = Y. Reframe by counter-example

Generalisations	Example	Intervention	Effect
Universal quantifier (all, every, never, etc.)	'This illness will never get better'	'Never?' 'What would happen if it did?'	Elicits counter-examples
Modal operator of possibility (can, can't, will, won't)	'I can't see myself getting over this'	'What stops you?' 'What would happen if you did?'	Recovers prior causes and future effects
Modal operator of necessity (must, have to, should)	'I have to look after my elderly parents'	'What would happen if you didn't?' 'Or ... ?'	Recovers consequences

Deletions	Example	Intervention	Effect
Simple deletion	'I feel uncomfortable'	'About what, specifically?'	Recovers the detail
Comparative deletion (better, worse, less, etc.)	'She's much better than me'	'Who is better?' 'Better at what?' 'Better in which way?'	Recovers the specifics of the comparison
Unspecified verbs	'He hurt me'	'How specifically did he hurt you?'	Recovers the details of the act
Lack of referential index (fails to specify person)	'People just don't like me'	'Who specifically doesn't like you?'	Recovers the performer of the act
Nominalisation (process words turned into nouns)	'Our relationship is not working out'	'How are you relating at present?' 'How would you like to relate instead?'	Turns the event back into a process, recovering deletions

One important use for challenging deletions is when you are helping someone to enter a resource state, or to recover more information about a pleasant experience. By going into detail in these circumstances you will help them to re-access the state fully in the here and now, and you can then redirect this for future utilisation. However, getting all of the details about their recurring depression is only likely to make them feel worse.

Use meta-model challenges sparingly, lest you become a meta-monster!

Meta-programs questions

In essence, this is an inventory of the types of meta-program questions that can help you to quickly identify and utilise a person's information-processing filters. You can use it as a 'tick sheet' to help you to cover all of the bases. And it's not only helpful during consultations. You can also use it for job interviews and even for assessing which member of staff is suited to which task.

Meta-programs profile		
1	Towards Away from	*'What do you want? And why?'* *'What's important to you in this situation?'*
2	Proactive Reactive	*'In the past, when you've had a problem, after sizing it up did you act quickly, or did you think in detail about all the consequences first, before acting?'*
3	Options Procedures	*'Why are you choosing to do what you're doing?'* *'Why did you choose that particular course of action?'* (Options give you criteria, procedures tell you 'how')
4	Match Mismatch	*'What's the relationship between what's happening now and what happened previously?'* (i.e. similar or different?)
5	Internal External	*'How do you know you've made the right decision?'* *'Where (in your body) do you know that?'* (Internals point to inside, externals don't understand the question)

6 General Specific	*'When you're planning to do something, do you want to know all the details, or do you prefer the big picture first?'*

7 Convincer
   See
   Hear
   Do
   Read
	'How will you know when this problem has been solved?'
	'What would be your evidence?'

8 Convincer
   Automatic
   Number of times
   Period of time
   Consistent
	'Once it has been solved, what does it take to convince you that's the case?'
	(Answers range from just knowing automatically, to being convinced several times, to being convinced over a period of time, or never being totally convinced)

9 Thinker Feeler	*'Tell me about a particular event that gave you trouble'* (Watch to see if they remain dissociated or associate into it)

10 Time
    Past
    Present
    Future
	Notice from your interaction with them which time-frame appears to be most relevant to the presenting issue

11 Self Other	Check for the presence or absence of the appropriate behavioural responses

20-Day skill builder

Whilst you have probably integrated much already, having gone through all of the exercises, it is often useful to have a skill-building programme to focus on day by day over a period of time. The following programme is for four weeks, five days per week, although if you wish you can continue to develop skills at weekends. If you are really keen you might even work out another four-week programme to carry on your development afterwards.

Each day, while you concentrate on one specific area, you can rest assured that beneath the surface everything else will be integrating nicely. Then, of course, you can forget about it all for a while and allow yourself to be delightfully surprised after you have spontaneously demonstrated the skill automatically.

Week One	
Monday	Develop your *consulting flow state* anchor. Consciously 'top it up' and use it before each consultation today.
Tuesday	Develop your *break state* anchor. Use it in tandem with your *consulting flow state* before and after each consultation today.
Wednesday	For the first 30 seconds of each consultation, *match and mirror* the patient's physiology (posture, gesture and breathing rate).
Thursday	As the patient makes their opening statement, listen to their voice qualities (tone, pitch, volume and tempo). *Match* these as you proceed.
Friday	Listen to the patient's opening statement. As you *backtrack* the main points, calibrate to their *yes-set*.

Week Two	
Monday	Access and anchor your *peripheral vision state* to your *consulting flow* anchor. Consciously 'top it up' prior to each consultation.
Tuesday	Listen to the patient's *predicate* words. Note down which ones are predominantly *visual, auditory* or *kinaesthetic*.
Wednesday	Draw a picture of the *eye-accessing* schematic. For each patient today, notice which ones they access most.
Thursday	Notice where patients *project their experiences in space* as they talk about their problem. Is this the same or different when they are speaking about solutions?
Friday	For each patient today, make sure that what they want instead fits with the *well-formed outcome* criteria.

Week Three	
Monday	Choose three additional states from Appendix 1 and anchor them to your *consulting flow state*. Use them prior to each consultation today.
Tuesday	Choose three *meta-programs* (*towards/away, general/specific, match/mismatch*), and notice patient preferences in each consultation.
Wednesday	Explore each patient's *beliefs and expectations* about their problem. Ask *'What do you think has caused that?'* and *'What do you think this means?'*.
Thursday	Write out a list of *softeners*. Use at least one of them in each consultation today.
Friday	Use the following *meta-model* questions in each consultation. *'How specifically does X cause Y?'* and *'How specifically does X = Y?'*. Use softeners!

Week Four	
Monday	Choose another three states from Appendix 1 and add them to your *consulting flow state*. Use them with each consultation today.
Tuesday	From today's consultations, find three examples of *limiting beliefs*. Afterwards, take each one through the *verbal reframing* format.
Wednesday	Give your explanations today using all of the *convincer channels*. Draw a diagram and talk your patient through it so that it feels right and makes sense.
Thursday	Use the *SCORE model* to summarise for each patient what has happened to them and what the next steps will be.
Friday	In each consultation today, cover the various *'what-if' scenarios*. If you are feeling adventurous, do a *future rehearsal*, too.

Listed below are some additional skill builders that you can incorporate into your ongoing practice. You can always have a go at making up your own exercises based on what you have read so far and your own training experience.

1   Take a patient whom you know well and with whom you already have good rapport, but who is 'stuck' with an issue. Ask them the *miracle question* and help them to formulate a well-formed outcome.
2   Review your consultations for one morning or afternoon. At which *logical level* did the problem arise? At which level was the resource you chose to use? Was it at the same or a different level? Could you have used another level of resource instead, or as well?
3   On a series of cards write out the following: posture, gestures, breathing rate, eye-accessing cues, volume of speech, tempo of speech, direction of past and future. Mix them up and turn them face down. As you call in the next patient, turn one over and focus on that for the next 60 seconds as you listen to their opening statement.
4   Notice when a patient displays simultaneous incongruence. Gently challenge it in one of the ways listed in Chapter 5 on building the relationship.
5   Notice when a patient has an issue of sequential incongruence (e.g. alcohol binges, eating disorders, etc.). Think about how you could approach this issue next time. How might you frame what you are going to say?

6   At the end of each consultation, notice how you managed to *break rapport*. What exactly did you do? What could you do differently in the cases which were more challenging?

7   For each patient whom you see today, notice from which *perceptual position* they are operating. Listen for *I, you, we* and *they* statements. Enlarge their perspective by including a position that they are currently neglecting. What would happen if they were a 'fly on the wall' or 'stepped into the other person's shoes'?

8   At the end of each week, using the four quadrants reflect on what went well. In which areas could you improve? What next steps will you take to put this into action?

9   For your answers to question 8 apply the *well-formed outcome* criteria so that you come up with a goal which you are committed to achieve.

10 Think of someone with whom you do not see eye to eye (or some other rep system!). Take your memory of a typical encounter through the *meta-mirror*. How has that changed your perspective?

Index